3-

W9-BCP-978

The Modern
Madame Butterfly

The *Modern Madame Butterfly*

FANTASY AND REALITY IN JAPANESE CROSS-CULTURAL RELATIONSHIPS

Karen Ma

Charles E. Tuttle Company
Rutland, Vermont & Tokyo, Japan

Published by the Charles E. Tuttle Company, Inc.
of Rutland, Vermont & Tokyo, Japan
with editorial offices at
2-6 Suido 1-chome, Bunkyo-ku, Tokyo 112

© 1996 by Charles E. Tuttle Publishing Co., Inc.

LCC Card No. 95-60955
ISBN 0-8048-2041-4

First edition, 1996

Printed in Japan

 Contents

Acknowledgments

This book would not have been written without the participation and support of many people. I want to express special thanks to Catherine Osborne for first inspiring me to write this book and for her steadfast support and belief in the project. I am indebted to my good friend Diana Hume, who stood by me as my adviser and provided generous editorial help with my earlier drafts. My thanks also go to Mitsuyo Arimoto for her research work in the U.S., to Professor Chizuko Ueno of Tokyo University for the informative discussions we had, to Professor Fumiteru Nitta of Kibi International University and to Dr. Yuko Franklin of the California Institute of Integral Studies for their invaluable comments on Chapters 6, 8, and 9; and to Elizabeth and Itsuo Kiritani, Jonathan Lloyd-Owen, Sam Kohn, Abby Deveney, Patrick DeVolpi, and Mami Hidaka for reading my manuscript at its various stages of development.

I am grateful to the Association for Multicultural Families (AMF) and to the Association of Foreign Wives of Japanese (AFWJ) for their generous research assistance, and to the many anonymous volunteers who spent hours sharing their personal stories with me.

I would also like to thank my brother Man Li for his endless help with the technical aspects of the manuscript's preparation and to my husband Mark Magnier for his patience and emotional support throughout the project.

 *Introduction*

The Modern Madame Butterfly is an attempt to revise some of the outdated Western stereotypes that prevail about Japanese women and intercultural marriages in general between Japanese and Westerners.

At the heart of these stereotypes, I've found, is the *Madame Butterfly* myth that has dominated the Western psyche for over a century. According to this belief, the Japanese woman is a passive and selfless creature who is easily exploited. This, as I hope to show, is far from today's reality. Although I started out wanting to focus on debunking the *Butterfly* myth, I found that I was faced with many tangents and loose ends along the way, all of which seemed in one manner or another to be related to *Madame Butterfly*. I therefore chose to explore the subject from all angles. Consequently, to complete the analysis, I decided to include also the growing trend in relationships between Japanese men and Western women.

My fascination with the *Madame Butterfly* myth began when I first came to Japan as a student in 1977. As a bright-eyed college student studying Japanese society and culture in Japan, I had always been intrigued by the inner strength of Japanese women. When I grew up in Hong Kong, I was often told of Japanese women's low status in their society. It was not until I came to Japan, however, that I learned that as matrons from a culture rooted originally in a matriarchal society (which lasted until A.D. 650), Japanese women have been accorded a kind of emotional autonomy from their men that is not readily understood by foreigners. The society is, for example, epitomized by the mother-child relationship, not that between man and wife. This makes Japanese men somewhat peripheral in matters except in their roles as sons—-a factor that is still not widely recognized outside of Japan.

The idea of writing about the stereotypes of Japanese women, however, did not come to me until I went to the United States to further my studies. Once in North America, I found myself and many of my Asian female friends the target of similar stereotypes that portray all women from the East as docile and subservient.

The notion of an impoverished Asian mail-order bride clamoring for a Western husband also remains strong among foreign observers, particularly those with limited contacts with Asians. Asian women are assumed to be easy targets because, as one woman put it, "our standards are supposedly lower." I remember once reading an article by an American woman of Korean descent who recounted how she was often mistaken for a mail-order bride while studying as a freshman at the University of Missouri in 1990. She wrote: "Occasionally, when I'm with my [Caucasian] boyfriend, total strangers walk up and ask him where I'm from, if I speak English . . . " What's more, she continued, "If you're vaguely Asian or slightly Hispanic, people automatically label you as fresh off the boat, even if your family helped welcome the Mayflower."[1] Such treatment is not unique. In fact, one of my Japanese friends was called a "boat person" to her face.

Another friend, a dynamic Japanese businesswoman armed with an MBA from a prestigious U.S. university, was told point-blank by an American woman, "You know, you Japanese women really ought to stop scrubbing your men's backs in the bath." While Japanese women have come a long way, many Westerners continue to believe Japanese women to be submissive servants to their men. It is incidents like these that made me realize how badly the images of the East are in need of updating.

Shortly after my return to Japan in 1986, I began writing for a local English newspaper. In the course of my research about the many social phenomena affecting the development of Japanese women, I was surprised to see how much the women have changed from how I remembered them during my first stay. They have emerged from their protective cocoons to become real butterflies. They are the newsmakers and the trend-setters of a new era. Then, in 1991, after I completed a feature story for a local magazine on the cross-cultural dating scene in Japan, I found there was an overwhelming interest in the subject. That's when I began to formulate the idea for this book.

Getting started, I set out first to explore how Western stereotypes of Japanese woman have been formed over time; how most of these images are heavily influenced by a Western bias; and how they are supported by the Japanese themselves due to their own insecurity in dealings with the West. I continued by examining how these stereotypes differed from reality. Japanese women, I found, have undergone great changes. In many ways, these transformations are related to the many social developments that have taken place due to Japan's rise as an economic power.

Japan's economic success is having a tremendous impact on how intercultural relationships are perceived. I argue that the increasing numbers of Japan-based relationships—which have resulted, in part, from the draw of Japan's new wealth—are gearing the cross-cultural dynamics more and more in favor of the Japanese partner. Ultimately, living in Japan gives a Japanese woman more say in a relationship because she is living on her own turf. Likewise, I believe Japan's economic strength has enhanced the attractiveness of Japanese men, making them more desirable and accessible as marriage partners for non-Japanese women.

In my study, I have also sought to point out some of the common pitfalls and unrealistic expectations many cross-cultural couples have due to the perpetuation of stale stereotypes. By also presenting some examples of successful relationships, I hope to shed a balanced light on the key factors that such relationships have in common.

The Modern Madame Butterfly is divided into two parts. The first part deals with Western men and Japanese women and constitutes two-thirds of the book because this combination has been the most prevalent in Japan and continues to dominate the intercultural dating scene. In addition to explaining the rising phenomenon of cross-cultural love, I'll also take a look at the changing gender roles of Japanese women and how many are now looking at intercultural relationships as a way of resolving their own dilemmas with Japanese men.

The second part of the book concerns the topic of Japanese men and Western women. Although my main interest lies in explaining the *Madame Butterfly* myth, I have deliberately devoted a full chapter to the subject of Japanese men because I feel that the stereotypes of Japanese men are the very opposite of the stereotypes of Japanese women. Having clarified this, I shall follow by addressing the question of why an increasing number of Western women are finding Japanese men to be attractive partners—a phenomenon many of my Western male respondents found unfathomable.

Because this is a book about the fantasies and stereotypes held by Westerners and Japanese about each other as seen through the dynamics of intermarriage, I have excluded non-Western partners of Japanese from my analysis. And by Westerners, in this context, I refer mainly to Caucasians, to contain the scope of my research.

In my study, I have incorporated articles, studies, group surveys and interviews with specialists as well as with individuals in intercultural relationships. For the first section of the book, I conducted a survey of about 30 members of the Association for Multicultural Families, (AMF), formerly known as the Kokusai-Kekkon o Kangaeru Kai (KKKK). For the second section of the book I surveyed 125 members of the Association of Foreign Wives of Japanese (AFWJ), the counterpart of AMF.

One problem I encountered in conducting my surveys of the two groups of wives is the disparity in the number of respondents between them. I ended up with four times as many respondents in the foreign wives' group than in the Japanese wives' group. One reason accounting for the disparity is the difference in size of the two groups. With close to 600 members, the foreign wives' group is about 200 members larger than its counterpart. The foreign wives' group also appears to be more structured and, following their suggestion, I sent out some 360 questionnaires to cover all of their Kanto Chapter members. For the Japanese wives' group, however, I was able to send out only sixty questionnaires.

Moreover, in the course of my dealings with the two groups, I noticed foreign wives were more forthcoming with their responses. One American wife suggested that this could be because Western women are better at organizing activities and tend to be more verbal about their feelings and thoughts (about eighty percent of AFWJ members are from North America and Europe). I tend to agree with this suggestion. Yet I am also fully aware of the concern many Japanese wives have expressed of not wanting to become targets of social ostracism because of their marriage to foreign men. Their reluctance is understandable.

Aside from couples, I also conducted numerous individual interviews with single men and women involved in cross-cultural relationships. Some of these singles were recruited at random through the help of personal ads. Others were introduced to me by word of mouth. The majority of my interviews were with people in the twenty-five to forty-five age range. To ensure their privacy, I have changed the names of my respondents. However, official representatives, experts, and authors are listed by their full names where possible, since they are already in the public eye.

The project took me three years to complete and the total number of direct interviewees and informants I have talked to comes to about 180 (130 individuals and 25 couples). As for indirect informants (e.g., survey respondents, respondents recruited from ads, etc.), I contacted nearly 200.

Because the majority of my sampling was drawn from interviews with Japanese married to North Americans, this study is somewhat biased in terms of application. This, however, was not intentional because I did want a broader perspective that included all Westerners. However, as I continued to research my subject, I realized that American men and women still make up the largest percentage of the non-Asian marriage partners of Japanese. But I have also, whenever possible, included information from interviews with foreigners of other nationalities, which was as close as I could get to my Japanese-Westerner relationships goal.

An additional caveat: The changes I have referred to as occurring in Japan—particularly those involving Japanese women—are based on those living in Tokyo, which has the highest percentage of intermarriages per capita in Japan. Therefore, I do not intend to imply that my study should be taken as a direct reflection of the situation existing in other parts of Japan. Likewise, since most of the subjects discussed in the book are based in Japan, their experiences may not have any direct bearing on Japanese-Western marriages outside of Japan.

In the past, many books have been written on the subject of East-West romances (mostly in the form of fiction), but most are works by Western men. These works thus tend to suffer heavily from a Eurocentric prejudice which often serves to further propagate "Oriental" myths. Because *The Modern Madame Butterfly* is essentially an observation of the changing dynamics of East-West relationships through Asian eyes, I hope to counterbalance some of the prevailing Western views of things Asian in the current media scene.

As an Asian woman educated in Japan, I identify with Japanese women. I do not, however, share their cultural background. Therefore, I hope to offer a different perspective as an outside observer.

This project also has meaning to me on a personal level. As a Chinese brought up in three different cultures, this book is also a personal journey which encapsulates my own search for a happy medium of living in a cross-cultural environment, a way of life that encompasses elements of both East and West. Writing this book has confirmed my belief, once again, of the importance of recognizing the individual beyond the cultural surface. Ultimately, what matters most about people is not their culturally learned behavior nor their attributed national characteristics, but rather their innate value as human beings.

—KAREN MA

Tokyo

 CHAPTER ONE

Myth of
the Modern Madame Butterfly

There is nothing new about romance and marriage between Japanese women and Western men. Ever since Commodore Perry forced Japan's doors open in the mid-nineteenth century, high-profile unions between the East and the West ranging from those of Lafcadio Hearn to Edwin Reischauer to John Lennon have been an established fact of modern history. These romances have also sparked many literary and art works in the West, perhaps the most enduring of which is Puccini's *Madame Butterfly*. Yet the West's romance with the East tends to be heavily weighted by stereotypes and fantasies that have changed little since those early years.

To the thinking of many Westerners, as expressed in English books and popular literature, Japanese women are still little more than compliant, doll-like objects of fantasy, as epitomized by the "geisha" image. When Japanese synchronized-swimming star and Seoul Olympics medalist Mikako Kotani wore a kimono and attended an International Olympic Committee meeting in Birmingham, Alabama, she was promptly described by a local reporter as a "geisha girl serving tea."[1]

The idea of a subservient, self-sacrificing Japanese wife may be even more prevalent. This image is imprinted in the minds of Western men and women alike. In a way, it is easy for people to assume Japanese women to be submissive. Compared with their Western counterparts, Japanese women (and men, for that matter) are not as verbal and tend not to assert themselves in a public setting. They are usually very polite and appear deferential toward others. When Westerners encounter this, they are likely to see these traits as evidence of subordinate behavior since in North America (and in many other Western societies), to be polite and deferential is often mistaken for weakness. This may be one reason why many Western men, discouraged by what they perceive as the assertive and confrontational manner of Western women, seek out Japanese wives.

An Australian fisherman in his fifties who recently visited Japan on a five-day trip told me over a beer at a Tokyo bar that he had recently divorced. Assuming I was Japanese, he confided that he was convinced he should marry a Japanese "lady" the second time around because "she would be more devoted" to the duties of caring for the family and children. This man had no prior experience in Japan nor did he speak a word of Japanese. Yet he presumed he would have a better marriage with a woman from a country he knew nothing about after failing in a relationship with someone from his own culture.

I have heard similar comments about Japanese women from Western men since I began interviewing people for this book. Single or divorced, there is a prevailing assumption that a Japanese woman, by mere virtue of her being Japanese, will automatically make a better wife. This assumption is applied not only to Japanese women, but to Asian women in general, who tend to be regarded as being docile, self-sacrificing, and home-oriented. Among the members of this group, Japanese women are continually singled out for particular attention. Perhaps this is because they most closely match the Judeo-Christian ideal of the perfect woman.

An old saying has it that a man is in heaven when he has an American house, a British salary, a Chinese cook and a Japanese wife. The stereotype that Japanese women make the best wives in the world did not develop overnight; it goes back more than a century.

Roots of the Stereotypes

In a recent *U. S.–Japan Women's Journal* article, Yoshi Kuzume traces the beginning of the geisha and good-wife stereotypes to around the 1860s, when the U.S. first established official ties with Japan.[2] Kuzume, who suggests that American writings have had the greatest influence on the formation of stereotypical images of Japanese women, identifies four eras, spanning about 130 years from 1860 to 1990. He points out that the image of Japanese women as geisha girls prevailed between the 1860s and the 1900s, when Japan hosted her first Western visitors. These visitors were predominantly American and English Victorian-era males stationed in the East to make the most of the trading opportunities that were developing with the opening of Japan. In those early years, foreign men had few chances to come into contact with Japanese women, save for those from the lower classes who worked as servants or prostitutes. In comparison with the virtuous, virginal, holy-mother pedestal upon which they placed their own women, these men saw Japanese women as being vulgar and sexually promiscuous. Because prostitution was legal in Japan and foreigners were given full access to "special quarters," many followed the custom of keeping a "local wife" or concubine. This is believed to have been the case with Townsend Harris, the first consul general from the United States, whose three-day liaison with Okichi, his laundry woman, became the source of a popular Japanese legend about a poor, helpless young woman separated from her fiancee by local officials and made to serve a strange foreigner. After her shame and ostracism by the community, she became dissolute, opened a bar, and eventually committed suicide.

Parts of Japan were very poor in those days, especially in the farming communities. Consequently, some Japanese women were forced to go abroad to earn money as prostitutes, such as the *ameyuki-san* (literally "America-goers"). During the Occupation years, the Japanese, fearful that the occupying forces would commit indiscriminate rape, made it easy for American GIs to gain sexual access to prostitutes. In May 1946, for example, there were an estimated 668 brothels staffed by 8,000 women in Tokyo alone. This further reinforced the image of Japanese women as sex objects, exciting a fantasy for the Western male that promised freedom from the sexual prohibitions placed upon him by his own culture. This was the beginning of the geisha-girl stereotype, which, to these first foreign males in Japan, defined Japanese women as the ultimate sex symbol.

Interestingly enough, the stereotype of the Japanese woman as a devoted wife and mother, according to Kuzume, originated during the same period by Japanese scholars. This was, in part, a reaction to the growing negative image. To the well-educated Japanese who had contact with Americans, the notion of the geisha girl as the typical Japanese woman, Kuzume says, was embarrassing, as it served to suggest that Japanese society was culturally inferior. To replace this negative impression, scholars sought to show the soundness of their social mores by emphasizing the virtues of the samurai class in terms of the increasingly fashionable Victorian moral code. This was what motivated Nitobe Inazo, Kuzume argues, to portray Japanese women as being loyal, subordinate, and self-sacrificing in his classic work *Bushido: The Soul of Japan*, which was written in 1899 (subsequently published in 1905 in English by G.P. Putnam's Sons, New York). The women, in Inazo's words, were the "keepers" of the moral code.

Shingoro Takaishi, a leading Japanese journalist at the turn of the twentieth century, published a new interpretation of *Onna Daigaku* (or "Greater Learning for Women"), which was a set of instructive precepts written for the Japanese woman in the late feudal period (1600–1800). Takaishi was, Kuzume asserts, another defender of the Japanese moral code, particularly because he set out to prove in his work that Japanese women, far from being uncivilized, were model Victorian women. The pivotal change in the image of the Japanese woman, however, came as a result of the works of Lafcadio Hearn, a wandering Irish-Greek journalist who settled in Japan to become a well-known Japanologist and one of the first foreign men to officially marry a Japanese woman. In numerous works published in the late nineteenth century, Hearn described Japan's women as being unselfish, obedient figures tied to their social duty by strict Confucian codes. Not only did he change the image of the Japanese woman from a mysterious and sensual geisha girl to the selfless woman who would do anything to help her family, but he also added the image of her "moral charm." He described her delicacy, her child-like piety and trust, and her exquisite tactful perception of all things around her. All of which, while presenting a more positive image, served to further entice the interest of Western men.

From 1910 to modern times, Japanese women have

evolved from being seen as, in Kuzume's words, "miserable creatures who needed to be saved" (mainly by missionaries) in the pre-war period, to women awakening to new-found freedom in the postwar era, to "domestic feminists" with real power in the household during the seventies and eighties. Despite these changes, and the increasing independence of Japanese women in the nineties, the dated Western stereotypes of Japanese women remain firmly entrenched in print, broadcast, and film media. In the latter, especially, Japanese women are still routinely depicted with painted faces and geisha attire.

The prototype for all of these images was Cho Cho-san in Puccini's *Madame Butterfly*—the famous 1904 Milanese opera based on a story about a geisha married to an American naval officer who callously deserts her in the end. This classic portrayal has no doubt had a long-lasting effect on the psyche of Western males. The compliance and gentleness attributed to Japanese women have long struck a responsive chord in men used to self-assertive, confrontational, and independent Western women. As pointed out by social anthropologist Sheila Johnson in her book *The Japanese Through American Eyes*, the early postwar years "heightened [American men's] response toward Japanese women."[3]

The Impact of the American Occupation

The American Occupation, as did the years Japan first opened to the West, brought far more men than women to Japan. As Johnson notes, there were an estimated 465,000 American soldiers stationed in Japan in 1946 to disarm troops and administer the occupation. The bulk of the romantic cross-cultural encounters that occurred were, accordingly, between American men and Japanese women. A variety of motivations brought the two together. Many Japanese women had lost their husbands during the war and were desperately poor. The American men were far from their own wives and girlfriends for an extended period of time and had access to food and other scarce items. It is therefore not difficult to see why an estimated twenty thousand American GIs married Japanese women during the zenith of the U.S. occupation.[4]

The pleasure that American GIs found in their liaisons with Japanese women was vividly captured in James Michener's *Sayonara* (1964)—a best-seller that was subsequently made into a film. In his novel, Michener profusely extols both the strength and gentleness of the Japanese woman through his descriptions of two characters: the beautiful Takarazuka actress Hana-ogi and the rather homely Katsumi. Hana-ogi is the radiant heroine with an iron will who devotes herself to her art and profession and Katsumi is the comforting, wifely woman who could "take a wounded man and make him whole."

In many ways, *Sayonara* served as an updated version of *Madame Butterfly*. It further reinforced the myth of Japanese women's moral charm. In more recent movies, we continue to see shadows of the *Sayonara* heroines, such as Mariko in James Clavell's *Shogun* (1975) and Kumiko in the movie *Karate Kid II* (1986), both of which depict their Japanese heroines as being devoted, selfless, and brave. In these cases, however, there is also the subtle suggestion that the beautiful heroines are so suppressed and deprived by society that they must be saved from their own destinies by powerful, gallant Western lovers. This insinuation repeats the age-old rhetoric that Asian women are a deprived underclass that can only be rescued by the power of the Western world—a condescending view of the East held by many white males. The stereotype has changed little, despite the recent economic boom among East Asian nations and city states.

The Persistent Western View

Even Japan's economic success has not had much impact in terms of eliminating this condescending Western attitude toward Japanese women. In fact, contemporary literature pumped out by Western writers repeats the well-worn theme of virtuous Japanese women rescued from cold, licentious Japanese husbands and boyfriends by righteous, romantic white boyfriends. The story of a Japanese wife and mother hurrying home to fulfill her obligations after an afternoon of delight in the arms of a foreign lover is the theme of both Pico Iyer's *The Lady and the Monk* (1991), a book based on his own experiences in Japan, and in Clive Collins' novel *The Foreign Husband*, (1989).

Similarly, in Ian Middleton's *Reiko* (1990), the heroine of the title is described as "Japanese, fascinating, unique," and as someone whose "face, half-smiling, flowered in Andrew's consciousness." After lovemaking, one character in the book remarks "only a Japanese woman can have such a gift." *Reiko*, as one Tokyo book critic put it, "is but another link in a tradition of associations between Asian women, the exotic East, and the white men who rescue them."[5]

Meanwhile, the American musical *Miss Saigon* (1991), by Alain Boublil, based on *Madame Butterfly*, renews the stereotype of the destitute, helpless, and ultimately disposable Asian woman who pins her only hope on a foreign lover. (It is interesting to note how, in both *Miss Saigon* and *Madame Butterfly*, the hero happens to be American.)

Miss Saigon was well received in Japan. Complete with a Japanese cast, it played for a full year at the Teigeki Theater in Tokyo. While few in Japan questioned the inappropriateness of perpetuating this dated image, in the United States the production had outraged many in the Asian community, David Mura among them. One of the founders and leaders of the Twin Cities-based Asian-American Renaissance, a group formed to give Asians a unified voice through art, Mura raises a key question in regard to such works: "Is it possible for the white male to imagine the world through the eyes of the Other, i.e., the non-white?"[6]

Japan: The Indirect Reinforcer

That Japan is oblivious to the Oriental myths created by the West is not surprising. In fact, Japan has indirectly helped to perpetuate the stereotypical view of Japanese women. As foreigners in Japan often notice, women are frequently exploited sexually on late-night television. Programs with both male and female cast members explore on any given night everything from panel judging of "the most pleasing" nipple size and color of several smiling, G-string-clad young women, to "scientifically" assessing how to erotically stimulate a naked, "hypnotized" young female subject.

The comic books read by men in their twenties to forties are also full of sexually explicit illustrations (albeit with genitalia obscured for censorship reasons). The male-dominated mass media continue to feature, ubiquitously and nearly across the board, scenes of women displayed and trussed up like meat rolls—i.e., rendered totally passive for male will and desire.

Meanwhile, daytime soap operas targeted at housewives continue to extol the ideal woman who knows that her proper place is at home. NHK's highly publicized TV drama *Oshin* is a story about the trials and tribulations of a poor young woman set in the immediate post-war years.

The program has given thousands of overseas viewers the false impression that Japanese women today are still subjected to severe deprivation and are demure, obedient maids willing to put the needs of others above their own. In reality, however, there is a vast discrepancy between today's Japanese woman and the officially endorsed model image that continues to meet the public eye.

There is another factor for Japan's reinforcement of Western stereotypes: The Japanese have always been more interested in Western approval and acceptance than in their own views of themselves. In fact, the Japanese, to use the expression of some critics, are "obsessed" with the West. This is illustrated by the Japanese penchant to seek out opinions expressed about them by foreigners. Japanese newspapers often carry opinion columns by Caucasian critics. Similarly, on prime-time TV, several American *tarento* (literally talents, or TV personalities) have become regulars, where they are invited to express their views about virtually anything Japanese. In contrast, Asian specialists have rarely been asked to cite their opinions, although this tendency is slowly beginning to change. Since 1993, some NHK radio programs, for example, have begun to invite Chinese and Korean journalists to talk about Japanese politics and social issues for their New Year's specials.

There is also a tendency for Japan to compare itself with the West through international surveys. Countless Japanese-American or Japanese-European comparative surveys on social trends have been conducted by the Japanese government and major Japanese enterprises. Some of the more obvious examples are *Amerika chosa—nichi-bei seikatsusha no ishiki kurabe,* a detailed comparative survey of Japanese and American families conducted in 1990 by Hakuhodo, Japan's second-largest advertising firm; and *Tokyo, nyu yoku, rondon tomokasegi kazoku no seikatsu hikakuchosa,* a comparative survey of dual-income families in Japan, New York, and London, which was conducted in 1990 by Asahi Kasei, a chemical firm. It is interesting to note that few of these so-called international surveys include comparisons with other Asian nations. This says a lot about who the Japanese identify with when ranking themselves with the outside world.

"Deserting Asia, Joining Europe"

Japan, as a hierarchical society, appears more than other nations to venerate nations perceived as being above her and disdains those perceived as being below her. Perhaps this, as well as Japan's self-imposed mission to compete with the West, is behind her dual attitude toward the world—revering the West and disdaining the East. In fact, *datsua nyūō*, literally "deserting Asia and joining Europe," was a notion strongly advocated by the prominent Japanese educator Yukichi Fukuzawa as early as 1885.[7] In order to compete with the West, Fukuzawa saw that it was of utmost importance for Japan to first seek its acceptance. At the same time, it would have to isolate itself from Asia so that it would not be mistakenly lumped together with the "backward" East.

This attitude, critics observe, has continued until today. One writer for a major Japanese language journal noted that many Japanese have developed the habit of reversing the order of their names from the traditional form of family name first to family name last when they introduce themselves in English, or write their names in the roman alphabet.

"But Chinese and Koreans never do that and have always followed their own traditions of placing their family names first, even when they have to write their names in

English," says the writer.[8] The result, he notes, is that in English-language newspapers, the names of Chinese and Korean leaders are written as Li Peng and Roh Tae Woo with their family names first, while Japanese names are reversed, such as Kiichi Miyazawa and Tomiichi Murayama. The writer, quoting another expert, commented that, "While the Japanese felt the need to appease Westerners, they made a deliberate distinction between themselves and Asians. This shows an inferiority complex on the one hand, and a superiority complex on the other."[9]

Although many Japanese deny having such a double standard, given the changing world order and the rise of many Pacific Rim nations, a few have become more honest about it. Explaining why it has been so hard to convince Japanese radio stations to give more air time to Asian popular music, Koji Niwa of WEA Music, in an interview with NHK in 1994, put it very frankly: "The Japanese have a long history of aspiring to and following American trends, especially in music. It's a kind of prejudice. The Japanese don't really want to admit they are Asians."

Internationalization

The stereotype of a helpless Japanese woman who needs to be rescued by a white lover is further exaggerated and compounded by the popularity that Caucasian men enjoyed with women in Japan in light of *kokusaika*, or internationalization, a social movement that began in the midst of the 1980s.

During the dawning of the eighties, when Japan was emerging as a world economic power and beginning to look increasingly toward changing its image in the eyes of the West, it took on the task of "internationalizing" its society. In fact, internationalization has become a buzzword for advocates of all kinds of reforms, from the shortening of the "salaryman's" work week to the restructuring of the Japanese economy. Other notable reforms include an increase in the number of foreign students in Japan, and the modification of road signs throughout the country to help foreign drivers. Many Japanese equate the elements of internationalization with the promotion of the English language.

On another level, internationalization really means nothing more to most Japanese than simply looking Westward. According to a poll conducted by the Economic Planning Agency, two out of three Japanese think internationalization means developing more contacts with the United States, Europe, and Australia in the form of travel. Only one in four associate the term with other countries in Asia.[10]

Some say that this response to the meaning of internationalization can be traced historically to the Tokugawa period (1603–1868), when Japan was closed to all but a smattering of tightly controlled foreign contact. This notion seems to be deeply rooted in the Japanese mind. The very word *gaijin*, or foreigner, literally means "outside person." But, as has been pointed out by many Japanologists, rather than meaning "non-Japanese," it is normally employed to mean people with visibly different features from the Japanese, i.e., Occidentals. East Asians such as Koreans and Chinese are not called *gaijin*, a term which some Japanese explain as being the short form of the "official" word *gaikokujin* (*koku* meaning country). These Asians are referred to more specifically as *kankokujin* (Koreans) and *chūgokujin* (Chinese). The word *gaijin*, moreover, was often equated with *amerikajin*, or Americans, by many Japanese until the 1980s. Canadians, Australians, and Europeans, often mistakenly called *amerika-jin* by the Japanese, are particularly offended by what they see as being a very narrow understanding of the outside world.

An explanation given by Masato Sato of Sony Corporation's Personnel Division may be even more convincing. Calling it a "foreigner complex," he attributes the phenomenon to the inability of most Japanese to speak a foreign language, particularly English, which they study for over six years in junior and senior high school. Despite a high literacy rate, (over ninety percent of Japanese are said to have a basic twelve-year education), the average Japanese is unable to speak even survival-level English. For a nation aspiring to Westernization, this is indeed ironic, which explains why most Japanese respect anyone capable of speaking the language well.

Learning English from native English speakers has naturally become a major task of the effort to improve Japan's image. While the Ministry of Education began recruiting thousands of native English speakers to teach English in junior and senior high schools as Assistant English Teachers (AETs), the number of roadside English schools targeted at young office ladies (OLs) and businessmen also burgeoned. In 1990, at the peak of the English boom, there were an estimated eight thousand English-language schools in Japan.

This zest for the West, along with Japan's expansion as an economic power, prompted a growing need for the English language in other areas, such as in the mass media, communications, law, government and public services, and financial fields. Suddenly, there was a rush to hire English-language "specialists."

The Rise of the Token Gaijin

At the height of the English-language fever in the late

1980s, having a Caucasian friend was the thing to aspire to. This trend, however, was common only among younger Japanese people in their twenties and thirties. As many government surveys have indicated, the majority of Japanese, notably the older generations, remain reluctant to associate with foreigners. Because many Japanese are under the impression that all Caucasians can speak English fluently (although this misconception has decreased dramatically in the wake of the great influx of other nationalities), having a Caucasian friend would often earn a person double-edged status—implying that he or she was either very good at speaking English, which would automatically garner a great deal of respect, or that he or she had an exclusive opportunity to practice speaking English and thus become internationalized.

So fashionable was this idea at the height of the bubble economy, that many companies even hired *gaijin* staff as showcase employees to highlight the extent of their *kokusaika*. Native English speakers could therefore, on language alone, secure jobs that they would not otherwise be qualified for in their home countries. This has allowed some foreigners to virtually re-create themselves—leaving their past behind or embellishing it by starting a new career.

This is symptomatic of men and women alike. One former New York art gallery employee who had recently arrived in Japan was, by chance, asked to write an article in English on a prominent foreign artist. From there, in her own words, she "reinvented herself." She then found a job at a prestigious museum as a foreign correspondent on art—a job that, in the West, would be held by a professional with years of experience and post-graduate credentials.

This chameleon-like tendency on the part of foreign job-searchers has led to misconceptions on everyone's part.

It has given many foreigners a false sense of importance and accomplishment, and has made them seem to the Japanese like magicians with supernatural powers. This was particularly true during the bubble years of the Japanese economy in the late eighties. It's no wonder that the Japanese, seemingly bewitched by the foreigners' apparent powers, have been so intent on cultivating friendships with them.

So eager are they for their doses of "internationalization" that the Japanese sometimes go to extremes to woo total strangers into becoming their friends, lavishing them with gifts and compliments. There is, however, a flip side to this attention. One American friend who used to teach English as a Second Language (ESL) at a college once put it to me this way: "Many of my Japanese friends told me that they liked me before they even knew me." Although she did not mind being friendly, when her neighbors started pressuring her to attend social functions with them, she felt like a token "blue-eyed" foreigner, and decided to put a stop to it. She said that at times she felt like a package of exotic fruit on display in a department store.

Her experience reminded me of what writer Ian Buruma once said about the Thais—which, with the substitution of Westerner for foreigner, well applies to the Japanese. In *God's Dust: A Modern Asian Journey*, he explains that they think of foreigners as God. However, "This does not always mean foreigners are liked. Gods are outsiders with great and unpredictable powers. They are to be appeased by all means lest they mean harm and do damage. It is better still, if their powers can be exploited. Therein lies the key to your own survival."[11]

This pragmatic attitude toward Westerners has become even more institutionalized since the beginning of the *kokusaika* movement in Japan. And with Japan's burgeoning economic success, Westerners are coming to Japan in ever-rising numbers. Even the dwindling economy did not seem to have deterred more from coming. According to Ministry of Justice figures, between 1988 and 1993, the number of foreign residents from North America and Europe jumped twelve percent. Indeed, international exchanges between Japanese and foreigners have been made even more convenient than before. In the seventies and early to mid-eighties it was mainly young people traveling through Asia who stopped to pick up some lucrative work in Japan on their way through. In those days, it was easy for unqualified native English speakers to get jobs as English teachers or copywriters.

Though a few non-degreed native English speakers are still slipping into some teaching positions, and others, barely armed with entry-level working experience, may not be qualified for the jobs they get, those coming from English-speaking countries today are generally more informed about Japan and more apt to speak Japanese. Attracted by the higher salaries and the opportunity to experience the dynamism of the rising East, more and more are seeing a stint in Japan as a launching pad for jobs back home.

Meanwhile, in the midst of Japan's enthusiasm for *kokusaika*, learning English (and other European languages) has become one of the fastest ways for women to get ahead in Japanese society. It is in this climate that many trendy young Japanese women are encouraged to search for a Western boyfriend through English schools, international parties, singles' bars in the *gaijin*-packed Roppongi area and at overseas travel destinations. The age-old taboo of dating foreigners, which had meant social ostracism as late as the Occupation, suddenly came to be the "in" thing to do. Although parents generally still frown on cross-cultural marriages (particularly in areas outside city centers), they are generally more willing to bend the rules if their prospective son-in-law or even daughter-in-law is Caucasian. *Kokusai-kekkon*, or international marriage, has therefore become almost as fashionable as *kokusaika* itself.

The Western male who is new to Japan, not realizing the source of his overwhelming popularity, is likely to obtain an exaggerated view of his importance from all the unexpected attention he is given by young Japanese women. He may even become so elated that he itches to spread the word back home about his incredible experiences. The *Madame Butterfly* myth has thus come full circle.

The Changing Butterfly

As mentioned earlier, young Japanese women today are strikingly far from yesterday's stereotypes. Rather than the victimized, exploited, and suppressed Oriental woman—an image that many Western journalists and scholars are slow to part with in their observations of Japan—quite a few of them have grown to become, as noted by Sumiko Iwao, professor of psychology at Keio University in Tokyo, "women who are aggressive, desire gratification of their own, know their minds, and can express themselves clearly."[12]

Unlike their grandmothers and mothers, who experienced war and poverty, the generation of daughters born after 1956 (the year Japan announced its emergence from the moribund state of the postwar period and began to recover its self-confidence) generally have been brought up in affluence and spoiled by a lack of sibling rivalry. Furthermore, being better educated, they no longer believe in suppressing their own desires and definitely do not wish to follow in their mothers' footsteps in their relationships with men. Not only has their higher education made them increasingly more difficult to exploit, they are in fact, in Iwao's words, "waging a quiet revolution against their own men." The labor shortage of the late 1980s and the Equal Employment Opportunity Law enacted in 1986 have also worked greatly in their favor, boosting their status to a new high (although some of the effect was subsequently blunted in the early nineties by Japan's economic slow-down).

What's more, as some critics have pointed out, a certain sub-group of young Japanese women have gained attention within Japan for their aggressive sexual pursuit of white, black, and other non-Japanese males. Dubbed "yellow cabs," these young women maintain an aggressive kind of sexual behavior which, as one American critic describes it,"defies standard Orientalist understanding." (See Chapter 3.) It looks as though the mainstream mass media in Western countries have yet to adopt a contrary interpretation to the age-old sterotype of a passive, self-sacrificing Japanese woman.

True, compared with their Western sisters, Japanese women may still appear to be overly meek and agreeable. But superficial appearances can be misleading. Some critics are quick to point out that disappointment abounds in cross-cultural relationships involving Japanese women and Western men, as they tend to be initiated by radically different assumptions and serious mutual misconceptions. The Japanese woman's soft-spoken manner and distaste for confrontation can easily mislead the unfamiliar Western male into assuming that she will make a more dutiful and obliging wife than most Western women. A businessman from Ohio told me that when he married his Japanese wife he had expected her to be less materialistic yet more compromising than American women. "Not only was she as materialistic as can be, she was also unbendable like steel," he said.

After fourteen years of marriage, he finally divorced his wife. He said he came to the realization that all the Madame Butterfly stuff was just on the surface. "Once you are married, everything is different. It becomes *kakādenka* (a family where the husband is henpecked)," he added.

Indeed, today's Japanese women are far from many of the existing Western images. In fact, the traditional Japanese woman has undergone great changes and has evolved to become, to cite Iwao, "one of several breeds of women in a society that is growing increasingly pluralistic." Those Westerners who are unwilling to take a closer look at these changes will undoubtedly fall into the same trap as did the Ohio businessman.

 CHAPTER TWO

The Modern Japanese Woman

In the late 1970s, when I first came to Japan to study, young Japanese women who worked as OLs, or "office ladies" (women who do clerical office work), brought tea to their bosses and co-workers as a matter of course. They were still called "office flowers" and, as the stereotype has it, they giggled at every comment with their hands modestly covering their mouths. In those days, equal opportunity was not sought after and sexual harassment lawsuits were unheard of. Aspiring to be a "good wife and wise mother," young women were more interested in attracting suitors and marrying than in pursuing a career or cultivating their own interests in life.

One summer day in 1977, a young American man who was studying at the same Japanese language school in Osaka as I joined a few fellow foreign students for a leisurely lunch break at a nearby park. A couple of young women from an adjacent women's college came along. Without having been asked, they brought jars of cold water wrapped carefully in handkerchiefs which they offered to refresh my school friend and the other male students. "See, only Japanese women are thoughtful enough to do a thing like this. Japanese men are so lucky," my friend marveled. Indeed, in those days, a Japanese man had his pick of a crop of doting women. Since the mid-1980s, however, the tide has turned. As we shall see in this chapter, it is now the men who must woo and win the Japanese woman of their choice.

Although many Western critics still believe them to be "shamefully exploited and suppressed by their menfolk,"[1] local newspapers and magazines catering to male readers have been pumping out stories warning about how "strong and unmanageable" Japanese women have become. Young working women, they say, are spearheading a revolution in work habits and are waging a rebellion at home by postponing marriage, initiating divorces, balking at having babies, and fighting in court to keep their maiden names.

Today, nearly 40 percent of Japanese women remain unmarried at the age of twenty-nine. The divorce rate, though low by U.S. standards, is more than four times the Japanese rate of the 1950s, and over half of all divorces are attributed to the woman's initiative. Perhaps the most disturbing evidence of the rebelling woman is Japan's dwindling birthrate, which in 1993 dropped to its lowest point ever—1.46 births per woman, on average.

Marriage and motherhood, once their raison d'être, is now only one of several options open to women. If Megumi Kawashima, thirty-two, had been born ten years earlier, she would most likely be a mother with at least one child. But today, the freelance interpreter and researcher remains single, traveling around the world whenever time and money allow. "Marriage? I haven't really thought about it," she says casually.

Her attitude, though still somewhat rare, is becoming more and more common these days among single women. Several recent social and economic changes are thought to be responsible, including: 1) an increase in the number of women with higher education, which makes them less tolerant of traditional marriage arrangements; 2) the growing economic independence of today's women, which has been encouraged by a persistent labor crunch in the late eighties and a recent change in employment laws; 3) improved job opportunities for women due to a rapid growth in the information, new businesses, and service-oriented markets which have an increasing need to use women's insights and skills for specific consumer demands; 4) the fact that many working women continue to live with their parents, enjoying a pampered, sheltered home life; and 5) a surplus of men between the ages of twenty-six and thirty-four, all of which have brought the turnabout that has seen women move from the chosen to the choosers in the marriage market.

Impact of Higher Education

Of the many forces operating behind the changes in Japanese society today, the impact of higher education on Japanese women is of particular importance. Since the 1960s, the number of women enrolling in junior colleges has quadrupled while the enrollment of women in universities has tripled. According to the Ministry of Education, only 3 percent of all female high-school students went on to junior college in 1960. By 1993, that percentage had jumped eight times to 24.4 percent. Similarly, in 1960, only 2.5 percent advanced to four-year universities. By 1993, this figure had soared seven times to 19 percent. What's more, in the same year the number of female high school students going on to junior colleges or universities surpassed that of male students for the first time since 1990.[2] The college advancement figures of women are some of the highest in the world. During these relatively prosperous times, when parents have fewer children and can afford to educate all of them, the trend toward higher education for women is likely to continue.

Higher education for women, once employed to assure the right credentials for marriage into a good family, is now having an unintended opposite effect—it is highly supportive of change in women's roles. Women are learning that not only should they be given equal opportunity as men, but their increasing involvement in their studies is leading them to new expectations. This means that they are less willing to accept traditional marriage arrangements that would restrict their freedom and interests outside of marriage. Armed with the knowledge that they can support themselves with the degrees and skills they acquire from a university education, they are more prepared to choose to stay single.

Growing Economic Independence

The mass media often refer to the 1980s as "the Era of Women." It was in this decade that Japanese women made the greatest strides toward job equality. Until 1986, most Japanese women were deprived of a chance to demonstrate their abilities as capable working members of society in traditionally male-oriented jobs. As recently as the mideighties, seventy to eighty percent of all Japanese companies refused to hire female graduates of four-year universities as full-time employees. Regarded as part-time or temporary workers, women worked mostly as tea servers and office helpers, receiving only forty-five percent of the average male salary. Women also had little hope of advancing into more important positions since the *sōgōshoku*, or managerial track positions, were reserved for full-time male employees. Until recently, it was not uncommon for companies to ask their female employees to sign an agreement to retire upon marriage or when they attained thirty years of age.[3]

What paved the way toward broadening the employment market for women in Japan was the International Women's Year of 1975 and the United Nations declaration of 1976–85 as the UN Decade for Women. Responding to pressure from activist groups and the need to boost its international image by ratifying the UN's Convention on the Elimination of All Forms of Discrimination against Women, the Japanese government committed itself to taking a token step toward providing equal employment opportunities for women by 1985. In April of 1986, the government passed the Equal Employment Opportunity Bill (EEO), which basically enjoined corporate Japan to attempt to provide women with equal chances for training and promotion.

Coupled with the passage of this bill was the problem of a worsening labor shortage heightened by the economic boom of the late 1980s, a declining birthrate, and the graying of the population. A Labor Ministry survey of 15,000 companies in 1989 found that there were about 130 available jobs for each 100 job applicants. The government was suddenly thrown into a panic about not having sufficient labor to shoulder the welfare and pension burdens for the years to come. This resulted in a dramatic expansion in employment opportunities for women, more of whom were placed in *sōgōshoku* positions. Consequently, the number of working women has doubled over the past twenty years, most especially over the last decade. According to Management Coordination Agency figures, in 1993 the total working population was 64.5 million, of which women accounted for 26.1 million, or 40.5 percent of the total.[4]

At the peak of the bubble economy in 1989, companies had to fight to hire fresh female college graduates. They were lured by promises of longer vacation time and better benefits. In 1989, Asahi Breweries received a lot of coverage when they announced that they planned to hire five hundred female sales managers over the following three years. Meanwhile, fifteen of Japan's biggest electronics companies, including Hitachi, NEC, and Matsushita, decided to offer one year of maternity leave along with social security and health benefits.[5] These benefits, however, are no longer considered special today as a new law that became effective in April 1992 requires all businesses to offer child-care leave to working mothers. Women have thus gained more on-the-job protection and privileges over the years.

Along with the urgency to employ more women as full-time workers came a boom in new job-hopping and flex-time-oriented magazines resulting from the new bubble-economy prosperity. Magazines such as *Salida, Torabayu,* and *Arubaito Nyusu* targeted young college graduates of both sexes who preferred jobs with shorter working hours and less responsibility. They were full of alluring ads promising: "Meet your friend at Hachiko (a favorite meeting place in Shibuya, Tokyo) at 5:30 sharp," and "We offer 123 days off out of 365." According to Toyoji Yamawaki, managing director of the Association of Job Journals of Japan, there were nineteen such help-wanted magazines in 1988 carrying a total of 1.2 million ads. The number of magazines and ads grew steadily, peaking in 1990 with thirty-six magazines carrying 2.5 million ads.[6]

In the late eighties, many of my Japanese girlfriends

aspired to become *furiitazu* (temporary workers who work whenever they like by registering with different short-term job agencies) instead of working full time for a company. In those days, they could pretty much name their jobs.

Capitalizing on the Consumer Age

Although Japan's booming economy in the eighties gave rise to new employment opportunities for Japanese women, the situation in the traditional job market quickly began to reverse as Japan entered the worst recession since World War II. Fortunately for them, the trend toward service-oriented jobs and a knowledge-and-information based society is providing some of the more talented women with new employment niches in the harder times.

1. Effects of the Economic Slump

As the job market tightened in the face of the recession which began in 1990, the labor crunch came to an abrupt end. In their enthusiasm to cut manpower, many companies reverted to their old, discriminatory practices, despite the EEO law. (Although the law states that companies must open jobs to both sexes, there are no penalties for violations.) In the massive hiring freezes that followed, women who were entering the job market for the first time were the hardest hit. According to Recruit Research Co., in 1993 a male college graduate had twice as good a chance to be placed in a job as his female counterpart.[7] Another Recruit survey of 1,292 companies in 1993 found that roughly one out of every two companies planned to employ fewer women in 1994 than the year before, or to employ no women at all.[8]

The survey also found that women and older workers

were the first to be dismissed or pressured to retire. One forty-nine-year-old woman was forced to quit her job when her company moved her from a clerical job to heavy manual labor at its factory. Her letter to the *Asahi Shimbun* is particularly revealing of the bitterness many women feel when confronted with job discrimination:

> During the good economic times, they said they were making use of women-power, but when there is a recession, women are fired first. In a small company like the one in which I was working, equal opportunities for men and women are two different worlds. The gap in wages and promotions still has not been corrected.[9]

Perhaps the real difficulties in the so-called "Ice Age" of employment are faced by those women without any particular outstanding characteristics or skills who might have succeeded in more favorable times. But in the prolonged recession, many of the traditional "pink collar" jobs (low-level clerical work for women) are fast disappearing.

Many capable women, however, manage to survive the hard times by making use of their intelligence and hard work. Many more are also quick to realize that they can rely on their feminine sensitivity to cash in on the booming new businesses targeted specifically at young female consumers. Talented young working women discover that while they may be spinning their wheels in the conservative, male-dominated business world, they do have a competitive edge over men in trades that set their sights on the women's market. Takie Lebra, in a study of successful professional women, found that many women manage to succeed by carving out new niches. As one of her interviewees puts it, "From now on it will be the female perspective that opens up new fields of business, because the male perspective has already been exhausted."[10]

2. *The Feminine Perspective as a New Resource*

The working woman is a newly discovered market within Japan's economy. The forty-odd percent of women who currently hold jobs are creating new needs and bringing ever-greater purchasing power to the consumer industry.

In the midst of the Japanese economic boom, many business segments discovered that OLs, with their large disposable incomes, were the forerunning trendsetters and the largest group of spenders among all consumers. According to a 1990 survey conducted by Dentsu Inc., a leading Japanese advertising company, OLs "injected nearly $56.2 billion into the fashion industry, $18.7 billion into the travel industry, and $13 billion into the publishing industry."[11]

During the last decade, working women and housewives were also responsible for turning culture centers (for traditional arts such as flower arrangement and Japanese dance) and language schools into big businesses. According to a 1990 *Newsweek* article, culture centers across the nation raked in at least 30 billion yen a year (about $300 million).[12] Similarly, the English-language school market was estimated at $22.6 million a year at its peak during the early 1990s.[13]

To keep pace with the demands of the burgeoning women's market, some manufacturers have chosen to pick the brains of special all-female project teams. One such team, at Otsuka Pharmaceutical Co., devoted a full year to developing a high-fiber drink called Fibe-Mini that was an immediate hit with young women. Another all-woman team at Matsushita Electric helped create a line of TV sets, cordless irons, and other appliances that emphasize chic design for young single women between eighteen and twenty-two. Tadashi Saito, the editor-in-chief of *Crea*, a women's magazine featuring articles on politics, economics, and other hard-news subjects, said he met with three hundred working women to develop the magazine's concept.[14]

3. *Bilingual Ability for Bridging Cultural Boundaries*

Lebra also pointed out that foreign language skills are one of the most powerful resources Japanese women found they have over men when competing in the male world. By mobilizing linguistic and other communicative skills, many women are finding their niches in areas that help "bridge cultural boundaries."[15]

In fact, according to a Teikoku Databank survey, in the face of the recession-based discrimination in hiring, there is an increasing trend for women to start their own businesses. By the end of 1992, more than one in twenty Japanese companies were being headed by either a woman president or owner.[16] Among these owners was Yoko Seya, a former stewardess turned businesswoman. Seya started Office Y's three years ago to provide corporate training and consulting services to companies both in Japan and abroad.

Likewise, Unical International Inc., a multimillion-dollar communications business providing data and linguistic services in sixty foreign languages, was started by Kaori Sasaki , a former freelance broadcast journalist and interpreter.

According to Sasaki, although the recession has had an impact on certain areas of her business, the workload of the one thousand registered interpreters and translators at Unical International remains unchanged. In fact, she says that her top-notch interpreters have gained more job assignments than before the economic slump as companies that spend money on language services now tend to be more selective and want the best value for their money.

Other women are finding their niches during the recession by switching from interpreting and translating to research work. According to Sasaki, the recession has produced the biggest research boom in history as companies, in their attempt to survive the fierce competition, need to find out what other companies are doing. This was how Megumi, the freelance interpreter and researcher mentioned earlier in the chapter, was able to survive the recession. Although blocked from the typical male paths to success through steady promotions at a traditional Japanese company, she has managed, like many other women, to "convert a misfortune into a blessing" (*wazawai o tenjite fuku to nasu*) by cashing in on her linguistic skills and creative ability.

Family Support for the Working Woman

If everyday working women are discriminated against through lower salaries, lack of housing allowances, and the denial of other such benefits,[17] then most manage to survive the situation by staying home with Mom and Dad. As statistics show, although more and more single Japanese women are working, the majority continue to live with and be supported by their parents. A *Mainichi Shimbun* survey in 1990 found that only one out of five single women was financially independent from her parents.[18] Meanwhile, a 1994 *Mainichi Daily News* article revealed that 70 percent of single women continued to live with their parents.[19]

One factor that contributes to this home-support phenomenon is the high-rent situation in major cities, particularly in the Tokyo area. Another reason is the tradition that encourages single daughters to continue to live with their parents until they marry. Many big companies are said to prefer to hire women who live at home, because employers can pay them a considerably lower salary. Added to this is the fact that the older generation still consists largely of full-time mothers who feel obliged to tend to the needs of their husbands and children. With fewer children, family funds are more generously available to these stay-at-home daughters.

Most home-dependent singles seem happy with the arrangement because they pay only a token rent or none at all, and are not required to contribute much toward living expenses. One survey conducted by Dai-ichi Kangyo Bank in 1994 found that single women who stay with their parents saved at least $500 a month on food and rent alone. Given that as of the early nineties, an average OL makes anywhere between $1,600 and $2,100 a month, depending on her age (25–30) and job specialty, women who live with their parents also have $7,000 to $12,000 more in total savings per year than those who live by themselves.[20] This means that home-dependent women have a lot of disposable income they could not otherwise enjoy. Best of all, many don't even have to do much to help out with the household chores.

"Yes, my mother sometimes irons my clothes for me and will do my laundry when I am busy," admits Motoko, a thirty-year-old secretary working for a foreign liquor importer. She says that when she finishes work and returns home, she is greeted with a hot meal on the table.

This pampered lifestyle has created a new breed of comfort-seeking young women, often called *dokushin ki-zoku*, or "single aristocrats" by the mass media, who look only toward perpetuating their leisurely and opulent lifestyles.

Too Many Men

Adding to the marriage bargaining power of single Japanese women is the general belief that young, single Japanese men outnumber single Japanese women quite significantly. In 1990, for example, one estimate has it that the number of young single men exceeded that of women by about 350,000.[21]

This is particularly true when the population of men between the ages of 23 and 35 is put alongside that of women between the ages of 20 and 32. The argument for this seemingly odd comparison of the two groups is that Japanese men on the average tend to marry women three years younger than they are.

Although some critics argue that this gap in demographics will eventually balance itself out,[22] they don't doubt the fact that Japanese men will continue to have a hard time convincing Japanese women to marry them. Sociologist Chizuko Ueno pointed out in a lecture sponsored by a youth marriage counseling center in Tokyo that "As long as women can support themselves, they will continue to choose only the most eligible men as partners. What this means is that women will start crowding over a few very eligible bachelors and totally ignore the other, less attractive men," she explained. "Competition for marriage partners among men will therefore become keener, and the losers of the game will be left to themselves," she added.

In short, Japanese women's hard-won economic independence brought on by a higher level of education and an improved working status, as well as their pampered, home-support lifestyle compounded by a surplus of available men, is rapidly changing their overall view on life, relationships, and marriage. There are a lot more options available to Japanese women now, and many are more prepared to stay single if they do not find an appropriate suitor.

In the past, when jobs for women were limited, marriage was the only way for them to survive. No matter how unwilling, daughters were often driven to the altar to ease their parents' financial burden. "In that sense, marriage was not a choice available to women, but a necessity," says Yoriko Madoka, a specialist researching modern family problems and an organizer of the *Niko-niko rikon kōza* (Divorce with a Smile) course, designed to promote a better understanding of divorce.[23] Many women in those days had no choice and learned to accept married life as their destiny. Two decades ago, most women still proudly wore their aprons to market as the badge of their marital status, aspired to *san shoku hirune tsuki* (three meals a day and a midday nap) and willingly referred to their husbands as *shujin*, or master. These days married women are more likely to refer to their husbands behind their backs as *otto* (my husband) or simply by their first names.

Widening of the Marriage Perception Gap

As recently as ten years ago, women were still abiding by an unwritten rule to marry by the age of twenty-five lest they be labeled "Christmas cake"—too old for the market on the twenty-sixth. These days, more and more women are opting to hold out until *ōmisoka* (New Year's Eve), or by age 31.[24] Ministry of Health and Welfare figures show that this trend is increasingly popular among young women now. While in 1970, for example, only 18.1 percent of all women in their late twenties were single, by 1990 that figure had risen to 40.2 percent among the same age group.[25] Meanwhile, according to international statistics and governmental figures, Japanese women marry at an older age than their counterparts in the United Kingdom and the United States.[26]

Single Japanese women are well aware that despite the fact that more women are participating in the work force, most men continue to view housework and the raising of children as being strictly a woman's responsibility. A 1989 survey conducted on single men by Altmann Co., Ltd., a large computer-dating service based in Shinjuku, found that only 31.5 percent believed that they should help with the housework after marriage.[27] Another survey found that while Japanese working women do about three hours of housework daily, their husbands pitch in a mere eight minutes a day.[28] As the couple's parents grow older, it is the wife who is expected to care for both his and her parents. "Because men have not caught up with the changing times, most husbands are still leaving the household chores to their working wives. Married life for the working woman, in many ways, has become a three-tiered burden of work, child care, and housework," says Yoko Itamoto, director of the Nihon Seinenkan Kekkon Sodanjo, a youth marriage counseling center that also runs a special workshop to raise men's awareness.

Once married, neither can women look forward to romance. Because most Japanese men tend to work an average of fourteen hours a day (including commuting time), by the time they return home all they want to do is to take a bath and go to sleep. According to Itamoto, when it comes to marriage, most men still expect to find a housekeeper. True, some younger men are struggling to change with the times, but they are limited by their social environment, so the changes that they are making often come too late (see Chapter 7).

Added to this is the factor that a traditional Japanese

marriage was a business partnership between two families, so the concepts of love marriages and romance after marriage are new and have no role model to follow.

The hard facts of reality have destroyed any dreams single women might have had about marriage. No wonder many young Japanese women are trying to escape from their expected role of marriage for as long as they can. In October 1990, Dai-ichi Kangyo Bank surveyed 500 employed Tokyo women between the ages of twenty and twenty-nine. When asked to choose three things they were most interested in, 47 percent cited traveling and 38 percent mentioned hobbies and sports. Marriage came in third, named by only 33 percent of the respondents.[29] When asked to describe marriage through a variety of words and phrases provided in the questionnaire, many respondents used the terms "reality," "hardship," and "graveyard of life." The bank's conclusion was that although marriage is still a focus of interest, it is no longer the first priority. Women today who view commitment to marriage as something leading to "restrictions" and "an end to youth" are more concerned with immediate gratification and leisure time for themselves.

Life as "Single Aristocrats"

Today's young males and females were raised in the bosom of the nuclear family when Japan's economic growth was roaring along in high gear between the years of the late 1950s and the "oil shock" days of the early 1970s. This sheltered generation has been showered with material wealth and excessive parental attention since birth. As singles, however, today's Japanese women have a definite advantage over their male counterparts in one important aspect—they have both the wealth and the free time to indulge themselves in consumerism to the fullest. As psychologist Sumiko Iwao observes, "The position of Japanese women outside the mainstream of society . . . has exempted them from having to fit into the frameworks set down by [corporations] and has allowed them the margin of freedom to explore their individuality in ways not permitted to men."[30]

Armed with a large disposable income and lots of free time on hand, many single women aspire to the flashy lifestyle of the shopping-crazed, gourmet-dining, travel-happy *Hanako*-zoku, or *Hanako* clan, which became a hot mass media topic in 1989. The name was derived from a Tokyo town magazine that was extremely popular with single women for its reports on fancy restaurants, exotic tourist resorts, high fashion, and luxurious goods. So popular was the magazine that many new women's magazines followed its lead to cash in on the OL consumerism phenomenon, thus creating a solid OL subculture that has become the envy of many salarymen.

Motoko, the thirty-year-old secretary mentioned earlier in this chapter, is one example of today's new women who are taking full advantage of their single status. A typical OL living with her parents and a younger sister, Motoko makes about $2,400 a month. Except for contributing $400 a month toward food expenses, the rest of her income is her own. Out of this, Motoko says she spends roughly $300 to $500 a month on clothes and other expenses. Eating out is also a favorite pastime. Although her mother would be willing to make dinner for her every night, she says she still ends up going out for dinner and drinks with friends at least twice a week. Her monthly expenses for dining out come to about $300.

On weekends she likes to join friends for an occasional visit to a karaoke room to sing away the week's frustrations and fatigue. She also manages to save for bigger things, too, like an occasional trip abroad, a Spanish language course, and a personal computer. Motoko says she takes an overseas trip about once or twice a year, spending between $1,500 and $2,500 each time. Three years ago she went to Guam and last year she went to Arizona. For the upcoming New Year's holiday, she was thinking of visiting Australia, a popular destination for both young Japanese singles and honeymooners.

Not all single women live with their parents and maintain such extravagant lifestyles. For example, Megumi, the thirty-two-year-old freelance interpreter, lives by herself and pays her own bills. Given her language ability and the availability of communication-related part-time work, however, she also manages to lead a fairly carefree and independent lifestyle.

During the boom years, Megumi made between $2,500 and $3,500 a month, depending on her workload. Since the burst of the bubble economy in 1990, she has been making a little less than $2,500 a month, doing freelance research and translation assignments. One saving grace is that she doesn't have to pay rent because her mother helped her purchase a condominium. Megumi spends about $1,200 a month on food and transportation. She spends very little on clothes, but she does like to spend an occasional night out with friends. Thanks to her savings, Megumi says she has no problems making ends meet .

Megumi prefers to save most of her money for taking extensive trips abroad. During the good years, she managed this easily by working intensively for two or three years, then taking off on month-long trips. Five years ago, Megumi spent $7,000 on a two-year trip around Europe, Africa, and Israel. Demonstrating the outer limits of today's more self-motivated woman, she says, "I worked as an occasional interpreter along the way, camping out and hitchhiking a lot like most Europeans do."

Changing View of Marriage and Relationships

The carefree, leisurely lifestyles of young singles such as Motoko and Megumi are making women think more carefully about marriage. What concerns them most is whether they can continue their current standard of living and lifestyle. "If I got married, I certainly would not want my living standard to fall short of what I have now," says Motoko. These kinds of worries make them highly selective about potential marriage partners. Already Motoko has been through two *omiai* (arranged meetings for potential couples with marriage in mind). She turned both of them down.

When marriage is a luxury, women can afford to be picky. Now they say "unless I find someone nice, I am not going to hurry," says Katsuko Suzuki, a spokeswoman for Altmann Co., Ltd. This company, which researches young singles, found that young women's demands for a marriage partner were getting higher and higher. And what do young women look for in a husband these days? Suzuki says most are looking for a man with *sankō*, or the "three highs": high salary (seven million yen or more a year), high education (graduate of a name-value university, preferably Waseda, Keio, or Tokyo), and a height of not less than 178 centimeters, or 5 feet 10 inches. True, as some social critics have pointed out, the significance of the "three highs" has been exaggerated by the mass media; however, their wide and instantaneous acceptance does suggest that they have struck a common chord in many of today's women. The importance of the trend is that, in the marriage market, it is women who do the picking, not the men.

Many single women, especially those between the prime ages of twenty and twenty-five, seek to take advantage of this role reversal. As long as they are young and pretty, they know they can get away with it. Japanese corporations, after all, still see marriage as being a stabilizing factor for their male employees, and as they do not usually promote single men, this has put many men in a bind. To try to woo a wife, single men will go to great lengths to please, sometimes spending the equivalent of hundreds of dollars on a single date.

Some women with multiple suitors assign purpose-specific roles to their men. The "Treat Boy" (*messhii-kun*) for example, will take her to fancy restaurants, while her "Gift Boy" (*mitsugu-kun*) will buy her presents, and her "Driver Boy" (*asshii-kun*) will chauffeur her around town. She will give these men the run-around until Mr. Right (*honmei-kun*) comes along.

This calculating, manipulative attitude is encouraged by young women's magazines. In the February 1990 issue of *Caz*, a magazine catering to young single women, an article titled "The Age of Men Being Utilized According to Their Worth" coached readers to court men for their own benefit. So strong is this trend that many men feel obligated to buy expensive gifts to win the hearts of their girlfriends. The *Asahi Shimbun* report that many young men were lining up outside Mitsukoshi Department Store to buy pricey "open-heart" Tiffany necklaces for their girlfriends for Christmas, therefore, came as no surprise.[31] Prices for the necklaces ranged up to $2,500. According to the same report, some of these men demanded rain checks as proof to their girlfriends when salesclerks announced that stocks had run out. [32]

Since the burst of the bubble economy, however, many young men have had to slow down on their extravagant spending in their pursuit of a matrimonial partner. But the sight of these men carefully carrying the handbags of girlfriends on subway trains and on the street is still very common. To be sure, in the leaner years of Japan's economic downturn, competition in the dating game will become even keener for many of them.

Marriage: The Final Escape

Despite their new freedom, most single women have only delayed marriage rather than ruled it out. As much as they like to think that marriage is no longer the focal point of their lives, it continues to be an esteemed goal reinforced by family and society. True, over the last two decades, as I have mentioned, there has been a dramatic rise in the number of single women in their late twenties. However, the number of single women between the ages of thirty and thirty-four has increased more slowly, from 7.2 percent in 1970 to 13 percent in 1990. This indicates that although society is more accepting of women who marry later in life, this acceptance is limited to women of up to about age thirty. This explains in part why many free-floating single women after thirty are less choosy about their marriage partners and more enthusiastic about arranged marriages. Another reason is that although women are having fewer children, childlessness is still frowned upon. The young women's challenge to Japanese gender roles thus does not entail a total rejection of marriage, as they realize that the leisure and wealth they enjoy as OLs is still well within the boundaries set by Japanese society.

There is yet another important reason for the marriage option—it provides a final escape from the hardships of the working world. Given the pressures of work, many career-track women have grown tired of working as front-line pioneers in the work force, fighting shoulder-to-shoulder with their male counterparts as "corporate warriors," and are actively seeking a way out through marriage. Since the introduction of the EEO Law in 1985, the first batch of *sōgōshoku* career-track women are finally waking up to the hard reality that their working under similar conditions to those of their male colleagues means putting in at least sixty to seventy hours a week, risking *karōshi*, or death from overwork, and having very little social life. Worse yet, the equality under the EEO law is in name only—it is not enforceable. In reality, there remains a disparity in salary and promotion opportunities between full-time male and female employees. According to a 1990 survey on wages by the Labor Ministry, most full-time women workers were earning only 60.2 percent of what men were making, and only 57.1 percent when overtime was included.[33] Also, in to a report on the effectiveness of the EEO Law, most management-bound women say their male superiors are prejudiced against women and do not make enough use of their abilities.[34] Life as a career woman, many soon find out, is not as rosy as it once seemed.

The emergence on the office scene of *oyaji-gyaru*, women who not only act and talk like middle-aged men who barely have time to slurp down a bowl of noodles at their desks during lunch breaks and have to gulp down fortified health drinks, is telling. The fact that they also have to visit acupuncture parlors and treat their stiff shoulders with medicated plasters to keep up with their work is clear evidence of how burned-out and frustrated some career women have become. Before it is too late, and they are confined in their forties and fifties to barren, dead-end jobs under the "glass ceiling" of gender discrimination, many are opting to retreat into married life.

A woman who was hired for a career-track position by a major bank in 1987 found herself suffering from thyroid, stomach, and intestinal problems. Just like her male counterparts, her typical day started at 7:00 A.M. and rarely ended before 11:00 P.M. After only three years, she decided to quit, and got married.

Another woman, after working five years in the planning section of a major car manufacturer, willingly stepped down from her career-track position to take an OL position in the personnel department of the same company. "I invested $5,000 in a computer course for a better chance to advance in my career, but I am too tired for that now," she says. The thirty-three-year-old woman admits to turning her energies to finding a good husband through an arranged marriage.

Younger women, watching their predecessors on the career path, are wising up about how they want to pursue their lives, and many are asserting their freedom to the limits while they can. Says Mari, a twenty-two-year-old university student, "I am not going to worry about becoming a career woman—the price is too high to pay. I would rather settle for having fun." Mari, who says she finds Japanese society oppressive, is planning an extensive tour through Europe after graduation. "I think I'll take up Spanish or something," she says, her eyes opening wide. She can afford to, as her parents are behind her and have promised to help out with her expenses. She says that when she returns, she will join an elite company to look for an eligible bachelor. She winks as she fluffs her long, permed hair, and jokingly says her dream is to find a match who is "part career man, part house-husband," i.e., one who makes good money at work and is also good at doing things around the house.

Not many are as lucky as Mari. Still, they are finding ways to escape, for as long as possible, what they find to be an oppressive social environment. A few do this by vacationing at foreign resorts, and some also engage in sexual adventures with local bartenders and beach boys. In the past, it was the Japanese businessmen who traveled in groups to Thailand, the Philippines, and other Asian locations for sex. The tables have certainly turned.

The travel-for-sex phenomenon was captured in Shoko Ieda's *Yellow Cab* (1991) and subsequent best-sellers which spurred numerous magazine articles and even TV programs, giving rise to what some critics call the "Yellow Cab hysteria." One factor that contributed to the travel-for-sex phenomenon, as mentioned in the upcoming chapter, is the desire of some young Japanese women to assert their power and freedom, which they cannot do to any such extent in their own territory. On a deeper level, it is also suggested that some have an unspoken agenda of wanting to rebel against the prevailing Japanese gender hierarchies at home through an active engagement with foreign lands and relationships.

 CHAPTER THREE

The Easy Sex Syndrome

They leave Japan loaded with cash with only one purpose in mind—to have steamy, everything-goes sexual encounters with foreign men. They lavish gifts of cash, jewelry and expensive clothing on foreign lovers who strike their fancy. The preferred destination for these women is New York City where they can revel in the drug culture of certain Manhattan after-hours clubs. They show a distinct preference for black men—the less like Japanese men, the better. Many of these women have paid the price for their sexual adventures, having become carriers of the deadly HIV virus. [1]

These women may not sound like your average OLs who travel overseas to study and work, but they are quickly becoming a stereotype for the vast number of women who journey to foreign destinations every year. Although the stereotype was initially circulated among the Japanese media, mostly in magazine stories, it eventually spread outside of Japan and caught the attention of some overseas publications, including the U.S.-based *Transpacific.*

The stereotype had been in the making since 1987, but was further boosted by author Shoko Ieda's best-selling *Yellow Cab*, published in 1991.[2] The title and nickname for these women, "yellow cabs," was taken from the name of the taxi company in Manhattan. It implies that many Japanese women living overseas, in Ieda's words, "can be ridden anywhere, anytime."

Ieda supported her reports on the yellow cabs with a later book, *Genshoku no ai ni dakarete* (Resort Love), wherein women she calls "resort lovers" travel on short stays to Hawaii for the specific purpose of boy-hunting.[3] According to this book, of the 4,500 Japanese tourists who visit Hawaii daily, over fifty percent are Japanese women. Many of these women, Ieda asserts, actively hunt out or wait to be picked up by local foreign men at shopping malls, discos, bars, and on the beach.

The so-called "Yellow Cab phenomenon" soon became a popular subject on talk shows and TV documentaries which sparked frequent debate among readers of the local press.

Problems with the Yellow Cab Reports

There are a few problems with the yellow cab reports. First of all, the origin of the yellow cab term is questionable. In the book, Ieda suggests that it was originally used by African-American men referring to Japanese women they had numerous sexual encounters with. Yet this was found to be ungrounded. A New York-based group calling themselves the Iero Kyabu o Kangaeru Kai (Association to Think Over the Yellow Cab Issue) conducted a survey in Manhattan in 1993 to see how widely known this term was and, not so surprisingly found that none of the two-hundred Americans picked at random from the white pages had ever heard of the phrase used in reference to anything other than a taxi.

Another problem is Ieda's methodology. The nine women interviewed in the book, for example, have either taken up unorthodox relationships with African-Americans, been raped, had money conned out of them, or push or use drugs. These examples, as many critics have already pointed out, are extreme. Even Ieda herself admitted that such women constitute "less than ten percent" of the Japanese women in New York."[4]

What's more, many of the quotations given in Ieda's book, to cite a source in a 1993 news article, "have apparently [been] modified."[5] One New York–based Japanese counselor who was interviewed gave support to that obseveration when he said in the article that Japanese women in New York who get into trouble with drugs or sex are "about one in a hundred."

Japanese Male Reaction to the Yellow Cab Reports

Despite the problems with Ieda's reports on the yellow cab phenomenon, her accounts of her fellow countrywomen's wanton behavior were immediately accepted as evidence of a general trend among young women and reported as such by the male-dominated Japanese mass media, which eagerly sought to play up the phenomenon.

Accounts of the sexual adventures of these women, which were largely related back to Japan second- or third-hand by overseas journalists, were readily picked up by the Japanese media to fuel the hype. And where hard evidence was absent, they filled the gap with exaggeration and sensationalism. A July 1992 Asahi TV broadcast on the subject, for instance, was later found to be staged. A spokesman for the production company confessed as much when he later said they were forced to set up scenes because many of the people the company had contacted refused to appear in it.[6]

Before long, the term "yellow cab" was being used indiscriminately to describe any Japanese woman who had gone overseas for any length of time or been romantically involved with foreign men. The Japanese press and men's magazines were full of writers criticizing these women, whom they saw as being immoral. Meanwhile, the infamous sex tours of Japanese salarymen to Southeast Asia and Taiwan, widely practiced in the seventies and early eighties, went unmentioned. It is clear that a double standard was at work here.

Interestingly, the male response to this phenomenon dwelt exclusively with the women's promiscuity. To Japanese men, the only desirable attribute of the *gaijin* (i.e., Western) male imaginable for women is their insatiable sexual appetite, which has been emphasized in Japanese ideology. In the guise of analyses of the yellow cab phenomenon, male journalists repeat the same rhetoric. Their tone of voice runs the gamut from mockery to disdain, from scorn to pity. In the September 11, 1987, issue of *Shukan Hoseki*, for instance, there is a report on the sexual travels of OLs and college students overseas. The anonymous reporter writes:

> As summer vacation comes to an end, planeloads of OLs and female college students chat enthusiastically about their sizzling summer experiences during the flight home. Listening in, you'll hear them say they were with the pretty boys in Paris, the passionate local tour guides of Hawaii, and the black (sex) technicians of New York. "Well, I really feel like flying back overseas . . . " Thanks to them, the tem-

perature of Narita Airport goes up every time a plane-load of these girls returns from overseas.[7]

Similar features ran elsewhere. The August 1989 issue of *Shukan Gendai* featured a report on the extravagant "pre tend-study" trips abroad made by female Japanese students. In the July 1992 issue of *Shukan Shincho*, there was a "sex hunt" report on Japanese women traveling to Hawaii. To top off these reports, the June 1993 issue of *Hiragana Times* when it featured a story on how Japanese women pick up *gaijin* men domestically. The article was entitled "The 'Yellow Cab' Is True: Japanese Women Are Like Prostitutes."

As many critics have noted, the reaction of Japanese men to the phenomenon is way out of proportion, particularly considering that most of these reports are anonymous anecdotes related indirectly from overseas. The media showed more enthusiasm for investigating this issue than they have ever had for any of the country's countless political scandals.

The controversy led to the formation of the New-York–based Iero Kyabu o Kangaeru Kai. In an interview, the group told me what they found particularly objectionable was the suggestion that yellow cab behavior was typical of all expatriate Japanese women living in the U.S. They pointed out that in January 1993, two years after Ieda's book was published, a Japanese TV network (TBS) broadcast a ninety-minute documentary entitled "Yellow Cab." All five Japanese women interviewed in the program live in New York and they all have African-American boyfriends. Once again, sex, AIDS, drugs, and foreign boyfriends were the main themes.

To the New York group, this overreaction by the Japanese media suggested that the very term "yellow cab" may have been a Japanese invention. The group believed that the mass media, with the help of Ieda, wanted to use the criticism of supposed yellow cab women as a means to vilify and control their women.

The deliberate focus of Japanese mass media on women who date or marry African-American men, the group says, also carries another message—that these women are uneducated and inferior. And they add that Ieda, a self-promoter who was married to a black American serviceman, was conveniently manipulated by the Japanese media to be their legitimized mouthpiece to ostracize the Japanese women who dare to leave their native country and pursue a different and freer lifestyle overseas.

Japanese society, the group adds, expects Japanese women to marry Japanese men, raise their children, and support national prosperity. That's why the mass media finds fault with women who associate with foreign men, rejecting Japanese males and the traditional *ryōsai kenbo*—good wife, wise mother—ideology expected by society.

Yellow Cabs and Japan's Gender Battle

It is clear that the "yellow cab phenomenon" has been used to heat up a feud between Japanese men and women in the midst of what can be viewed as the most apparent gender debate we have witnessed in decades.

On the side of the men, led mostly by conservative male journalists, the yellow cab is the epitome of the Japanese woman who has taken her freedom too far. Perhaps that's why they play up the phenomenon: to justify their need to criticize and contain Japanese women in general.

On the side of the women, led mainly by the New York group, the criticism of yellow cab women by male journalists is evidence of the men's jealousy of the women's new-found liberation. The group's immediate response is thus to show that the yellow cab is a hyped, and largely fabricated, myth created by Japanese men.

The yellow cab phenomenon may not turn out to be what the media have been reporting, but evidence shows that there is a rise in the number of Japanese women consciously seeking foreign men for casual sexual encounters at resort sites—a trend that may not be limited to women from Japan but apply to those from other rising Asian nations as well.

In Hawaii, for example, several sources in 1993 confirmed that Japanese women were engaging in short-term sexual relationships with local foreign men on Waikiki beach and the men are just as likely to be white as black. Karen Kelsky, a Ph.D. candidate in anthropology at the University of Hawaii, who has done extensive research on the sexual encounters of Japanese women with Western men on Waikiki Beach, estimated that there were twenty to thirty beach boys there specializing in picking up these women.[8]

So conspicuous was their behavior in 1992, that Megumi Baba, a sex counselor at the Waikiki Health Center, felt compelled to start an STD/AIDS Japanese Outreach Program—a volunteer sexual counseling service in Japanese, to help educate Japanese tourists about the danger of sexually transmittable diseases and AIDS. According to Baba, the group has since been involved in giving away free condoms on the beach to visiting Japanese.

These women not only travel to New York and Hawaii for their sexual adventures, but have also been seen at other resort destinations such as Thailand and Bali. Word has gotten around, and local Balinese and Thai tour guides have quickly learned that they can make a living on the side as holiday lovers for female Japanese tourists.

This was confirmed by Thai researcher Dr. Sairudee Vorakitphokatorn's report at the tenth annual International Conference on AIDS held in Yokohama in August 1994. At the conference, she said that she had interviewed Thai beach boys at the popular southern Thailand resort of Phuket, seventy percent of whom claimed they had had sex with female Japanese tourists. What is alarming is that most said they rarely used condoms and were seldom asked to.[9]

Unfortunately, a large number of Japanese women, caught in their gender battle with Japanese males and fearing for more discrimination against women, reacted emotionally to Dr. Vorakitphokatorn's report, seeing it as support for the claim of a yellow cab problem. They fiercely protested the report and demanded an apology from the doctor. Their denial was both alarming and disconcerting.

As pointed out by the doctor, young Japanese women, when far from home and suddenly freed from supervision, are more likely to venture into friendships with local males. They are thus more vulnerable to the danger of HIV. What's more, Dr. Vorakiphokatorn said that since Japanese women are more protected at home they may be less observant of danger signs. They may also often find it difficult to refuse sexual overtures because of a lack of social skills. But unless Japanese openly address the existence of the problem of casual sex, Dr. Vorakiphokatorn warned, there is little hope of AIDS education being satisfactorily carried out in Japan.

The Implication

For the purposes of this book, the fact that these women exist is less significant than their minority "sub-culture" behavior, which seems to be connected with a larger pattern of social unrest among young Japanese women today. What, then, is the implication of yellow cab behavior? More importantly, what prompted the appearance of this travel-for-sex syndrome among young women and what factors led to its occurring now? Different critics interpret the phenomenon differently. To me, however, whatever the reasons, it is undoubtedly connected with Japan's new-found economic wealth.

1. Japanese Women's Rising Sense of Independence and Freedom

Some critics say that the easy-sex phenomenon indicates a rising sense of independence among young Japanese women today in the wake of Japanese economic success and greater freedom to travel.

"Now that they have more independence and money, they are looking for a little bit of excitement and danger," says Keiko Iigata, editor of *Mr. Partner*—a magazine noted for its sponsorship of international parties aimed at bringing foreign men and Japanese women together. Megumi Baba agrees and adds that the strong yen also gives Japanese women who travel overseas a sense of power and freedom through financial independence they do not experience at home.

Women I interviewed supported this claim. Atsuko, a kinky-permed OL who works at an event-planning company, admitted to having gone out with local tour guides when she was in Bali, saying that this was a way for her to "mingle and blend in" with the local people. Like many of her friends, when traveling, she looks for experiences that cannot be gained at home. "To me, this is the best way to expand my horizons," she said matter-of-factly.

Another OL I spoke with said that going out with *gaijin* men is in fashion. She pointed out that many of her girl-friends feel that having a foreign male on their arm while traveling in an exotic land is not much different from wearing Chanel perfume and carrying a Louis Vuitton bag. These days, young OLs like to travel to tropical areas such as Australia and Hawaii where it is much easier for them to act out their fantasy of falling passionately in love with a gorgeous man under the palm trees. "It's like fancying yourself a movie heroine." Women who fall for this kind of fantasy naturally want to seek out Richard Gere, Tom Cruise, and Keanu Reeves look-alikes to make their dreams as real as possible.

While it is true that this kind of fantasy about Hollywood stars is not unique to the Japanese, somehow, in Japan, the women's dreams are exaggerated by their obsession for name brands. In fact, many tend to treat their foreign boyfriends more like merchandise than as real people.

Another factor is that Japanese women are hungry for a romantic experience based on the Western ideal. Frustrated by the existing model of romance at home, they are easily enamored of the Hollywood versions of romance as well as the many sexy, attractive male stars featured in the roles of modern Don Juans.

2. *The Rebelling Japanese Woman*

There are indications, however, of other substantive reasons for the "yellow cab phenomenon." Some critics suggest that the willful flirtation of Japanese women with things foreign and with socially unacceptable behavior is their way to engage in an indirect discourse with Japanese men—they are expressing their frustration and dissatisfaction with the place assigned to females in Japanese society. As Karen Kelsky of the University of Hawaii suggests, by challenging masculine ideals of appropriate female behavior, they also seek to criticize "Japanese male norms of work, recreation, romance, and marriage."[10]

There is obviously some truth to Kelsky's suggestion. We don't have to look far to see that young Japanese women are doing their best to tease and annoy their male counterparts, while stretching Japanese notions of female sexuality to the limit. At home, Japanese women are causing a commotion by dancing on platforms while wearing skimpy outfits and gyrating in seductive movements at local discos and bars. Dressed in stretchy, body-hugging mini skirts or skin-tight bikini briefs that bare their legs, midriffs, and cleavage, they appear on TV shows to compete in "sexiness" contests. So prevalent was this trend among young teenage girls and OLs that Juliana's, a once-famous but now defunct disco in a warehouse district near Tokyo Bay, became a popular and fashionable stage on which these women, nicknamed *otachidai gyaru* (platform girls), performed.

By strutting their stuff on stage, women are allowed to display their frustration against the tight social roles expected of them. But it also serves another purpose—it's a statement of their wish to defy the expected norm: Japanese men prefer their wives and girlfriends to be cute rather than sexy. Therefore, baring their body in front of male onlookers is a challenge to male standards, a stamping of the feet and thrusting of the hips against prevailing mores.

Admittedly, by resorting to such subtle rebellions, Japanese women may appear passive to some Western critics, as they are unable to confront their society directly and demand change. One female journalist from the U.S., in fact, said these behaviors are nothing more than passive-aggressive acts of self-escapism.

3. *The Need for Self-expression*

Other critics, however, say it is dangerous to read too much into the social rebelliousness of younger Japanese women. Tamotsu Sengoku, director of the Japan Youth Research Institute and a social critic, believes most young women remain oblivious to their plight and are more interested in seeking immediate gratification. Rather than a conscious will to rebel against the society, the travel-for-sex behavior, much like the Juliana's boom, "is more directly connected with young women's longing for self-expression," says Sengoku. Many if not most of the Juliana's dancers, for instance, were not there because they were hoping to seduce a bedmate. For the most part, they more often returned home after midnight or slept over with girlfriends. Their behavior, therefore, was motivated more by a desire for attention, a wish to be seen as a "somebody," or a star. All the attention these women received provided them with quick jolts of self-esteem. It gave them the satisfaction of being different and exhibiting a measure of individuality.

Since the late seventies, when the Japanese started breaking away from the century-old mentality of *gaman*, or endurance, amid the rise of modern consumerism, young people—especially women—have been looking for various ways to express themselves. Forms of self-expression, noted Sengoku, have historically come and gone in the guise of short-lived trends. In the late seventies there were the Takenoko-zoku who roamed around Harajuku (a trendy area of Tokyo frequented by the chic young) in outlandish outfits and danced to loud street music. Then in the late eighties came the Epicurean, shop-till-you-drop *Hanako-zoku* (pg. 53).

Although Juliana's is now history, there are signs that a few discos in the Akasaka and Roppongi areas of Tokyo are quickly becoming the new hangouts for what are known as the *para-para* girls—young women in their late teens and early twenties dancing in unison in Japanese dance steps to the sound of fast-tempo Euro-beat. *Para-para* dancing is not a new invention: it dates back to the early eighties. During the Juliana's boom, however, it simply didn't gather the attention being paid to it now. Like fashion, Sengoku says, such fads no doubt will continue to drift in and out of the Tokyo scene in the years to come.

4. *The Quest for Better Sex*

Tamotsu Sengoku also noted that some women are even going beyond strip-tease flirtation to flaunt their personality. Many go as far as posing nude for popular magazines.

Nearly nude photos of provocatively posed young women are the stock in trade of a multitude of weekly news and sports magazines targeted at men, and have been for many years. However, since teen idol Rie Miyazawa shocked Japan by publishing *Santa Fe*, a book of nude photos, in 1991 when she was only nineteen, young women have learned that there is nothing wrong with flaunting a beautiful body. Later, when *An-An*, a well-established woman's fashion magazine solicited nude photos of readers for publication, more than a thousand young women responded. What's more, they began to speak with less inhibition about their own sexuality, making no attempt to hide from public view the kinds of suggestive sex scenes featured in women's magazines with titillating titles such as "Light Sex, Real Sex and Overly Real Sex," "The 100% Orgasm," and "Slimming with Sex."

This sort of article has become more popular since 1989, when *An-An* took the lead with its feature story, "Sex Makes You More Beautiful." Since then, *Crea, Clique,* and *Frau* have been trying to outdo each other with ever-more-provocative features. In these articles, they teach women bedroom techniques, how to make the most of sex, how to reach orgasm, and the appreciation of male nudity.

Why the sudden rush of sex-related articles in women's magazines? Editors say they have a lot to do with women's rising social status. With greater economic independence comes a greater say in sexual equality. After decades of repression, Japanese women are finally beginning to realize that sexual enjoyment is something they are entitled to and there really is nothing wrong with being direct about sex. In *Flash*, a weekly tabloid, one anonymous male writer made the following observation: "In the past, women were taught to wait for sex to be done to them. Now they are taught how to initiate it."[11]

All the talk about AIDS and safe sex, some observers say, has also helped make conversation about sex easier for women. "Yet no doubt the richer lifestyle of Japanese has also prompted many to look deeper for better quality of life. And having better sex and better body communication with one's partner have very much become a part of that quest," says Yuko Tanaka, an editor for Kawade Shobo Shinsha Publishing. The publisher put out in 1993 a sex therapy book under the title *Beautiful Love*, complete with soft-touched photos on how to better communicate through touching and love-making. Actually a translated version of Anne Hooper's *A Sex Therapist's Guide to Better Communication and Better Sex*, it became an instant best-seller.

But all the talk about sex is making Japanese men uncomfortable. No wonder the writer of the *Flash* article writes worriedly, "For today's Japanese women, sex has become a daily topic as common as wearing fancy clothes, eating at gourmet restaurants, and flying to exotic resorts."[12]

To be sure, women who assert their sexuality are intimidating to Japanese men because they usurp aspects of the masculine hierarchy in Japanese society and thus become a worrisome issue. This is precisely why the yellow cab phenomenon, the epitome of feminine deviation away from Japanese social norms, is to many Japanese men a threatening trend that must be contained.

Another reason why this overt sexuality is threatening some men is because today's young male may not be either physically or psychologically able to respond. An August 1994 editorial in the *Asahi Evening News* (translated from the *Asahi Shimbun*), reflecting on changing views of sex over the last fifty years, affirms the increasing awareness of women toward seeking sexual fulfillment. However, it says that along with this has come a disturbing new problem: impotence. Experts agree, according to the article, that Japanese men "have lost their vigor as males. Many patients suffering from impotence have strong maternal ties and receive little paternal influence,"[13] this being a result of their fathers' spending most of their lives and energy at work.

However true this may be, Japanese women can no longer be controlled as before. The riches of Japan have afforded them with the means to better their lives. With an airplane ticket in hand and an exchange rate in their favor, many women have found both short- and long-term escapes from Japanese men and from the suffocation imposed by a conformist society.

Amy Yamada and the "Gaijin-Men-Only" Japanese Women

Through their romantic involvement with *gaijin* men, many women also experience something they cannot find at home. In fact, this is precisely how author Amy Yamada (Yamada Eimi in Japanese) explained her attraction to black American men, although in her case, she sought out these men not in foreign destinations, but mainly at local U.S. military bases.

Yamada, an award-winning novelist who specializes in writing about black American men and their romances with Japanese women, made her debut in 1985 with *Bedtime Eyes*. The novel, which is about a bar singer's romance with a black military man nicknamed Spoon, shocked the literary world with its explicit depictions of sexuality. Yamada, who is married to a black American serviceman, is also credited as the first author to write about the military base scene and about the romances between Japanese women and black American GIs. She has since written over twenty novels, many of which are about African-American men's lives and based on her own encounters at the military bases.

In a March 1991 interview with *Tokyo Journal*, a Tokyo-based monthly magazine, Yamada is quoted as saying her attraction to black men has a lot to do with her having felt like an "outsider" in Japanese society when growing up. Because of her father's job, she had to move with the family around the country and had to change schools six times in her elementary school years alone. And following each move, she would be picked on by her new classmates because she spoke in a different dialect.

Later, as an older teenager, she started to hang around the military bases. Although initially she was drawn there because she was a "black music freak," she soon found the bases to be the closest thing to a foreign land available in Japan, where she could be herself and behave freely.

Bedtime Eyes, which was subsequently made into a movie in 1987, no doubt struck a resonant chord among many young Japanese women. Although there is no clear evidence that the novel (and subsequent works by Yamada, such as *Soul Music Lovers Only*) directly led to a sudden increase in the number of young women hanging around military bases[14] and night spots like Roppongi, it is clear that many of these women were closely following Yamada's distinct fashion style of only wearing black. Calling it *Yamada Eimi o shiteiru* (going Amy Yamada), these young women also tended to sport dark suntans and lots of cheap-looking jewelry. Meanwhile, according to Kawade Shobo Shinsha, the publisher of *Bedtime Eyes*, the novel sold over 260,000 copies in hard cover alone, with most of the readers reportedly young women in their twenties.

The Roppongi Scene

I spoke with a few such young women around the U.S. military base in Yokosuka and at discos in Roppongi—a popular night spot in west Tokyo which, with its flashy bars and chic discotheques, attracts a constant flow of foreign residents and tourists. One of the women I met is Asami.

Although Asami, a plump nineteen-year-old college student I met at Gas Panic (a popular Roppongi bar), insists that she's not there to pick up *gaijin* men, she adds that it is a perfect escape for her from unchallenging schoolwork and boring Japanese men. "None of the Japanese guys I have gone out with know how to flirt with girls. All they can talk about is work," she complains.

Asami is typical of most Gas Panic patrons—young, bored, and looking for action. Asami moved out of her family's home when she started college. She works at a fast-food restaurant and cannot really afford to frequent bars in Roppongi. Yet she claims she goes there three times a week and says she likes "wild" bars such as Gas Panic, Gaijin Zone, and Deja-vu, that play loud rock and pop music.

When I first met her at Gas Panic, the first thing she asked was if I could loan her some money for another drink.

Asami says she and her friends often hang out at these bars until 2:00 or 3:00 A.M. Then they take a taxi and camp out together at a friend's nearby apartment. It was after she became a Gas Panic regular that she met the African-American man she now lives with. A rebellious teenager who resents her strict upbringing and feels that she doesn't really belong to society, Asami says her boyfriend makes her feel more a part of the local scene.

When asked what she likes about Roppongi, she says it makes her feel like she is in another country. She can let her hair down and really have a good time in the presence of "cute" foreign bartenders and the heart-thumping beat of the music.

Some American men I have talked to say they can understand women like Asami. "You can't blame the women," says Ted, an American serviceman. Japanese women, for one thing, "have much more free time than the (Japanese) guys." Most of the men, he pointed out, are off swilling saké with their company colleagues. This means that by 6:00 P.M., "the Hard Rock Cafe in Roppongi is crowded with OLs and relatively few Western guys."

Gate-Girl Fever

The U.S. military bases have always been a haven for young women seeking Western men, especially those infatuated with black Americans. Nicknamed the "gate girls," these women hang around the gates of army bases to wait for their dates. A few of them without dates also stay around in the hopes that a serviceman will "escort" them to one of the clubs on base.

The gate girls apparently fall into two distinct groups—those interested in white men and those interested in blacks. One interesting point about these women is, depending on their color preference, they have different dress codes. The early nineties style was: those who liked African-American men tended to dress in all-black mini skirts and tank tops and wore heavy make-up—a style invented by Amy Yamada. They bleached their hair and wore a toasty-brown suntan. Those who preferred white men were generally more casual, with long hair, blue jeans, and cowboy boots.

I met a couple of "gate girls" in front of Club Alliance at the U.S. Navy base at Yokosuka. Naomi, twenty-one, and Kyoko, twenty-seven, who were escorted into the club by an acquaintance of mine, told me that they come to the base about three times a week to look for men to go out with. Both women said they prefer *gaijin* men because Japanese men are "too boring." Kyoko, who claimed that her parents were too conservative, said she is looking for a blond-haired, blue-eyed sailor boyfriend because she wants to live in the United States. "I'd like to live on the West Coast," she says. Kyoko's fantasy is a measure of independence from a conservative upbringing. The black sheep of her family and self-proclaimed social rebel, Kyoko also says that being with foreign men makes her feel comfortable. She says that she wants some "emotional and mental excitement" from life, something she believes she can't get from the average Japanese male.

A romance with a *gaijin*, these women believe, means being treated with more respect and kindness (*yasashisa*), and being more accepted for who they are. Better yet, they hope, it means learning about a whole new world with an exciting person as different as can be from the dull, everyday Japanese *salaryman*. Whether this belief is grounded in reality is debatable, but the fact remains that the opportunity to go out with foreign men does provide Japanese women with a new experience—something totally refreshing apart from a mundane norm.

The Rise and Fall of the English School Boom

Not many young women are as adventurous as Asami, Kyoko, and Naomi; nor are they able to be. Most young, single Japanese women still live with their parents and often have to observe curfews. They are also concerned about how they appear in the eyes of their parents, neighbors, and colleagues. Despite their outward conformity, there is evidence to show that some of these women, too, are looking for foreign boyfriends. Instead of hanging out at military bases, however, the women attend fashionable *eikaiwa* (English conversation) schools and salons, which have been described by cynics as "pseudo-dating services" for foreign teachers and their Japanese students.

That many language schools sell English through sexual innuendo is no secret, at least to foreign nationals residing in Japan. Sex sells, and many *eikaiwa* managers are eager to use sex to help boost enrollment. The provocative ads put out by many of these schools during the peak of the bubble years readily suggested this. One, showing a young Japanese woman removing her T-shirt, exposing her naked back and the curve of one breast, read "Japan's New Era: Let's Change into Bi-Lingual"; another displayed a Japanese girl about to kiss an attractive young *gaijin* as she wonders whether he really loves her. In another ad, suave, Ivy-League American youths walked among a bevy of admiring Japanese students across a sprawling campus lawn.

There was even an ad featuring a naked young blonde hugging her knees under the banner "Heartful Language."

Although in 1992, at the peak of the English school boom, there were an estimated eight thousand English-language schools in Japan, and the market was thought to be worth three trillion yen (thirty billion US dollars) annually, there is no easy way to find out who the main customers were. The English-language industry in Japan had been totally deregulated; it was only in late 1992 that the Japan Foreign Language Education Promotion Association was formed after considerable prodding by the Ministry of Education.[15]

Individual school surveys, however, indicate that young OLs and homemakers in their twenties and thirties make up a sizable portion of the market. In 1993 at PREP, an English-language school located in west Tokyo, about sixty-four percent (or roughly 130 regular pupils out of 200) were OLs in their early to mid-twenties.

Not surprisingly, the foreign male teachers working at these schools usually outnumber the female teachers. One school manager went so far as to say that older teachers were not welcome because "they're not popular among (female) students."[16] According to the manager, most of the teachers were male, with an average age of twenty-seven.

Although the manager of this school insisted that it does not allow any dating between teachers and students, less-structured schools admit openly that affairs have been common. Few of the women who study at such schools admit to any involvement with their teachers. Some former English teachers interviewed, however, were frankly honest and admitted to having had affairs with their students.

Tony, a blond, blue-eyed American in his late twenties

who taught briefly at a small English school in Tokyo, said he used to get frequent invitations for dates from young female students, including some married women. Once he arrived at a housewife's home for a private lesson and was totally shocked when his "student" greeted him in a bathrobe.

Of course it would not be fair to say that most women who attend *eikaiwa* schools go with the ulterior motive of finding a *gaijin* boyfriend. One of the few ways for a woman to get ahead in Japanese society is to have an exceptional knowledge of a foreign language. In all fairness, the majority of women who go to language schools do so because they want to improve their lot in life. Moreover, the Japanese are programmed from an early age to attend cultural centers to study arts and other subjects. To the Japanese, studying outside of one's school or college is almost a national pastime.

Yet in the free-floating, fast-wheeling lifestyle of the late eighties and early nineties when money was coming in easily to everyone, it did appear that sex between foreign teachers and students was practically rampant at many of these language schools which, to quote a Chinese saying, sprouted out like bamboo shoots after a spring rain.

But the English school scene is changing quickly, and these changes are sure to have an effect on dating between teachers and students. Since the economic slowdown of the nineties, many of the larger English schools have closed shop, including big names like ANA Stanton and ASA. Even the much-publicized Bi-Lingual that boasted an enrollment of 40,000 students at its peak announced bankruptcy in 1993.

Along with the decline in English-language schools is the tarnished image of dating English teachers. These days, dating services claim they prefer not taking English teachers as clients, and some teachers have found that their dating chances improve if they pose as bankers or lawyers when they go to Roppongi.

A Fixation on Gaijin Men

Even if the *eikaiwa* scene is facing a rapid decline, it doesn't discourage some of the more persistent women from looking elsewhere. Unfortunately for the women, in their eager pursuit of a foreign romance, many of them have fallen victim to the exploitative agendas of certain unscrupulous *gaijin* men. Japan, a financial "revolving door" for many visitors, has often attracted *gaijin* who stay for short-term gains. Some of these men consider women to be a convenience along their way. A few women I spoke with recounted incidences of date rape, verbal and physical abuse, lies, and even swindles perpetrated by their uncommitted foreign lovers who, after a while, disappeared altogether.

According to a 1993 report in the *Tokyo Journal*, in one extreme case, a few unsuspecting young Japanese women were videotaped by a hidden camera after they had been taken home by foreigners they met at international parties. These tapes were then circulated among the party-going men as pornography.[17] The report further describes one *gaijin* man actually offering a reporter disguised as a party-goer the opportunity to watch one of these videotapes. As he made the offer, he pointed to one of his victims, who was sitting naively next to him, and said, "Check her out." The woman, who spoke no English, had no idea what was going on and smiled during the negotiations.

True, incidents like these are as likely to occur in New York as they are in Tokyo. Yet many Tokyo *gaijin* do tend to take on a cavalier attitude with the local women as they carefreely roam around the Big Mikan—one of the last heavens, they believe, left on earth for men.

Despite incidents like these, many Japanese women insist, "But *gaijin* men are so kind and gentle . . . " One woman I met told me that her Japanese girlfriend seems to have this "thing" for *gaijin* men. Although the woman has been repeatedly treated like dirt by several, she still insists on dating only *gaijin* men.

It's only logical to question why some Japanese women have a blind faith in *gaijin* men. Critics say the women's optimism is rooted in their subconscious need to experience the exotic, a longing to emphasize their own individuality. Tamotsu Sengoku of the Japan Youth Research Institute, for one, insists that this desire is nothing more than a fad which will fade, in time, like the Juliana's phenomenon.

Yuko Tanaka of Kawade Shobo Shinsha disagrees. She suggests that young women, wanting to break away from frustration at home and having had no role models for their relationships with men up to now, are at a crossroads. As such, they are trying their best to find answers through trial and error with new things. If women think favorably of foreign men, it could be that they need to believe that *gaijin* men are better. At least they promise these women a chance to work out fresh possibilities.

There is evidence to prove Tanaka correct. One indication is the increasing use of international dating services by Japanese women. This may suggest that many Japanese women are serious about their relationships with foreign men and their interest goes beyond just fashion.

The next chapter will focus on the increasing use of international dating services by both Japanese women and Western men as well as the mutual attraction that serves to bring the two groups together.

 CHAPTER FOUR

Mutual Attraction

International Companions Services (ICS), based in Covina, California, is a dating company in the business of matching American men with Asian women. According to Billy J. Miles, who manages the company, of the 450 regular female members, about three-quarters are Japanese. Although many of these Japanese women live in the United States, the company is getting an increasing number of calls from women in Japan—many of whom are young and well educated. Many of these women, in their search for an American husband, promote themselves in *Matchmaker Single*, a quarterly put out by ICS. Their ads range from wistful to wishful:

> MAMI, 5 feet 1 inch tall, 105 pounds, 20 years old. Lives in Orange County.
> From Japan, Mami is single, a student at an L.A. university, and lives with an American family. She wants to marry an American and stay in the USA.
> RIEKO, 5 feet 2 inches tall, 103 pounds, 23 years old. Lives currently in Japan.
> A Japanese girl, Rieko is single, has just graduated from university with a B.A. degree . . . The man must be single, no more than 32 years old, and have a very bright future.

Many similar dating services are catering to Japanese women. For example, in *Los Angeles*, a monthly magazine, there are at least three or four dating services advertised that act as East-West matchmakers. In Tokyo, the *Tokyo Journal* and *Tokyo Classified* frequently run ads for people who are looking for international partners. Many of these ads are targeted at Japanese women. *Shukan Hoseki*, a popular weekly men's magazine, estimates that as many as four thousand Japanese women make use of such services annually.[1] The rising popularity of these services hints at the fact that the fixation of Japanese women on *gaijin* men is not limited to those who "just want to have fun."

In the Third World, marrying a Western man can pave the way out of poverty or an unpleasant or dangerous political situation. Japan, however, has become one of the world's largest economic powers and is still one of the safest countries in the world. Economic and political motives are thus not a major factor in Japanese–Western couplings. In fact, as testified by many women interviewed by Ieda and other writers in America, their moves overseas have almost always amounted to a step down in their standard of living, leading to employment uncertainty and a struggle with the language barrier. The question consequently arises: What reasons motivate Japanese women to actively seek marriage with *gaijin* men? Conversely, what are the attractions that lead Western men to date and marry Japanese women?

Chance and Availability

According to Billy J. Miles, one of the biggest changes in women who make use of international dating services is that their average age is becoming younger. Miles, who has been matchmaking Asian women and American men since

1979, says that while most Japanese women registered at his association used to be between thirty and forty and working in the United States, there has been a gradual increase in the number of non-residents in their twenties.

This is largely related to the travel and study-abroad booms among Japanese women that peaked during the bubble economy of the late 1980s. According to the Ministry of Justice, of the 4,253,859 Japanese women who traveled abroad in 1990, more than 40 percent were between the ages of twenty and twenty-nine, and most were traveling abroad for sightseeing or foreign study. This is 1.5 times higher than the same figure for men.

The proximity factor thus plays a big role in bringing Japanese women and Western men together. Overseas excursions made by young Japanese women provide them with an opportunity, even if not intended, to meet potential marriage partners. While overseas, one thing they have discovered, quite to their surprise, is that by virtue of being "exotic" Asians they receive a lot more attention outside of Japan than they do at home.

AKIKO WATANABE, owner and manager of East Meets West, a singles' social club based in Los Angeles, says that her seventeen years of experience in the business have shown her that, as an Asian woman, "You don't have to be a real beauty to be appreciated overseas." In fluent English, Watanabe explains that Japanese women who are not so pretty by Japanese standards may still have a good chance with men in the United States because "they are often considered to be exotic, no matter how plain they may seem back home."

Watanabe said that this difference in perception may also have to do with what Japanese and Americans perceive as being attractive in a woman. While Japanese men place youth and physical beauty as top priorities in their choice of girlfriends, American men, she says, tend to look a little deeper at personality and intelligence.

RUMIKO, a former pharmacist living in west Tokyo who is in her late forties, agrees. Rumiko, who was single until she married an American at age thirty-eight, says she once thought she would never have a chance to marry. A visit to the United States, however, changed her thinking. Within a few months of her arrival, she found herself the romantic target of five suitors. In the end she chose Henry, she says, as she thought he was the best looking and most wholesome. When I asked Henry what attracted him to Rumiko, he said that aside from her gentleness, he was also very impressed by her artistic ability—a quality he found refreshing. Rumiko, an accomplished *sumi-e* painter, had participated in some major exhibitions in the United States during her stay. "So many Americans I knew had tried to make it to those exhibitions and failed, and then there was Rumiko, who got in on the first trials," Henry says proudly.

SAEKO had a similar experience. Five years ago, she was working as an assistant manager for a small editing production firm in Japan. Though she found her job challenging, it wasn't making her happy. At age thirty-seven, she found that, as a woman, she was being ignored by the men around her. In fact, many of her male colleagues called her *obasan* (auntie) behind her back. She was so annoyed that she left her job for a chance to advance her education at a U.S. university. There she met a thirty-two-year-old American who fell head over heels in love with her.

He fulfilled Saeko's romantic dreams. Once, when she returned to the United States after a brief visit to Japan, he greeted her with an apartment full of balloons. When she worked late, he would come to the office to wait for her. Saeko was so taken by his thoughtfulness that she decided to marry him. She says that she feels American men have greater depth than the Japanese men she knew who tended to only look for youth and beauty in a woman.[2]

Dreaming the American Dream

The travel and study-abroad booms of the 1980s also inspired many Japanese women to seek better career opportunities and a new identity free from the constraints of a highly conformist society. Smart, high-powered women in Japan are often left to themselves. Because Japanese men tend to find them intimidating and they, in turn, find the men boring, they have slim hopes of finding a suitable life partner. Except for the most driven, they often end up in dead-end company jobs. These factors have led a number of women to head straight for Western cities, particularly New York, where they feel better able to realize their ambitions through their belief in the American dream.

True, this dream has lost its luster for many Americans. But it has certainly gained new life among goal-oriented immigrants, including some single Japanese women. As many critics have pointed out, if Japan is still believed by Westerners to be a man's heaven, there is a similar myth held among Japanese women regarding America—as a woman's paradise.

A seemingly endless number of Japanese books laud the romance and success to be found in the big international cities of Europe and the United States.[3] This is particularly true of New York, which to many Japanese OLs is still the pinnacle of opportunity. This may explain why, of all the destinations chosen by OLs for overseas study, the United States is the most-visited country.[4]

Many professional Japanese women who have experienced gender discrimination on the job say they left Japan to seek a more equal working environment. Midori is a member of the Iero Kyabu o Kangaeru Kai who has been living and working in New York as a freelance editor for the past five years. She told me that she left Japan because she felt that women are treated as outsiders. As long as women were excluded from the "private club" of Japanese men, Midori says, she felt she did not want to be a part of the Japanese working scene. In New York, she says, everyone seems to have an equal opportunity, regardless of age or gender. "That is why I decided to leave Japan and settle here."

Other Japanese women travel to New York just for the experience. In 1992, *Spa* carried an article on the lifestyles of young Japanese women living in New York. One interviewee, a twenty-four-year-old former fashion design student identified as A. M., said she had been in New York for a year and eight months, supported by money sent from home. When asked why she chose New York, she said she hated Japanese people and Japanese society.[5] She said she came to New York in the hopes of improving her English-speaking ability and perhaps to find a *hakujin* (white) husband.

Another twenty-five-year-old OL interviewed in the same article said she went to New York because her mother told her that she would never be able to amount to anything as an OL in Japan. Supported in part by her mother's savings, this woman decided to study jazz and popular music. Meanwhile, she hoped that she could learn more about life and herself.

While in New York and other American cities, Billy J. Miles of International Companion Services says, many women are naturally tempted by the freer, wider, more abundant qualities they see as being characteristic of the American lifestyle. Miles says that many become interested in dating American men when they see how active the men are outside of their work place, how spacious their houses are, and how they appear to treat women with more equality and respect.

Miles has a point here. Japanese men typically work late and have very little daily communication with their wives. Compared with their Western counterparts, they are also limited in how they can express themselves. Because men of few words are still considered to be masculine in Japan, many find themselves reluctant to bare their innermost thoughts and feelings. Thus incapable of paying their wives compliments and voicing expressions of endearment, they nevertheless expect their wives to tend to their emotional needs through unspoken, intuitive understanding.[6]

Some young women, disillusioned by what they see as being unfulfilling relationships between their mothers and fathers, older sisters and their husbands, decide that rather than waiting for things to get better at home (as Japanese people are often told to do through the spirit of *gaman*, or endurance), they will seek a better life elsewhere. This, too, helps explain why, of the 450 women registered at ICS, close to three-quarters are Japanese.

RIE is one such marriage hopeful. A twenty-five-year-old OL who works at a major Japanese public relations firm, Rie took a six-month English program in Seattle two years ago and, ever since her return, has been resisting her parents' enthusiastic matchmaking efforts. Though Rie admits that she has not dated any Western men, she says she was impressed with the lifestyle of the American couple with whom she spent her six-month stay. She says she was particularly envious of how they shared household chores, including cooking and washing, and how they enjoyed themselves by throwing parties on weekends. A few months ago, Rie signed up with a local international dating service. She says there is very little doubt in her mind now that she will marry a Western man.

The Kindly Gaijin

The hot pursuit of *gaijin* men also has a lot to do with the Western chivalry fantasy prominent among Japanese women. Watanabe, the owner of East Meets West mentioned earlier in this chapter, says that if there is one single myth that Japanese women believe about Western men, it is their *yasashisa*, an expression that embodies tenderness, kindness, and is often used to refer to the "ladies-first" attitude of Western men. This claim seems to match Ieda's findings. In a survey conducted for her book *Yellow Cab*, Ieda found through a survey of seventy-five Japanese women that the *yasashii* quality was the most-cited reason for their being drawn to Western men, followed by the belief that they are "good at sex" and "considerate."[7]

Quite a few women that I have met also cited the *yasashii* quality when I asked them to describe Western men. So strong is their belief in this attribute that they tend to apply it indiscriminately to every *gaijin* man they meet. But where did this blind faith originate?

"Japanese women, who are ignored by their workaholic Japanese boyfriends and lovers, have this craving for 'physical warmth.' Since they are not getting it at home, they are looking for it overseas in *gaijin* men," a Japanese female friend of mine once explained.

Essentially, she was suggesting that it is the workaholic attitude of Japanese men and their incapability of expressing affection that have driven many Japanese women into the arms of foreign men. But this is only part of it. The real reason, I believe, lies even deeper within Japanese culture.

As Sumiko Iwao, a psychologist teaching at Keio University in Tokyo points out in her book *The Japanese Woman: Traditional Image and Changing Reality,* if Western culture can be called a "couples" culture, then Japanese culture can, in contrast, be labeled a culture of "singles." What she means is that while Westerners tend to devote their energies to attracting the attention of the opposite sex, Japanese tend to center their activities on (and receive support from) members of the same sex. Moreover, Japanese are more concerned about impressing members of their own sex than those of the opposite sex.

Evidence shows that the Japanese singles culture is reinforced from early childhood by a series of gender-specific events. The celebration of *shichi-go-san,* literally "seven-five-three," for example, is one such event in which families with female children commemorate their having reached the ages of three and seven, and families with male children celebrate their having reached the age of five. For this event the children are dressed up and taken to a shrine to be blessed.

Similar traditions can also be traced back to the traditional Boys' and Girls' Day celebrations. Until July 1948, when the Prime Minister officially designated May 5 as Children's Day, girls celebrated their girlhood on March 3 with displays of special dolls. Boys celebrated their boyhood on May 5 with displays of swords and armor and, later, carp streamers, as carp are respected for their endurance and strength. Though May 5, a public holiday, has been Children's Day now for many years, the separate celebrations continue.

Before World War II, upon reaching the age of seven, boys and girls were seated separately in class and often went to separate high schools. Although most schools in Japan are now co-ed, young children still receive a lot of pressure from teachers, their parents, and peers to mingle only with others of the same gender.

The result of this separation of male and female cultures from an early age is a huge gap in understanding and communication between the two sexes, a circumstance that has remained relatively unchanged despite the changing times. Western men, who are trained when young to watch their appearance and behavior around women, appear to be more understanding, which easily impresses Japanese women.

Speaking of the blind faith of Japanese women in *yasashii* foreign men, Hideyuki, a thirty-three-year-old Japanese male acquaintance, said to me half-jealously and half-mockingly: "Japanese women just get hypnotized by all the attention they get, that's all."

There are plenty of women who love being "hypnotized" by *gaijin* men. Mariko, a young OL who worked at a health club, is one of them. "Jeff was very nice, very *yasashii*," says Mariko reflectively. Mariko dated Jeff, an American, for about a year before he left Japan after a two-year stay teaching English. But Mariko is not discouraged. In fact, she vows that she has not given up on him and said she will only go out with *gaijin* men from now on. Mariko says that Jeff always pulled her chair out for her at restaurants and always held her hand wherever they went. Mariko says she couldn't help but feel a sense of superiority when riding on the train with him; she felt as if she were basking in the admiring glances of her fellow passengers. Unable to forget Jeff, Mariko is now concentrating on saving enough money to travel to the United States to be with him.

YUKI, a twenty-nine-year-old jazz dancer, has a lot of nice things to say about the black American man she has been seeing. "Ralph is really kind; he always asks, 'What do you think about this, Yuki?' or 'How would you like to do that, Yuki?'" Yuki's eyes sparkle as she talks enthusiastically about this man she has been dating for the last eight months.

To her, there is very little comparison between Ralph and her ex-boyfriend Kenji. For one thing, Kenji never bothered to ask for Yuki's opinion about anything. "Whenever I volunteered an opinion, all Kenji would say was, 'What good does it do to complain? You can't solve anything anyway.'" Yuki says she used to get very irritated when Kenji said things like that. As far as Yuki is concerned, not only was Kenji incapable of respecting her opinions, he was also a coward "who gave up before he even tried."

NORIAKI FUSHIMI, a singer and a gay writer, sees it differently. In an interview with the magazine *Shukan Hoseki*, Fushimi explains that if Western men seem to be more free-spirited to Japanese women, it could be because they can afford to look at their jobs as being only one part of their lives; they are free and have time to pursue other interests. Japanese salarymen on the other hand feel they must give their all to their companies. "If they (Japanese men) themselves feel suppressed by society, they have all the more reason to feel threatened by women who appear to be 'liberated,'" Fushimi says.[8]

The Romantic International Marriage

Because most Japanese men are so wrapped up in their work, Fushimi says the very thought of marrying a Japanese salaryman has an unromantic image for many young Japanese women. Such marriages are simply too predictable. They know that after marrying they will have one or two children, their husbands will have moderate success at work, and they will experience completely separate lives. Then when they get old, they will have nothing in common. These images wipe out whatever romantic notions they have about marriage to a Japanese. In recent years, though more young men in Japan court their girlfriends with expensive gifts and treats at fancy restaurants, many have yet to learn how to capture their hearts.

Marriage to a foreigner is a totally different story. The expression *kokusai-kekkon*, or international marriage, used mostly by Japanese women to designate pairings between Japanese and Westerners,[9] tends to have a very exotic image. This is because "a cultural gap in expectations," according to Fushimi, "allows them to project their own fantasies onto reality." When two people have different cultural, racial, and linguistic backgrounds, he says, it is easy for them to "tailor-make" their own ideal partner. If love is an illusion to start with, then when the mate is a foreigner it is all the easier to fall into the trap of fantasizing. This is because the gap in communication and understanding is likely to be filled by each person's own imaginings and expectations. A quiet pause in the conversation after one has asked a question, for example, may be thought to indicate acquiescence instead of a lack of understanding.

The term *kokusai-kekkon* also carries the image of *kokusai-ka*, or internationalization. If traveling and studying abroad are considered to be part of internationalization (see Chapter 1), then speaking English and having a foreign boyfriend or husband is also seen as being international by many Japanese people. Of course, Japanese women in international marriages also carry with them the stigma of being different. Some women, out of a desire to flaunt their individuality and worldly sophistication, however, are more than happy to play the part of the "nail that sticks up," refusing to let society pound them down.

Going for the Image

Many women will play along with being different as long as it enhances their image. This is why the image-seekers do not marry just any foreigner. He must fit a certain image; i.e., be a Caucasian man from an advanced Western culture. Tomiko Sato, a marriage consultant at Beavers—an oddly-named Tokyo-based dating service that matches Japanese with foreign nationals from both Asia and Western countries—says that she has been getting calls from a lot of women who specifically say that they want to meet Caucasian men. Sato says that when she suggested that they might also consider eligible men from China or the Philippines (who, in her opinion, make better husbands), these young women show no interest.

Their excuse, she says, is that going out with an Asian man simply does not have the same cachet as going out with a white man. They say that if you tell your friends you are going out with a Chinese or Filipino, all they say is, "Oh." But if you say you are going out with an American or a Frenchman, they are more likely to say, "Really? Tell me more . . . " Sato, who praises the patience and kindness of Filipino and Chinese husbands, says she is disappointed that most young Japanese women who go to her seem to have implanted in their minds the notion that international marriage means marrying a Caucasian. She says that over sixty percent of the women registered with her are waiting to be matched up with men from North America or Europe.

Chizuko Ueno, assistant professor of sociology at Tokyo University and Japan's most prominent feminist scholar, says this tendency may have to do with an intermarriage pattern called "hypergamy." The term was coined by French sociologist Pierre Bourdieu, who theorizes that there are race and class hierarchies behind people's decisions to marry. It refers to the tendency that, when considering marriage, people try to improve or maximize their status by marrying someone in a better socioeconomic position. Ueno says that this tendency is quite strong in a society like Japan, which ranks its citizens by hierarchy, race, and gender.

Ueno, pointing to the high intermarriage rate of Asian-American women to Caucasian men in the United States, says that Japanese women in Japan may have also been affected by a similar, however subtle, racial hierarchy within Japanese society. In today's Japan, because of a persisting *gaijin* complex left over from the Occupation days, the white race, particularly North Americans and Europeans, rank at the top of the foreign social scale (which is, however, totally separate from the Japanese social scale). Ueno says that this "social climbing" tendency is strong among Japanese women considering a mixed-marriage partner. Given a choice between a non-Japanese Asian man and a Caucasian man with similar attributes and economic clout, more Japanese women would choose the latter because of his higher social status.

This socioeconomic interpretation may seem heretical to Westerners, particularly Americans, who tend to idealize equality and democracy in love. In the context of Japanese society, however, which is still very hierarchical, there is evidence to support Ueno's point. In Japan, there have always been both overt and covert preferences for Caucasians over Asians and other ethnic groups from choosing a foreign student in a homestay program, to hiring a private English teacher. Asian Americans and other nationals from English-speaking nations are routinely turned down for English-teaching positions because, as one third-generation Japanese-American (*sansei*) was once told, "You look too much like everybody else here."

It is therefore not hard to see why young Japanese women prefer going out with Caucasians. Mariko (mentioned earlier in this chapter) admits that it made her feel very special when her friends cheered her on with remarks such as *sugoi* (amazing) and *kakko-ii* (that's cool) when they found out that she was going out with an American.

Overcoming the "I May Never Marry" Syndrome

Kokusai-kekkon is sometimes sought by Japanese women who reject, or have been rejected by, their own society, though some of these women may be extremely well-educated and have extensive overseas experience, which Japanese men generally find intimidating. Conversely, these women may also find that they cannot relate to ordinary Japanese men, who seem to have a very limited outlook on life. Accordingly, they have to look outside their society and race for new possibilities.

Other women may be divorcees who feel their chance of remarrying a Japanese man is very slim. This belief is not entirely true as second marriages are not all that rare in Japan these days (particularly for women without children) and more specialized dating services are helping to bring these so-called *batsuichi* (men or women who have been divorced once) together.

Kokusai-kekkon is sometimes perceived by older women who have passed the favored marriageable age as being a last chance at matrimony. Though more and more Japanese women are marrying later, parents have largely not kept up with the changing times and continue to pressure their daughters of marriageable age to hurry up and find a husband. Ken Joseph, a Japan resident for twenty-seven years, runs a nationwide hot line that counsels foreigners and Japanese encountering problems in Japan. He says that this is particularly strong among parents whose daughters are between the ages of twenty-seven and thirty-two. So much pressure is put on these young women that many become quite desperate. Joseph says that he has received quite a few calls from worried parents who say their daughters have run away from home to avoid being forced into an arranged marriage.

Added to the desperation of the older women is the tendency for Japanese men to pick only young women as marriage partners. According to Yoko Itamoto, general director of a marriage consultation service for Japanese singles called Nippon Seinenkan, most Japanese men, including those in their forties and fifties, confine their search for marriageable partners to women in their early to mid-twenties. This has led many women in their thirties to worry that they may never have a chance to marry.

In Koseido's 1992 book, *Kokusai-kekkon Monogatari* (Tales of International Marriages), author Kaori Kawatake expresses this worry in her preface: "At twenty-seven, while I held steadfast to the hope of marrying, I found myself a lonely *hai misu* (old maid), feeling like I had passed the marriageable age."[10] Kawatake said she was very relieved when she finally met by chance a handsome, gray-eyed *gaijin* who reminded her of Mickey Rourke. Small wonder that she felt compelled to give him her telephone number. Lucky for Kawatake, he called and, after dating for a while, they married.

The Feeling Is Mutual

If Japanese women are enthusiastic about Western men, then these men are equally, if not more, responsive to Japanese women. In fact, interracial dating between Japanese women and white men is one of the most visible of the *kokusai-kekkon* trends in Tokyo. So prevalent is it that many Western women in Japan feel totally ignored. Some jokingly refer to Japan as a "romantic wasteland" (see Chapter 8). This is not an exaggeration. A look at the personal ads section of the *Tokyo Journal*, for example, gives the reader a good idea about the dating scene in the Big Mikan. Consider the following:

> American Man, 29, seeking Japanese woman 22–32 for relationship. I like jazz, classical and rock music, art, movies, travel, hiking, swimming, and tennis.

> Business-oriented young man, 31, intelligent, loyal, responsible, honest seeks nice Japanese lady for serious relationship.

> American Male, white, 29, Hawaii resident, seeks shy, quiet Japanese female for lifetime partner.

One very noticeable thing about the ads is that most are placed by American men. Some ads are sent from the United States, from as far away as Alaska, not to mention the many more sent from both coasts. It is very evident that the American–Japanese attraction is strong—a phenomenon due very much to the repercussions of a legendary romantic fantasy that dates back to the Occupation days.

Fantasies of Japanese femininity, as I mentioned earlier in Chapter One, have been imprinted on the psyches of Western males, particularly Americans, for almost fifty years, due to the U.S. occupation of Japan. In 1958, for example, there were 87,000 U.S. troops stationed in Japan and Okinawa. During the zenith of the U.S. military presence in Japan, an estimated 20,000 American GIs married Japanese women.[11]

This attraction shows few signs of waning. True, there has been a decline in Japanese–American marriages since the height of the U.S. military presence in Japan, but marriages involving an American husband still represent a sizable percentage of all intermarriages in Japan. According to Ministry of Health and Welfare figures, of all the intermarriages between Japanese brides and foreign grooms in 1992, some 21 percent involved an American groom, the second-highest figure after 44 percent for Korean grooms.[12] This trend has continued since the early seventies, making American men the most likely candidates from a different ethnic group to marry Japanese women.

Another reason for this persisting attraction between American men and Japanese women may have to do with recent demographic changes in the larger Japanese cities, which have seen a steadily increasing influx of American residents as a result of the strong political and economic ties between Japan and the United States. According to Ministry of Justice figures, in 1992, there were 42,482 American residents living in Japan—this accounts for the largest proportion of Western residents in the country. (The figure is 3.5 times that of the British and nearly seven times that of Canadians.) Chance and availability are thus major factors in marriages between American men and Japanese women.

But there is another, more subtle element involved—the feminist movement. While American men I have spoken to in Japan do not actually come out and attack the movement, there is an undercurrent of discomfort with this continuing and strengthening trend among those men who show a definite preference for Japanese women. One former engineer from Houston who said that he had "burned out on American women," including his wife, came to Japan to "look for something different" since he'd been told that Asian women are more appreciative of their men. He found Japanese women in general to be beautiful, very kind, and loving. After two years in Japan, although he is still looking for the right woman and has had a fair amount of difficulty meeting Japanese women due to what he sees as cultural differences and a gap in expectations, he said he doesn't think that he will "ever go back to American women."

Some of the North American men I have talked to think of American women as "angry men-haters" who make an issue of everything. "They are really mixed up these days and don't know what they want. They want a relationship, but they don't. They want a nice sensitive guy but they also want a brute," says one frustrated American male. "You open a door to let a woman leave first and you are likely to get sneered at. They say, 'I don't want your help, I can get it myself,' recounted a Canadian lecturer from Toronto. This man said that at least Japanese women give him a break because they "don't get caught up in all that." The question remains whether these men will understand Asian women if they have difficulty with those of their own culture.

Old Fashioned, "Home-grown" Girls

American as well as other Western men get a few breaks because, as one man puts it honestly, "Women's standards are lower here." Many men believe that because Japanese women are used to being treated so badly by their men, they do not expect much in the way of kindness or consideration. In fact, the one quality that is most attractive about Japanese women for these men is their Japanese upbringing. After all, Japanese women continue to retain the image of being the *Yamato-nadeshiko,* or the "old-fashioned girls of Japan," to the West.

ICS's Billy Miles says that most of his male clients specifically ask to meet Japanese women brought up in Japan because they feel that second- or third-generation Japanese women raised in the United states tend to be "spoiled," having the same attitude as Western women. This makes them "irresponsible, self-centered, and greedy." These men believe that only Japanese women who are brought up in Japan can live up to their ideal image of being "honest, understanding, and home-oriented," the three qualities Miles says are the most sought after by Western men looking for a Japanese wife.

This view is echoed by Boye De Mente, a longtime Japan resident and author of *Bachelor's Japan* (1991). According to De Mente, most Japanese women are more graceful, petite, sensitive, and poetic-minded than their Western counterparts. "Trained to respect and cater to men, they are seldom abrupt, negative, or assertive. All of these features combine to make Japanese women . . . appear the epitome of femininity and charm to Western males . . . so long as they are not Westernized or removed from their own cultural setting."[13]

The "Ultimate" Femininity

In their search for ideal, untainted femininity, many Western men feel they have no choice but to find it in Japan, which explains why so many personal ads addressed to Japanese women are from Western men from all over the world. Just what do Western men mean by femininity—a quality many lament Western women gave up in the name of feminism? To early Japanologists such as Lafcadio Hearn, it has to do with the Japanese woman's success in "winning affection by gentleness, obedience, kindliness"—virtues that "only a society in which all self-assertion was repressed, and self-sacrifice made a universal obligation" could have produced.[14] It is this type of idealistic image of Japanese women that has drawn so many foreign Japanophiles into falling in love with Japanese women.

For the more conventional sojourners to Japan today, the femininity of the Japanese woman takes on yet a different meaning. In *Bachelor's Japan*, for example, De Mente asserts that the average Japanese girl, along with her other feminine attributes, "is more willing to prove her 'ultimate' femininity than most of her Western sisters," by which he means to say that she will not say no to a Western man. "The popularity Japanese girls enjoy with foreign men," De Mente continues, "is primarily founded on the ease with which they can be had."[15]

To be fair, one problem with De Mente's book is that it is outdated. The book was originally published in 1962. Even with subsequent new editions, most of the information included in the book is at least four decades old. Today's Japanese women, as I mentioned in earlier chapters, are going through major changes and their choices for affiliating with *gaijin* men are often motivated by very different reasons. Consequently, while the form still appears to be there, the substance has changed entirely.

Unfortunately for Japanese women, the international "yellow-cab" fever and the domestic Roppongi craze are actually enhancing the old stereotypical image of Japanese women being easy. In fact, many Western men admit to having preconceived ideas about Japanese women before coming to Japan. An American journalist friend formerly married to a Japanese woman once put it like this: "For many foreign men, sex is a big incentive in their coming to Japan." He admitted that sex was on his mind when he first came.

A similar confession was published in 1992 in the "Letters to the Editor" column of the *Daily Yomiuri*, where a writer confessed that he had come to Japan "with high hopes" of being "a big hit among the women."[16] Meanwhile, in a *Tokyo Journal* article that appeared in December 1991, one English teacher was quoted as saying that Tokyo life was easy for him because "I only have to teach about ten hours a week . . . and I always have at least three women."

The Superiority-Inferiority Complex

Another reason for the attraction of Western men for Japanese women, De Mente points out, is an inherent superiority-inferiority complex that many men feel toward Western and Japanese women. What he means to say is that not a few Western men feel superior in regard to Japanese women. This feeling, he says, is particularly true of the kind of Americans who are unsure of their prowess with the opposite sex from their own country. Afraid of shaming themselves in front of Western women for their shyness and ineptness, they find it a relief to be with Asian women—particularly Japanese women—because "they are outside of their own cultural sphere; the men are able to look at them in a more detached manner, often with a feeling of inherent superiority that, although perhaps racially motivated, is nevertheless satisfying and even sexually stimulating."[17]

Although De Mente was speaking from the experience of an expatriate living in Japan during the sixties, his observation of this particular psychology of Western males apparently continues to hold true even today, albeit with a new application to the current situation. To elaborate how this complicated sentiment has survived the times and been revived into the nineties, one twenty-nine-year-old journalist friend from Canada put it to me this way: "With Japanese women, I don't feel this sense of competitiveness the way I do with women in Canada."

While Japanese women tend to be more low-key about competing with men largely because the traditional gender roles are still very much honored by society, the journalist points out that women in North America, on the other hand, have become increasingly competitive with men in every way, including sex, love, and employment. To demonstrate his point, he reminds me of a song (sung by a female artist) titled "I Love Better Than You."

Even the relatively smaller size of Japanese women, my friend was quick to admit, appears to have "an interesting effect" on him, making him feel bigger, stronger, and therefore more confident.

Other men I interviewed echo a similar feeling of ease and comfort with Japanese women, although this sense of superiority also seems to be rooted in the fact that America won World War II and occupied Japan afterward for several years. If America's position as Japan's conqueror and savior helped to reinforce a general sense of awe and respect among Japanese people toward Westerners, then it also produced a colonial attitude among many Western men who, as the Canadian journalist puts it, believe they can easily "lord it over" the Japanese.

As Hiroshi Wagatsuma pointed out in a scholarly study in 1973, Japan became the self-appointed champion of white Asians at the turn of the century, boldly trying to win a place in the coterie of white imperialists. After their bitter failure culminating in the loss of World War II, the Japanese found themselves receiving a "democratic education" from their American teachers, "toward whom they felt great rivalry mixed with admiration."[18] This ambivalence fostered a strong association in the minds of Japanese people between a sense of respect and the skin color and other physical features characteristic of Caucasians. This is why some single Western men, after acquiring a taste for the preferential treatment they receive from the Japanese, have made it a rule to date only Japanese women.

This attitude has invited criticism from some feminists. In an article that appeared in the May 11, 1986, issue of the *New York Times Magazine* , Grace Lyu Volckhausen, a women's rights activist, charges that men who reject Western women and only wish to marry Asian women are basically "losers" who cannot face up to their own women.

A similar charge is echoed in a letter to the editor that appeared in the *Japan Times* on December 5, 1993. In response to a letter that was published earlier, an American woman suggested that the man, who claimed "women are happier at home," was one of those chauvinists "who have fled the West to be among so-called 'submissive' Oriental females because they could not abide the idea of women having an equal say and equal opportunities."

Michael, a New York trader who arrived in Japan in 1992 , sees it differently. He says that in New York, with all the sexual harassment lawsuits, men feel wary of even asking out any of the women they work with. In America today, there is a lot of confusion in terms of what men and women want and how they ought to behave. At least in Japan, because the division of sexual roles is still strong, "life is much easier for men here," he says.

Feminist accusations do not bother Eric, an English teacher from New Jersey. The brown-haired, dark-eyed cram school teacher admitted openly that he has dated one of his students and said coming to Japan was a form of escape from Western women. As long as he is living in Japan and going out with Japanese women, he says he doesn't worry about dealing with issues that are sensitive to women.

"Because Japan is at least thirty years behind in the feminist movement," he said, he can just relax and take it easy. "Let's face it, this is Disneyland."

Practical Reasons

During the U.S. Occupation in the 1950s, Japanese women were thought to be good marriage material because of their graceful, quiet, self-sacrificing spirit. But not all Western men attracted to Japanese women are driven today by these stereotypes and fantasies. Some are motivated by simpler, more practical reasons.

John, an editor from Britain, feels that in an intercultural relationship many men feel liberated from having to perform the roles expected of them in Western culture. In other words, he can relax more with a Japanese woman because the differences in their cultural backgrounds spare him the worry of being judged by a woman from a similar culture. The books he reads, the kind of car he drives, the college he graduated from, and the job he holds may all affect his relationship with a woman from home. In Japan, however, these things would have little effect on a relationship with a Japanese woman who is unfamiliar with Western culture—that is, provided he has a good-paying job in Japan and time to spend with her.

A Japanese woman, many men have testified, can also be a great help for the bewildered foreigner trying to make it in Japan. Jeff, an American friend, says that not speaking the language is often very stressful and frustrating. When a foreign man is going out with a woman from his own country, their relationship tends to suffer, he says, because the problems of everyday living are greatly compounded by their ignorance of the language and culture. "But going out with a Japanese woman is different because she acts as a stabilizing factor for the *gaijin* man," he explains.

What he means is that a Japanese girlfriend can act as an insider's guide to Japanese culture and help her *gaijin* boyfriend to gain access to otherwise difficult-to-come-by connections. She also acts as an interpreter when necessary and can help smooth things should the man encounter discrimination, such as when trying to rent an apartment. She is very much what Mariko is to Blackthorne in James Clavell's novel *Shogun*—the hero's guide to all things Japanese.

Then there is always the lure of the spouse visa—the ultimate incentive for some to marry a Japanese woman. Japan has been the land of opportunity since the 1980s and the situation is likely to continue for many through the 1990s. While Japanese women are looking to live their American dream by traveling to the West, thousands of Americans, Canadians, and Europeans, discouraged by the dwindling job opportunities at home, are coming to Japan every year to look for work, take advantage of the high yen, and live out the Japanese dream. According to the

Ministry of Justice, between 1988 and 1993, the number of foreign residents from North America and Europe jumped an average of 12 percent. Some of these men, who want to stay in Japan but do not want to deal with the headache of applying for a working visa, are actively seeking marriage with a Japanese. Keiko Iigata, editor of *Mr. Partner*, a matchmaking magazine that attempts to bring Japanese women and foreign men together, says she has encountered several European men who asked her to help them find a Japanese wife "because they want to stay in Japan to do business."

This has added a realistic twist to the racial fantasies— Japanese women are also desirable marriage partners because of Japan's rising socioeconomic status.

The Asian Aristocrat

That Japanese women enjoy wide popularity with Western men is reflected in the demand for them at cross-cultural dating services based in the United States. Miles says that his male clients often specifically ask to be matched with a Japanese woman. Miles himself is married to a Japanese and calls Japanese women "the top of the tree," adding that they are also likely to be the most sophisticated and best educated among the many women members registered with him.

Nick, an American banker who met his Japanese wife in New York, agrees. He says that although he has always found Asian women attractive, he never doubted that his heart belonged to a Japanese woman. This is because, compared with other Asian women, he finds the average Japanese to be "soft as a baby." While many other Asian women still suffer in one way or another because of less favorable social and economic environments at home, Japanese women, blessed with Japan's economic success, "are treated like little princesses and are totally spoiled and pampered." Consequently, he says, "there is not a single rough edge left on them."

Fumiharu Yoshimura, manager of Dandies Minami Aoyama, a Tokyo-based dating service that specializes in matching Caucasian men and Japanese women living in Japan, concurs. But he also added that Japanese women are favored because his clients feel that Japanese society is the most democratized society in Asia and, therefore, the closest to Western society. As a result, there is a belief that Japanese women think more like Westerners than other Asians. This is why these men feel they are getting the best of both worlds.

Caucasian men who use Yoshimura's service also repeatedly say they like Japanese women because they look young, slim, and beautiful. Rather than being especially beautiful, Yoshimura says, modern Japanese women are just better groomed. With their acute sense of "total" fashion, they have learned how to package themselves better. "In fact, this is why most foreign men who have just arrived in Japan are so struck by them," he said.

Whether it is real beauty or a superficial package Western men are seeing, Japanese women have definitely become objects of desire and status. Not only are they increasingly symbolic of the energy, wealth, intelligence, and economic vitality of Japan, but to Western men they personify the vital new power of Asia.

 CHAPTER FIVE

The Dating Game

Given Japan's moves toward internationalization and the curiosity and fantasies Japanese women have about Western men, many believe Japan to be a paradise for Western men. Tetsuo Koyama, a women's magazine editor familiar with the dating scene in Japan, once said that because Western men are in short supply, they never have to worry about getting dates with Japanese women. The editor estimated that at any given time a Western male is likely to have at least a dozen women to choose from.

This is true for some, but far from true for others. While Western men generally enjoy great popularity with Japanese women, and it is true that many meet prospective dates, girlfriends, and future wives through work, schools, parties, and friends, many—particularly the shy ones—do not find dating easy. How well a man fares in the dating game depends on factors valid in most other countries, namely, his profession, looks, personality, and ability to mix and mingle in the crowd. In Japan, however, how well a person speaks Japanese also can have a decisive effect.

This chapter will provide a cross section of the international dating scene between Japanese women and Western men in Japan's largest city, beginning with background on some of the most common meeting areas. This chapter will also look at some individual cases and concludes with an analysis of some of the common myths and stereotypes that can lead to disappointment and misunderstanding.

English Schools

As mentioned in Chapter 3, English teachers have perhaps the easiest time meeting women. The access they have to their students makes dating very easy. Many English teachers insist that their schools tolerate no dating between teachers and students and say that it is written into their contracts: If they are caught fraternizing with students they will be fired. However, even some of the more professional-minded English teachers admit to having dated students.

Many male English teachers interviewed, particularly those who teach at smaller schools, recounted incidences of having been approached by women, both single and married. Some do not hesitate to say that they feel many of their female students have an ulterior motive for attending classes. Tales of students going to their teachers' apartments for private lessons and ending up in bed with them are common.

Although most male teachers say that their students initiate invitations and encounters, evidence shows that the seduction comes from both parties. Ronald, an English teacher and businessman from Connecticut who has dated many of his students, says he often gives his phone number to those he wants to go out with. Nine times out of ten they will call. Another teacher, interviewed in the *Hiragana Times* (June 1993), claims he uses subterfuge to get female attention. For example, he'll pretend to be lost and approach an attractive young woman to ask for directions. Below are the stories of two English teachers.

• Ronald

Ronald came to Tokyo from Connecticut three years ago. A tall, good-looking man with blond hair and blue eyes, he worked at a large English school. For Ronald, meeting women in Japan was a breeze. Often, they would come to talk to him of their own accord at bars or on the street. But at age twenty-seven, he was not ready to settle down. He found himself going from woman to woman, often seeing more than one at a time. He didn't think he was being unfair; as far as he was concerned, a lot of them were just as promiscuous as he was.

Although one-night stands were standard fare for him, he also maintained steady relationships with women. These longer courtships, however, did not usually last for more than two or three months. It's true that a lot of these women were beautiful, but to Ronald they were either too weak or too possessive. Once he went out with a thirty-year-old who started pressuring him about marriage. When he decided to break up with her, she harassed him incessantly for several weeks before giving up on him.

Ronald did eventually fall in love with another woman. She was an attractive actress who maintained an independent lifestyle. But she had other boyfriends and was not always direct with Ronald. Once he made a date with her but she never showed up. When he confronted her, she said she was seeing someone else but did not go into any detail. When this happened a second time, Ronald was forced to give up. He now feels that the indirect, non-confrontational attitude of the typical Japanese woman can often be more hurtful than the straightforward approach of Westerners.

Not all English teachers are like Ronald and the teacher described in the *Hiragana Times*, whose driving interest is to see how many women they can talk into going to bed with them. Dan, for one, married a student he met just a month after he arrived in Japan.

• Dan and Noriko

Dan and Noriko met in 1992 at an English school where Dan was teaching. Before arriving in Japan, Dan worked for an insurance firm in Britain but found his job boring. When a good friend living in Tokyo told him he could work in Japan and make a lot of money, he gave notice, packed up, and moved. He started working right away for a major English school in Tokyo where he met, only a month after his arrival, the woman he says he knew he was going to marry.

Noriko is not your typical Japanese woman. At thirty-four, she had had a ten-year career working as a professional theatrical actress and was continuing to work as an occasional model for commercials. In 1989, when her theatrical group broke up, she decided it was time to move on to something new. She looked into becoming a beauty therapist. To secure the necessary qualifications, she went to London and enrolled in a special one-year beauty therapy course. Upon her return, she started working for a beauty salon. She also started going to the English school where Dan was teaching, as she did not want to lose her newly acquired English-language skills. She said that until she met Dan, marriage had never really crossed her mind as she was always so busy.

Some of the things Dan found irresistibly attractive about Noriko beyond her beauty were her intelligence and independence. Her English skills and experience living in Britain also helped make close communication possible and eliminated many obstacles in an international relationship where misunderstandings can easily arise.

As for Noriko, Dan was very mature for his age and a devoted partner. Best yet, Dan did not have any preconceived idea about Japanese women and was able to see Noriko for what she was. Dan continues to teach; Noriko is expecting a baby.

Roppongi Bars and Conversation Lounges

If English schools are still the easiest venue in Japan for local foreign men to meet women, the Roppongi district of Tokyo qualifies as one of the more immediate international "meat markets" in town. Myriad bars and discos in this district attract tourists and business people on short stays who are looking for action. GIs, foreign bankers, and stockbrokers stationed here congregate in Roppongi to enjoy themselves and, perhaps, find someone to take home for the night.

Roppongi regulars favor hangouts like Motown, Hard Rock Cafe, Java Jive, Buzz, Gas Panic, Lexington Queen, and the Drug Store. Roppongi is definitely not for the reserved or dispossessed; cover charges are high and competition is very keen. "In Roppongi, girls will not approach you unless you are very good-looking," says blue-eyed, blond-haired Ronald, the English teacher mentioned earlier. If you don't have the right looks, you have to take the initiative and approach women first. Appearance aside, it doesn't hurt to be wearing an expensive-looking suit and fancy watch to catch the eyes of Roppongi girls, he says, adding, "It's really tough out there."

Some men do not feel they are up to the challenge of approaching total strangers. They may, instead, find their way to one of the less competitive hangouts, called "English conversation lounges." Relatively new in Tokyo over the last seven or eight years, these lounges are quickly gaining popularity among young Japanese women as they provide a neutral ground where they can meet foreign men and practice their English. In Tokyo, there are about five or six such hangouts. Some of the better known ones are The Library, Mickey House, Corn Popper, and Gecko's Lounge. There is a relatively low cover charge of between ¥500 and ¥1,500, which includes a bottomless cup of coffee. Some of these places only charge Japanese customers, making the lounges all the more tempting for foreign men to forsake the expensive Roppongi scene.

Dave, an Australian part-time editor I met at Mickey House lounge, says he prefers the conversation lounges to Roppongi bars because "Here, I know I have a starting ground—at least I know that the women who come here are here because they want to practice English." With that, he says, the rest comes fairly naturally; all he needs to do is to speak English. In Roppongi, Dave says he feels he has to compete with bankers and other guys "who tend to be extremely aggressive."

Some salaried workers at trading firms, banks, and factories where women are few and far between also come to these lounges. Steve, an engineer, says he comes to the Corn Popper about once every other week to chat with visitors and read the newspaper in the library-style lounge. A relatively shy man who claims that after a year's stay in Japan he has yet to have a Japanese girlfriend, Steve says he greatly prefers the laid-back atmosphere of the Corn Popper to the cut-throat mood of Roppongi.

Mark, a bartender from Texas, however, claims to be a regular Roppongi bar hopper and party-goer. He also boasts that he has befriended quite a few Japanese and Western women. Here is his story.

- **Mark**

Mark is a twenty-year-old Japanese-language student who works as a bartender at a Tokyo restaurant and club. Two years ago, Mark came to Japan from Texas to experience life outside of the United States. But Japan was a bit of a shock to his system at first, particularly because he experienced some overt forms of discrimination against foreigners. Renting an apartment, for example, was often a major hassle because many landlords would not have anything to do with a foreign national. "In Texas, being a white male means you never have to experience any form of discrimination. In this sense, American women might be better prepared for life here than American men," he says.

But he quickly adds that he also sees why Japan is such a popular place for certain Western men. "A lot of guys love it here because they can get away with bullying the innocent and the naive," he says. After a pause, he continues, mentioning how when he first came to Tokyo and stayed at a *gaijin* house (low-budget housing for foreign tourists and people on short stays), he was shocked to hear two Canadian men bragging about "gang raping" a woman. "They actually said that it was like playing American football."

Mark, who is young and preppy-looking, gets all the dates he can handle whenever he makes the rounds in Roppongi. More often than not, he is the one who is approached by women—not all of them single—at bars. He says he has been invited to love hotels on several occasions by married women in their late twenties and early thirties. These women, he says, were usually the wives of fairly well-to-do businessmen "who knew what their wives were doing."

At the time we spoke, Mark did not have a steady Japanese girlfriend. In fact, he found himself going out with Western women more often than Japanese simply because "Japanese women aren't straightforward, and that isn't attractive to me." Besides, Japan is only a temporary stop-over for Mark. In two year's time he plans to leave for Europe.

International Singles Parties

Professionals who have little opportunity to meet women through work and are unhappy with Roppongi pick-up joints or the casual atmosphere of English-language lounges may choose to attend "international singles parties," which are often organized specifically for Western men to meet Japanese women. These parties may take different forms, depending on the organizers.

The first Japanese-sponsored international parties I know of began around 1989. I remember seeing an ad in a local English-language newspaper urging foreign singles to join an international party in Shinjuku (a major city center) organized by a local matchmaking magazine, where they could meet local women. The ad caught my interest and I decided to do a story for a local paper. When I called to make a reservation, however, they turned me down, saying that I had to be Japanese to participate. As it turned out, foreign women and Japanese men were not invited to these so-called international parties. After some coaxing, I managed to talk my way in. For ¥2,000 each, foreign men were provided with a chance to mix and mingle with about thirty to forty Japanese women. Participants sported name tags and were encouraged to match up as couples by writing down the name of their favorite partner on a piece of paper. To further encourage intimacy, couples that were successfully matched up were awarded a complimentary night's stay at a hotel. I met an American freelance writer who also went to cover the party and watched him walk away with a woman he had met there.

Evidently, this kind of party is still being sponsored by similar organizations (and a handful of other Japanese groups) although restrictions regarding nationality are no longer strictly enforced. Prices, however, have skyrocketed. One party I was recently invited to in Shibuya had an admission charge of ¥9,000, which covered music, snacks, and a curry dish. Prizes are no longer given. What's more, only female Japanese participants were charged admission. The men I talked to at the party said that when they were invited there was no mention of an admission fee.

Singles parties held by the foreign community tend to be slightly different. One of the better-known affairs was the now-defunct "Single in Tokyo" party. Organized by a businessman who felt it was difficult for businessmen stationed in Tokyo to meet people, he took it upon himself to invite, by word-of-mouth, friends and friends-of-friends to meet every last Friday of the month at a Roppongi club. For a while, the party was very popular among an "in-group," with fifty to eighty people attending each session. Although the organizer insisted that it was not a foreign-men-meet-Japanese-women setup, some of the regulars told me otherwise.

Although the "Single in Tokyo" party was discontinued early in March 1993, a few new ones have emerged. One is the "Second Friday Party," a rather tame gathering that meets at another club in Roppongi. The organizer, Kimihiro Okuma, says he conceived of these parties as a way for "decent people" to meet each other. In the five years since the first gathering, three couples have taken the road to matrimony. In addition, there is a "Beer Bash in Setagaya" and an "International Socializing Party." But as new international parties continue to pop up, the existing ones also quickly disappear from the Tokyo scene.

Yumi, an OL acquaintance, has been to a few such international parties among her attempts to find a Western marriage partner. They did not really work for her, she says. Her story below demonstrates the frustration a lot of marriage-minded Japanese women face.

• Yumi

Yumi is an OL who works for a foreign lawyer's office as a legal assistant. A somewhat overprotected daughter who lives with her parents and younger sister, Yumi says she did not have a lot of dating experience. In the beginning, her lifestyle seemed fine; she made fairly good money and didn't have to pay rent. She went out on weekends with friends and could afford a trip or two every year to Australia and the U.S. As she approached thirty, she says, she noticed that most of her college friends had married. Marriage suddenly became an issue she felt she had to confront.

Her aunt offered to be a go-between for an *omiai*, but this unromantic approach to marriage did not appeal to Yumi. She felt, however, that there were no other realistic options open to her, as Japanese men seemed to be interested only in younger women. She considered going out with foreign men, but most of those in her office were older and already married. After reading about international parties in various Japanese magazines, she decided to try them out. She says, however, that they were outrageously expensive. She also discovered that most of the men who attended were not very interesting. They were either older men or shy English teachers—definitely not what she was looking for. Eventually, she stopped attending.

When a twenty-eight-year-old British lawyer joined the law office, Yumi thought her chance had finally arrived. Working with him seemed to make her days pass by a lot more quickly. One evening, she went out with the staff—including the young lawyer—to Roppongi to celebrate the company's tenth anniversary. As the evening wore on, Yumi followed the men from bar to bar until she found she was the only woman remaining, along with the young lawyer and another colleague. She says she hadn't yet figured out what to do about returning home and, in the meantime, her train had stopped running. At midnight, she took a cab with the young lawyer to his apartment. Though it wasn't what she had planned, she says she wasn't upset about it either. They spent the night together and the following morning she asked him if he was serious about her. He promptly said, "No." He apologized for what had happened the night before and said he already had a girlfriend. Yumi says she felt terrible afterward, particularly as she still had to work with him. She fell into a deep depression.

A few weeks later, a friend took Yumi to a conversation lounge where she met an American English teacher, who was a divorced father with two children. They started going out about twice a week. After three months, Yumi started asking him about marriage, but he was not interested. In fact, he said he had been through one marriage and wasn't sure if he would ever marry again. Yumi was very disappointed at this turn of events and decided to end the relationship.

Although she has thought about giving up on the idea of marrying, she isn't sure if she could. "I've always lived with my parents and if I don't marry, I just don't know if I've got what it takes to lead a life on my own," she says.

Dating Services and Personal Ads

International parties can be just as boring for men as they are for women. At least Peter, an American friend, thinks so. A twenty-seven-year-old engineer who is determined to marry a Japanese woman before he returns to America, Peter admits that he had been a regular since coming to Tokyo six months ago. One problem with the parties, he says, is that after a while, he tended to meet the same people over and over again. He says he went out with a few women he met at these parties, but when he found that they were not what he was looking for, he returned to look again. His old dates, he said, had the same idea, which caused some awkward moments.

Those who fail to find what they are looking for at international parties may turn to one of the few professional international dating services in Tokyo.

There are said to be more than one hundred international-marriage brokers in Japan. Most, however, cater to Japanese farmers who have difficulty finding Japanese brides because of their isolated and labor-intensive lifestyles. These brokers set up meetings with women from less-affluent Asian countries (see Chapter 7). The number of international matchmaking services tailored to Caucasian men wanting to meet Japanese women is limited. In Tokyo, there are a handful of such services advertised in the yellow pages or in English-language magazines, e.g., Dandies Minami Aoyama, Beavers System International, Inter-Connect Systems, Transpacific Marriage Agency, and Freedom International Marriage Club. Although Dandies is strictly a local service that aims at bringing Tokyo-based singles together, some of the others attempt to match Japanese with prospects across the Atlantic and Pacific oceans. A few also provide a service that introduces Japanese men and foreign women.

Information gathered through interviews shows that registration fees vary from place to place. For Western men, the going rate is between ¥30,000–¥40,000. For women, however, ¥270,000 or more is charged. For the registration fee, a man can expect to be introduced to a variety of women. He must promise to foot all the bills for his dates. The introductions are supposed to continue until a match results. Fees for services to arrange a meeting with a prospective partner overseas can run to ¥500,000 or more.

Not everyone, however, is prepared to pay this kind of price for romance. For them, there is another option—placing a personal ad in a local English-language magazine like the *Tokyo Journal*—a popular monthly events magazine—or in one of the few Japanese-language matchmaking magazines like *Mr. Partner* or the *Hiragana Times*.

But how well do these services work? The following two case studies may shed some light.

• Peter

A former navy officer from West Virginia with extensive experience in the Far East, Peter says he has always liked Asian women. He didn't care for American women as much because he found many of them to be selfish and not oriented toward being wives and mothers. But more importantly, he says American women do not hesitate to say no. Whereas "a beautiful American woman knows she's beautiful and won't give you the time of day. But here, women are not as stuck up."

Peter says that, in the U.S., men have to be very aggressive if they want to go out with a beautiful woman. But in

Japan, most women don't seem to know they are beautiful and do not shun men the way American women do. Peter had hoped that meeting women would be easy in Japan. Employed as an engineer in a Japanese firm with a predominantly male staff, however, Peter found it difficult to meet women. He didn't particularly like the Roppongi scene, so he attended a few of the international parties. "All I want is someone who is good-looking, maybe a couple of years younger than I am, and knows how to speak English well," he said. However, he didn't meet anyone who quite fit the bill and became so frustrated that he even tried slipping a self-introductory note to a friendly shopkeeper at a local Seven-Eleven store. It didn't work; she refused to speak to him from then on.

Four months ago he met Mami, a beautiful Japanese woman who worked as a flight attendant for a foreign airline. She was everything he wanted: she was good-looking, spoke good English, and was only twenty-four. Peter, smitten, thought he had finally found his dream girl. Happily, she seemed to be just as interested. Everything went fine for about two months until he received a phone call from a mutual friend late one evening who broke the news that Mami was planning to marry and had been engaged all along to a Japanese man stationed in New York. When Peter confronted her she cried, saying that she had not had the courage to tell him about it, and hadn't wanted to hurt him.

As he was recovering from that devastating experience, Peter decided to give international dating services a try. During the initial interview at one such agency, he was shown pictures of several beautiful, "star-quality" women. He was warned, however, that he should reconsider his age requirement as the women who registered were likely to be older. After a screening test, he was asked to pay a ¥35,000 registration fee. Over the ensuing weeks, he met several of the women. Each time he had to foot the bill for the date. He says, however, that the experience proved to be a total disappointment as none of the women he met were as pretty as they were supposed to be, not to mention the fact that a couple of them also seemed to be overly anxious about wanting to leave Japan. Peter was not impressed. "I am not going to be a ticket for some woman who wants to get out of Japan," he said. After five weeks, Peter decided he was wasting his time and money and quit the agency altogether. From Peter's experiences, it seems that the "perfect woman" myth is perpetuated by those with unrealistic expectations.

On the international romance scene, it appears that the game can be as hard for women as it is for men. Junko's adventure with personal ads, in some ways, echoes the perplexing experience that Peter experienced with dating services.

● Junko

Junko worked for a foreign capital firm with a very small staff. At age twenty-seven, she says she felt some pressure to look for a husband. But she was not interested in Japanese men. "They are so immature and predictable. If you go out with a Japanese man, I bet he'll start off by asking questions like 'What's your blood-type?' and 'What's your zodiac sign?' It's so boring," she says. A pretty woman with long hair and good fashion sense, Junko always dresses sharply. She also speaks good English. She knows she has what it takes to draw the attention of Western men, but she has always been rather choosy about whom she dates. She had been seeing an American technical writer and claimed he had all the desirable qualities: a good job, a nice character, and fairly good looks. But she felt that something was missing. "Really, if you know anyone who's interested in meeting a nice American guy, I'll be happy to play the matchmaker," she said half-seriously.

After she lost interest in him, she worked hard, she says, to find a replacement. He didn't have to be extraordinary, "Just a Caucasian from North America or Britain with a good profession, preferably a lawyer or a university professor. But where do you find them? It's so hard to meet nice guys these days." Junko tried different ways of maximizing her opportunities to meet eligible men. She had been to several international parties and tried to visit different English conversation lounges whenever she had a free evening. But she wasn't impressed by what she saw. Although a friend who had registered with a local international dating service advised her to do the same, she felt the registration fee was too high. Instead, she decided to place a personal ad in the *Tokyo Journal.* From among thirty responses, she carefully selected one candidate: a British man working as a copy editor.

After dating him for a few weeks, Junko felt compelled to continue with her search for Mr. Right, for this man was set to leave Japan in four months and she felt he was only using her. So while she was seeing him, she kept her eyes open for a better candidate. In the meantime, she wondered if she was wasting her time as she didn't want to live in Britain, even if he proposed.

Other Options

Prior to the eighties, the kind of job openings available to foreign nationals in major Japanese cities had been limited mostly to teaching jobs at English schools and the odd in-house position with a foreign company. As a result of the bubble years, employment opportunities have expanded into other fields. With that change, the meeting grounds for foreign men and Japanese women have also extended beyond the scope of English schools and Roppongi bars to universities, business offices, and other places. Of course the U.S. military bases, as they have been since the fifties, remain a viable meeting ground for Japanese women and American GIs.

Chance meetings are made all the more easily as neither party feels obliged to observe the dating code of their own culture. Foreign men often say that they find Japanese women more open to the idea of asking the man out first—something they say most Western women are still not very comfortable with.

The following story concerns Rob and Yasuko, who met under rather unusual circumstances.

• Rob and Yasuko

Rob and Yasuko met three years ago at a restaurant—unintentionally. That day, while Rob and a friend were eating, they overheard a woman at the next table criticizing Americans to her friends, half in Japanese and half in English. Rob, a twenty-six-year-old English teacher from the Midwest, felt upset about the attack and decided to join in the conversation. The two ended up in an argument, but they also found the situation amusing and decided to go out afterward. To Rob's relief, Yasuko, who had studied in the United States for a year, spoke very good English. This created a common ground that was also part of the initial attraction Rob felt for Yasuko. "She's very smart, very strong," he says.

But Yasuko was not quite sure about Rob. The fact that he was an untrained English teacher and not a professional working for a big company bothered her. Yasuko, twenty-seven, was working at the time for a major Japanese bank handling foreign accounts. Before she met Rob, she had gone out with another American man named Rick for eight months. Rick, who had graduated from an Ivy League university, was in many ways "a lot more sophisticated." But Rick was also very demanding and critical of Yasuko. In fact, he tended to be rather cold and told her directly that she was too dependent on him. He was also very chauvinistic and never expressed thanks when Yasuko poured beer for him or waited on him. Before he left her, he made it clear that what he wanted was a strong woman who was both emotionally and financially independent. Until Yasuko met Rick, she said she had thought all Western men were extremely romantic and would take care of their women completely. "But I was wrong; that was a big illusion," she recalls.

Yasuko had no complaints about Rob as a person. Compared to Rick, he was a lot more sensitive and understanding. The problem was Rob's future prospects. She worried about his being able to find a job back in his own country, as he was not a professional ESL teacher. Although the two had discussed marriage, Yasuko was hesitant. Somehow, she couldn't bear the thought of marrying a man who might fall short as a breadwinner. It was not that she rejected the idea of working after marriage; it was just that she was not used to the idea of having to contribute in terms of finances as an equal partner.

Rob finally proved that Yasuko's worries were unnecessary. Rob quit his teaching job and left for the U.S. to look for a job. He found a position in California working as a journalist for a local newspaper—something he had always wanted to do. Yasuko was very pleased with the move and decided to join him in the United States.

This chance meeting worked out well for Rob and Yasuko. However, random meetings have not quite worked out for Naomi, the woman mentioned in Chapter 3, who frequents a navy base in the hope of finding a steady boyfriend or future husband. Here is her story in detail.

• Naomi

Naomi, a twenty-one-year-old with an innocent look and a broad smile is a junior high school dropout who works as a receptionist at a karaoke bar making about ¥800 an hour. A curious girl who knows little about the outside world, Naomi dreams of visiting foreign countries. One day, as she was walking through her neighborhood near the U.S. Navy base at Yokosuka, she was picked up by an American sailor. She soon decided to go with him to a nearby hotel.

Although the affair lasted only a few weeks before the sailor shipped out, the encounter changed her life. The novelty and danger excited her and she decided she would only date Caucasian men. Naomi started hanging out at Club Alliance near the gate to the base, waiting for GIs to pick her up. At times, she asked to be escorted to the club to maximize her chances of meeting men. In a year's time, she became intimate with more than twenty men, many of whom were one-night stands. "It's not that I didn't want to continue the relationships; it's only that these guys so often just come and go with their ships," she explains. She didn't particularly like the situation, but learned to keep cool and play the game. She says she wishes she could get to know men who are not related to the base.

Because she speaks very little English, she knows her options are limited. She thought about going to language school to study, but "that would cost a lot of money and time, and there's no guarantee that I would learn how to speak the language." She reckons it is better to just practice her English at Club Alliance.

Looking at the Big Picture

It is often said that, in general, people involved in cross-cultural romances are more susceptible to frustration and disappointment. If this is the case, then the problems are likely to be magnified in international relationships involving Western men and Japanese women. Differences in language and culture are two of the obvious contributing factors. More often than not, however, it is the mutually exaggerated expectations, based on myths and stereotypes, that are the causes.

Common Myths Concerning Japan's International Dating Scene

Perhaps one of the most prevalent myths among Western men is the belief that in Japan they can pick up women everywhere. Dan, the English teacher from Britain mentioned earlier in the case studies, for example, says he has never had any women approach him on the street or at school. In fact, he knew of a good-looking man from the United States who, during his eight-month stay in Japan as an English teacher, never had a single date. Peter, the engineer from West Virginia, has also had great difficulty meeting women. One thing that worked against both Dan's friend and Peter is that neither of them spoke much Japanese. Although more and more Japanese people are speaking better English, the hard fact remains that they are still in the minority. Therefore, it is not difficult to see why relationships can be quite limited in Japan unless the foreign man has acquired a certain fluency in the language.

Another factor has to do with appearance. As mentioned earlier, certain looks tend to be very popular among Japanese women. As a general rule, young Japanese women go for blond-hair and blue-eyes. This has to do with their *honmono shikō*, which loosely translates as "a desire for the real McCoy." Put another way, to the Japanese, people with blond hair and blue eyes are seen as being the ultimate *gaijin*. One Japanese woman explained it to me this way, "It's almost like buying a Gucci bag—since most Japanese women can't really tell the difference from one product to another, they go for the name brands—satisfaction guaranteed." This obsession with blonds is quite prevalent. One freelance sports announcer said that a frustrated foreign friend of his felt compelled to dye his hair.

A lack of language skills or the right looks have not, however, stopped certain types of men. The Australian teacher mentioned previously who was written up in the *Hiragana Times*, for instance, claimed to have had affairs with eighty women during his four years in Japan. His technique for picking up girls included playing lost at stations and intentionally bumping into a woman on a crowded train. He always apologized and secured his prey by asking for the woman's number.

According to Dr. Jim McRae, executive director and marriage counselor at the Counseling Center of Tokyo, this kind of foreign man is quite common. "Many Western men with sexual disorders come to Japan to act out their fantasies simply because they find it easy to do so in Japan," he says. These men, he adds, take advantage of the naiveté of Japanese women to get their way. Doctor McRae says he has treated several men with this type of disorder.

Another myth some Western men have about dating in Japan is that beautiful women are accessible to any foreign man. Peter, whose bride-hunt story through dating services was mentioned earlier as a case study, certainly was under this assumption, but his experiences proved him wrong. As one American lawyer said, ten to fifteen years ago when the foreign community was still relatively small, being a *gaijin* male would almost certainly confer a kind of celebrity status. But those days are over. I interviewed a thirty-two-year-old owner of a small communications firm, a woman who claims she has many foreign friends. She says that many of her male friends who have this attitude of being "God's gift to the local women" complain to her about their not-so-fortunate encounters with beautiful, young Japanese women. "What they don't seem to understand is that beautiful Japanese women don't have to pay court to them just because they are foreigners. After all, there are plenty of guys after them." She says that it is a big mistake for men to take the outward friendliness of a Japanese woman for interest, as Japanese people in general like to avoid a confrontation at all costs. Just because Japanese women don't come out and say, "Leave me alone; I'm not interested," does not necessarily mean that they oblige easily, she says. Her point is well taken, as an ever-growing number of men can testify based on personal experience. To their discomfort, they have found that the Japanese woman's indirect, roundabout way of saying no can be confusing and eventually much more hurtful than a straight refusal.

The other side of the story is that many women in big cities are also becoming more selective about whom they will date. Junko is one such example. Accustomed to the relatively affluent lifestyle that has accompanied Japan's economic success, many women want to ensure that they will live comfortably after marriage. This is why marriage-minded women tend to be very careful about ensuring that their potential husbands have good incomes. The "three highs," mentioned in Chapter 2, as qualities for a future husband, are a strong indication of how carefully they consider a potential mate's qualifications. Women generally receive far lower pay in Japan (about 40 percent less) than men for equal work. Traditionally, marriages were not based on romance but treated more as a business arrangement to further the fortunes of the family. The man brought home the rice and the woman controlled both the purse strings and the raising and education of the children. Rather than romance, it was a caretaker-housekeeper relationship.

A woman like Junko, who like many OLs does not have the solid working skills nor the means to lead an independent life, does not make herself readily available to just any man. She rules out those she thinks have few prospects of securing a good job in their own country. This attitude is obviously spreading among women who are seeking foreign husbands through international dating agencies. To meet his clients' high expectations, Fumiharu Yoshimura, director of Dandies Minami Aoyama, makes it a rule not to provide services to American GIs or foreign men working as English teachers in Japan.

The Changing Attitudes of Japanese Women

It is misleading, however, to assume that all young Japanese women are like Junko. Yasuko, mentioned earlier, represents the contemporary Japanese woman who finds herself at a societal crossroads. In some ways, Yasuko also wishes for a marriage complete with a meal ticket, but she is also looking for a more emotionally fulfilling relationship that the traditional Japanese marriage often lacks. What do you do if you can't have both? Should she trade financial stability for emotional support? One thing she has learned is that Western men are not as tightly tied to the breadwinner role. The equal rights movement in the

Western world has allowed men more freedom to make different choices in life. Furthermore, with more Western women working and contributing equally toward the household income, more men can afford the luxury of pursuing their own personal interests. What this means is that a Japanese woman who wants to marry a Western man may have to be prepared to become more financially independent and ready to chip in her share toward the household income.

Perhaps Noriko, as mentioned earlier in this chapter, is a more typical example of today's increasingly independent Japanese women. Although she is in her early thirties, she did not think about marriage until she met the right man. She also has a career and is very positive about her future. This seems to be a strengthening trend as more and more women are opting to have their own careers and lead independent lives; they no longer pin their entire future on men. I have come across quite a few women like Noriko in journalism, broadcasting, and academic fields.

A man like Peter, however, might not have been interested in an independent woman like Noriko because of the conditions he has set for his dream woman, including his insistence that she be very young. Most women, at age twenty-four or twenty-five, are not yet interested in marriage. Foreign men have repeatedly told me that Japanese women are often quite immature for their age. They say that those younger than twenty-six are not likely to have fully developed their own way of thinking and are therefore not very interesting to talk to.

Although this is a generalization, I believe it carries some truth, as most single Japanese women (unlike their Western counterparts) continue to live with their parents and never experience the struggle of having to fend for themselves. As long as they are young and cute, society allows them to maintain their childishness. Suddenly, when they approach thirty, they are forced to grow up as society pressures them to behave like adults and marry.

Marriage-minded women looking for Western husbands consequently tend to be in their late twenties and early thirties. In fact, according to Yoshimura, there are three types of women who are particularly interested in marrying Western men: women from wealthy families who are not interested in living a Japanese lifestyle; women with experience working and studying overseas, who look to benefit from this experience; and Japanese women who are looking for something different. Mr. Yoshimura says that, in general, the last group has the least knowledge and experience of the West and their enthusiasm for foreign men tends to be blindly based on myths generated by the mass media.

Are Western Men Really Yasashii?

One of the most common misconceptions the latter type of women have about Western men is that they are all good caretakers, *feminisuto* (feminists) and practice *rediifāsuto* ("ladies first," an expression used by Japanese to describe the chivalrous manners of the Western male). Naomi, who has had little exposure to Western culture, is the type most susceptible to this sort of myth. Even a worldly woman like Yasuko admitted to believing the myths to be true about Western men—until she met Rick, her former boyfriend. Takako Day, a U.S.-based Japanese journalist married to an American man, has written many articles about cross-cultural relationships. She says that this belief is widespread among Japanese women. It is encouraged, she argues, by Hollywood movies, which tend to show only the romantic, idealistic side of Western men. "I have been in the United States for more than eight years and have met many American men who would not lift a finger to help in the kitchen," she says. This is the side of the story that few Japanese women ever hear about.

Whatever good manners Western men may have upon their arrival in Japan often disappear within months. Why? "Because Japanese women are too eager to show them a grand time," says Rika Okada, who works for a local English newspaper. Many Japanese women, in their attempt to capture the heart of their Western boyfriend, bend over backward to wait on him. "The result is that he becomes spoiled and unappreciative just like a Japanese man," she adds. If Japanese women want to maintain the good qualities of the Western male, she says, they will have to learn not to pour him a beer every time he has an empty glass in front of him.

The *yasashisa*, or kindliness, of Western men is sometimes taken too much at face value by Japanese women. Ken Joseph says that he has received a number of phone calls from women who have been victimized by foreign men. In one case, a thirty-two-year-old woman was cheated out of 50 million yen (roughly US $500,000) by an unscrupulous American English teacher with whom she had a brief relationship. The man promised to marry her and asked to borrow the money to start a business. He left for New York and never called her back.

"Japanese women often equate kindness with goodness. They can't tell a nice guy from a jerk. What's more, they tend to take for granted the responsible nature of Japanese men (even though this also exists in foreign men)," Joseph says. Because Japanese women are often drawn to the flamboyant type of Western man who tends to be irresponsible, Joseph says they are extremely vulnerable to abuse.

A more experienced woman such as Junko is not likely

to fall into this kind of relationship as she knows how to protect her own interests. The only problem for Junko is her extremely high expectation of what a foreign man will be for her. It is an entirely different story with young women like Naomi, who pick up men at the military bases. She hangs on to her naiveté and allows herself, in her indiscriminate search for a boyfriend, to be taken advantage of. Unfortunately, women with little self-confidence think that sex is the only way to win a man.

Although there are no statistics to confirm this, promiscuity is believed to have become more common among women in their late teens and early twenties. One model who frequents Roppongi says he knows of a sixteen-year-old girl from a broken home who goes to a love hotel with two or three different men every week. What is even more alarming is that she does not practice safe sex. During the course of my interviews, I have been told several times that there is a wide assumption among foreign men that unprotected sex with Japanese women is safe as they are supposedly less promiscuous. This is untrue, says Doctor Yutaka Masuda, a sex counselor working at a Tokyo hospital. He also pointed out that Japanese women are often extremely naive or shy about asking their partners to use protection during intercourse.

Factors That Can Frustrate Romance

There are several factors that can make cross-cultural romance in Japan, particularly in Tokyo, an anxious experience.

1. Tokyo Transiency

Japan attracts foreigners from both East and West with promises of jobs and business opportunities. In the wake of economic affluence and internationalization, Japan's major cities were quickly discovered to be meccas for those seeking to make easy money. Because many are motivated by the lure of money rather than an interest in Japanese society and culture, their commitment to Japan tends to be very short-term. Japan, accordingly, becomes a playground for these foreign men on extended work-vacations. They bring a transient attitude toward life in Japan, and this carries over into their relationships. Also, many, when encountering freedom for the first time outside of their home countries where they don't have to worry about being judged by family and close friends, tend to be very irresponsible with themselves. Their behavior, in some ways, is not unlike that of the so-called yellow cabs.

For a Japanese woman, it will be a heart-rending experience falling in love with someone who is bound to leave in a matter of months or years, or, as one American man puts it, "is going through the phase of being the bad *gaijin.*" This is particularly the case if she is near thirty and desperate to marry. Not a few of these women devote themselves to their foreign lovers, volunteering their services as interpreters and guides to Japan. As such, many are unable to escape the fate of becoming contemporary Madame Butterflies.

2. *The Loneliness Factor*

The possibility of attraction between Western men and Japanese women is almost irresistible. One immediate force that brings them together is loneliness. A foreign man in a new environment who does not speak the local language can easily become angry and discouraged when faced with overt forms of discrimination such as signs that read "No Foreigners Accepted for Rentals" or "No Foreigners Admitted to Restaurant." He may consequently seek a Japanese girlfriend to give him a better fix on his new surroundings and help him communicate by acting as his interpreter. An American writer once explained the attraction in this way: "When you come to Japan, you don't want to go out with a foreign woman because that will only intensify the extent of your disorientation. A Japanese woman, on the other hand, can serve as a stabilizing factor during your stay— thus the attraction."

3. A Western Veneer

Finding a date is considerably less difficult than keeping a relationship going. Basic cultural differences and wide gaps in perceptions and expectations are the primary reasons for troubles and breakups. One of the most commonly cited cultural differences is in communication—the Japanese "yes" and "no." That many Japanese women (and men, for that matter) tend to nod yes without fully understanding what's being said or asked or because they are too embarrassed to ask, can often lead to misunderstandings and subsequent mishaps.

Foreign men also complain that their Japanese girlfriends are too indirect about saying no, which they confuse with dishonesty. They are puzzled as to when they should take a yes for a no, and vice versa. The most exasperating situation for Western men is when they feel Japanese women are vague about wanting to call it quits, which goes back to the Japanese tendency to avoid confrontation at all costs. Ronald and Peter both had this experience. In Peter's case, he had to find out about Mami's plans to marry another man from a mutual friend. "I wish she had told me from the beginning, then I wouldn't have fallen for her in the first place," he says.

An example of another kind of common miscommunication was repeated in a story in *Crea*.[1] This article told of an American man who invited a woman friend from work for a chat at his apartment. Her first visit ended up with her crying and him sending her home. She had begun to cry when he told her that he just wanted to talk with her, and that there were no other intentions on his part. What had caused her to cry? The writer says that Japanese women, while expecting to be led by a man on an occasion like this, may also feel a bit hesitant and scared. Ultimately they want the man to take the responsibility of asking them to bed. This allows the woman to say later that "It was you who wanted to sleep with me, so you have to make a commitment."

In this case, the woman cried possibly because she was disappointed that the American man did not assume the responsibility and consequently she was made to lose face. A Japanese man would take her tears and hesitation to indicate a "woman's pride" and would pursue her further. Conversely, an American man, who is used to a clear yes or no, would find the woman's behavior disturbing. This is why the American man in the article ended up sending her home. It goes on to say that this kind of miscommunication is not at all uncommon in international romances between Japanese women and foreign men.

Because of these kinds of communication gaps, Japanese women can fall victim to foreign men who willfully take advantage of their inability to say a clear "no" when they mean to say "no." Megumi Baba, coordinator of the STD/ AIDS Japanese Outreach Program at the Waikiki Health Center in Hawaii whom I mentioned in Chapter 3, once told me about a client who had broken down during a counseling session at the center. The young woman, who was living in Hawaii at the time, said she had been approached several times by an American man. Although she made excuses many times, he persisted in asking her out.

She finally felt "forced" into going out with him, which ended essentially in date rape, as she was unable to firmly tell him "no." Baba says that Japanese women need to be more confident and learn how to say "no" when they mean it.

4. *The Gap between Sex and Love*

Other problems that get in the way of most international relationships are the differences in the languages of love and marriage. There is a saying in Japanese that couples fall in love after they get married. This is not an exaggeration as, even today, many couples are brought together by the need to fulfill social obligations, rather than because of love. Romance, as has been pointed out by many social critics, is not traditionally a part of a Japanese marriage, no matter what the women's magazines promise. In the West, however, love is a highly valued motivation for marriage. Therefore, while marriage is the consequence of a couple's relationship in the West, the reverse is often true in Japan.

True, many more Japanese women are looking for romantic love and are shying away from the traditional *omiai* (arranged marriages). For those seeking cross-cultural romance, their search is complicated by the differences in Japanese and Western notions of sex and love. If carefree sex is more accepted in the West as something that can be enjoyed separately from love, then in Japan, sex, or physical love, has traditionally been very much an expression of love itself.[2] According to *Warera ga sei-mondai hakusho* (Our White Paper on Sexuality, Taishukan-shoten, 1993), in ancient Japan, there was no Japanese expression equivalent to the English expression of "I love you." The ancient Japanese way to express love was to say "I want you." In this sense, in the thinking of early Japanese, there was no love without sex and no sex without love.

If many Japanese women still feel that sex and love are inseparable, then many may expect that sex should inevitably lead to marriage. After all, sex is the expression of love, and love, as they have been seeing over and over again in Western movies and in foreign novels, is the reason for marriage.

Unfortunately for the Japanese girlfriends, many Western men often make a clear distinction between sex and marriage. One forty-year-old divorced American, who made up his mind to stay single, said he had to break up with two Japanese girlfriends because they both had wanted to get married. "Why can't they just enjoy the relationship and the good times?" he complained.

Aside from this strong link between sex and marriage, there is the social pressure placed on women to marry by a certain age. Though more Japanese women are postponing marriage, being an old maid still carries a strong social stigma. This is why women in their late twenties and early thirties seem particularly desperate to get married. This strong urge to marry explains why many Japanese women resort to hysteria when they realize they have no chance of receiving a commitment from their foreign boyfriends. This is the case with the thirty-year-old woman that Ronald went out with. When she found out that Ronald was not ready for commitment, she ended up haranguing him for weeks. In some cases, women even threaten suicide to try to force their foreign boyfriends to marry them.

5. Language —An Inevitable Issue

One reason that holds a Western man back from taking his Japanese girlfriend home to meet Mom and Dad is the woman's lack of English-speaking skills. I have been told many times by foreign men, particularly Americans, that they wouldn't marry a Japanese woman who had few marketable skills in their home country. "She's very nice and everything, but she hardly speaks any English. What could she do in the United States?" says an American technical writer. "If I wanted to stay in Japan, she would be perfect. But the problem is, I don't want to do that."

Likewise, language can also become a problem for some foreign men residing in Japan with Japanese wives, particularly those with limited Japanese skills. Often they feel resentful because they are dependent on their wives and are led to believe that they are being controlled by their partners. This may become a source of stress for both parties and a potential hazard in the marriage.

 CHAPTER SIX

Japanese Wives, Western Husbands

Intercultural marriages between Asian women and Western men trigger a variety of reactions. A common one among Western women is pity or empathy for the "victimized Asian woman." This attitude has been conditioned by the narrative convention of portraying Oriental women as being submissive and helpless while white men are seen as callous. There is also a deep-rooted assumption that an Asian woman, as a member of a deprived underclass seeking to improve her fate through her affinity for a Western lover, will almost certainly be exploited at his hands.

The following letter, sent by an American woman to the *Pacific Stars and Stripes* in 1993 is an example of this view:

> Millions of American men marry women who can't speak English, are from diverse cultures, are usually not close to their own age, and basically have nothing in common with them .
> Asian women marry these men not for love but for survival. They want these men because of what they have: ID cards and the accompanying benefits. The

men don't want partners who can think and share common interests; they want slaves.

Until Asian women wise up, become educated and do not marry/date sexist idiots, they will continue to be used, abused, and abandoned.

—*Name withheld, Yongsan, ROK*[1]

This view, while still very widespread, is proving to be more and more outdated, at least as far as Japanese women are concerned. Intermarriage has gone through great changes over the past two decades. Today, Japanese wives of foreign husbands have a much more liberated role in marriage.

Decline in American–Japanese Marriages

Until very recently, the Japanese have equated international marriages with alliances between Japanese women and American men—an image no doubt influenced by the U.S. military presence in Japan after World War II and best-sellers such as James Michener's *Sayonara* (1964). Indeed, until the early 1960s, over half of all cross-cultural marriages in Japan were between Japanese women and American men.[2]

This trend, according to Ministry of Health and Welfare figures, continued into the sixties. In 1969, for example, American husbands accounted for 51.6 percent of all husbands in intermarriages. This, according to Professor Fumiteru Nitta of Kibi International University, was most likely a repercussion of the American Occupation, which produced thousands of "war brides." The Korean and Vietnam wars also brought to Eastern shores many U.S. soldiers on leave or working on U.S. military bases in Japan who took Japanese wives.[3]

Since the mid-1970s, however, the non-Japanese husband was less likely to be an American. Government figures show that Koreans, many of whom are permanent residents of Japan, now make up the largest group of foreign men married to Japanese women. In 1975, for example, 55 percent of the 2,823 Japanese women who married non-Japanese men were wedded to Koreans, while only 22.4 percent were wedded to Americans. This was followed by 14 percent wedded to men from "other foreign countries," and 8.6 percent to Chinese.[4]

Although American men have remained at the top of the Western groom list, there are indications that intermarriages are diversifying. In 1991, 21.7 percent of all foreign grooms were from "other foreign countries," a slightly higher figure, for the first time, compared with the 21.3 percent who were Americans. By 1993, the percentage of foreign grooms from other foreign countries had gone up to 25.2 percent while that from America had dropped to 21 percent.

While a breakdown of nationalities was not available for the "other" category before, this began to change in 1992, where the category was further broken down into the "Philippines," "Thailand," "Britain," "Brazil," "Peru," and "Other." According to government-released data, among these new sub-categories, both Britons and Brazilians account for the two fastest-growing groups of non-Japanese grooms of Japanese women.[5] Meanwhile, according to the latest available guide, the Association for Multicultural Families (AMF), formerly known as Kokusai-Kekkon o Kangaeru Kai, has over four hundred Japanese women members married to men from some fifty countries.[6]

Diversification of Intercultural Marriages

The foreign groom is not only less likely to be an American, he is also less likely to be affiliated with the military, as the U.S. military presence in Japan has dwindled since the 1970s. According to Sheila K. Johnson in her book *The Japanese Through American Eyes*, there were between 210,000 and 260,000 U.S. soldiers in Japan in the early 1950s. From 1958 to 1970, that number dropped to below 100,000. Since 1975, the total number of American troops in Japan has "hovered at around 46,000 a year."[7] According to the public affairs office at Yokota Air Base, this number has remained about the same.

While the number of American GIs declined over the years, the number of Western civilians immigrating to Japan has continued to grow as more of them seek to improve their dwindling job opportunities and upgrade their lifestyles. Jobs requiring English-language skills have been plentiful in Japan, especially during the bubble years, and the salaries are much higher than those in North America or Europe for equivalent work. According to the Justice Ministry, a record 3.1 million foreigners entered Japan in 1994, with more than 130,000 coming specifically to work in different professions. (This represents an 18 percent increase from the 1991 figures.) These numbers do not include the many more on tourist or other visas who are working illegally in Japan, as well as those with spouse visas, which allow them to work.

Meanwhile, since the lifting of Japanese laws against foreign travel in 1964, more Japanese have been traveling and living overseas. Of the 687,579 Japanese recorded as living abroad in 1993, a combined total of over 48 percent lived in the U.S., UK, and Canada (36.7 percent, 8.1

percent, and 3.7 percent respectively). The result has been an increase in Japanese–Western marriages.

A Changing Nexus in the Balance of Power

One of the biggest changes in modern-day intercultural marriages is a shift in the balance of power. As Johnson pointed out, in the immediate post-war days many Japanese women married American GIs out of a desperate need to escape poverty. Marrying a man from the conquering nation was, not surprisingly, looked upon with suspicion and contempt by the Japanese community. What's more, because Japanese law decreed that Japanese women who married foreigners would automatically lose their citizenship, the decision to marry a non-Japanese meant having to abandon one's own country and identity. This law did not change until 1950, and it is why most Japanese war brides followed their husbands to the United States or stayed on U.S. bases.

In either case, most of these Japanese wives had little means of maintaining their autonomy. Largely ignorant about their new environment and culture, they had no choice but to make the most of their lot. In an American study on Japanese war brides, Gerald Schnepp and Agnes Masako Yui surveyed twenty couples in St. Louis, Missouri, and Chicago, Illinois, and found that "all the wives adopted American family rituals" and "all accepted American food and adapted themselves to it." They also had to depend on English to communicate, which tended to create difficulties "in times of crisis or emotional excitement and in such situations as the discussion of technical matters or joking."[8]

The post-war marriage, where the wife had very little independence, has little in common with the intercultural marriage of today. As mentioned earlier, more and more foreigners, particularly men, are coming to work and live in Japan. In the 1970s, when the exchange rate was at 360 yen to the dollar, foreign men usually left Japan after marrying or starting a family. Today, with the dollar almost at parity with the yen and little improvement in the Western economy, those who chose to stay, along with the many more who have entered Japan more recently, feel that they must commit to a longer stay. Japan's recession, it is true, has forced some less-skilled workers as well as high-salaried foreign expatriates to return home or move to other parts of Asia, such as Hong Kong or Singapore, where jobs can still be had. This has not, however, affected the number of foreigners who continue to enter Japan as spouses of Japanese nationals.

Figures provided by the Ministry of Justice show that 266 Europeans and 441 Americans entered Japan as spouses of Japanese nationals in 1988. Those numbers surged in 1993 to 335 and 1,025, respectively. Although the data do not indicate the gender of the foreign spouses, there is no question that the number of Western wives is still relatively small (e.g., the number of American wives married to Japanese in 1993 was 244). This may suggest that more husbands from the West are choosing to move to their wife's home country.

Meanwhile, recent revisions in the Japanese Nationality Law enacted in January 1985 changed the restriction preventing children born to a Japanese mother and non-Japanese father from gaining Japanese citizenship. This was, no doubt, a consequence of an increase in the number of international families. In fact, the change in the law was due to pressure from the Association for Multicultural Families which has over 400 members nationwide, including many overseas members.[9] This change, along with the increasing number of international couples living in Japan, offers Japanese wives a new kind of freedom and autonomy that their predecessors never had, as they are on their own home ground and know the language, culture, and social rules.

In addition, as ever more Japanese women obtain an overseas education, they are quickly learning Western ways and becoming better informed about the world outside of Japan. Further, since most of today's Japanese women no longer face the threat of being disowned by their kin or endure disapproval from their fellow countrymen for marrying a foreigner, they are free to stay in Japan. This is an attractive option, because the country's economic security also provides a safety valve for many Japanese women, who know that they can always fall back on returning home should their cross-cultural marriages fail. And in reality, many women do return after a period of living abroad with their husbands. This assures them more independence and security within such a relationship.

A Glimpse at Today's International Marriages

Just how are these changes affecting the everyday lives of Japanese women and their foreign spouses? While there are no sufficient empirical data available to adequately answer this question, my interviews with fifteen couples and thirteen individuals and a survey of thirty members of the Association for Multicultural Families suggest that the less military-oriented, increasingly Japan-based intermarriages are changing the whole dynamic of how couples relate to each other. I will discuss these changing trends through case studies, beginning with the stories of five Japan-based couples. I interviewed some of these couples together, others by themselves. One man is separated from his wife; another is a divorcé. Except for one couple, which leads a happily married life, the other four are experiencing problems.

To illustrate how potential problems in these intercultural marriages can be avoided, I will conclude with the case of a couple whose success may reveal some of the important ingredients of a happy marriage.

Speaking the Wife's Language

In the course of my interviews, one thing that stood out was how well many Western husbands speak Japanese. This was revealed in a survey I conducted of thirty members of the Kanto and Nagoya chapters of the Association for Multicultural Families in March and April 1993. Among the thirty respondents, well over half said that their husbands communicated with them in Japanese. For example, in answer to the question, "What language do you use when communicating with your husband?" nine responded "strictly Japanese," and nine responded "partially Japanese." In response to the question "How well does your husband speak Japanese?" thirteen answered "fluent" and eight responded "fairly good."

In the late 1970s when I first arrived in Japan, I did not remember meeting many foreigners who spoke fluent Japanese. One reason why more husbands are speaking the language today is that more foreigners are studying Japanese, both in Japan and in their home countries. In many foreign countries there is a growing boom in the study of Japanese language. According to a 1995 news story, the number of students abroad studying Japanese has tripled in the past decade.[10] Part of the reason for the boom, the article says, is because many students believe that learning the language will give them an economic edge. In the

West, Australians, Americans, and New Zealanders make up for the largest growing population learning the language. What's more, Japanese is now even being taught at some middle and high schools in these countries.

The result is that more foreigners are becoming skilled in the language—many even before they set foot in Japan. This seems to be particularly true of people under the age of thirty-five who, despite relatively short stays in Japan (i.e., less than four years), have acquired considerable fluency in Japanese. The survey found, for example, that three husbands between the ages of thirty and thirty-two, who have been in Japan for less than four years were described by their wives as speaking "perfectly fluent Japanese." One wife said that her husband had passed the highest level of the prestigious Japanese Ministry of Education's proficiency test of the Japanese language.

The importance of language is demonstrated in the case study of John and Yumiko, an upwardly mobile Tokyo couple.

• John and Yumiko

John and Yumiko live in a spacious apartment in quiet, secluded Setagaya: an expensive residential area in southern Tokyo. John, thirty-six, is a banker from New York and Yumiko, thirty-five, works part-time for a securities firm. The two met nine years ago through a mutual friend when Yumiko was in New York pursuing a second B.A. in communications and working as an intern for an American television station.

Yumiko describes John as being attractive and warm. But the main reason she married him, she says, was because "I fell in love with his parents." Yumiko says John's parents are very respectful of each other and were very supportive of her. Meeting John's parents helped her make up her mind to marry him, as she knew he had been brought up in a loving, understanding family. John, in turn, was drawn to Yumiko because she was cheerful and independent.

Four years after they met, Yumiko and John married. A few months later, they decided to move back to Japan. John, who had been an exchange student in Japan long before he met Yumiko, was keenly interested in Japanese culture and had always entertained the thought of returning. Because he spoke fluent Japanese and had worked as an interpreter while living in New York, he had no trouble finding a job. Yumiko continued to work for the Japanese branch of the securities firm she had worked for in New York until their first baby came.

Now with two children, Yumiko works out of her home as a part-time overseas agent for another securities firm. Although she does most of the housework, John helps take care of the kids when he is at home. Until they had children, John spoke only Japanese with Yumiko, even though Yumiko speaks fluent English. Now he tries to speak as much English as possible with the kids. Although they enjoy a comfortable lifestyle in Tokyo, they are toying with the idea of returning to New York when the children are old enough for junior high school. This is when John and Yumiko feel their children would best profit from a Western-style education, which stresses creativity over rote memorization.

When asked about the secret to their happiness, Yumiko says she has not tried to adapt herself to a Western lifestyle. She thinks too many Japanese wives try too hard to be American. Yumiko also believes that the fact that she and John both speak each other's language has been a great help toward their mutual appreciation and understanding.

This demonstrates both her strength as an individual and her confidence in John's understanding of Japanese ways. John not only speaks impeccable Japanese, but also has a deep admiration for the Japanese culture since childhood due to his study of karate and other martial arts. This is why, he says, he never presses Yumiko to do things "the American way."

Living on the Wife's Turf

Because more foreign spouses are choosing to stay in Japan, this again helps create room for greater autonomy for the wife as she does not need to depend on her husband to help her with communication barriers or an unfamiliarity with his culture. If anything, it is the husband who has to adjust to doing things the Japanese way. Unless he has been in Japan for a while and speaks adequate Japanese, chances are he will not even know how to pay his bills or file taxes. Having a Japanese spouse in Japan can also win the foreign husband greater trust from the Japanese, which translates into enhanced job or business opportunities. Renting an apartment can also become a lot easier. No wonder Keiko Iigata, the editor at *Mr. Partner*, says that many foreign men openly admitted to her that they want to marry Japanese women to increase their job options or obtain long-term visas.

The following account presents Alan, a Frenchman who separated from his Japanese wife because he felt she did not respect him and was virtually running his life.

• Alan

Alan, a French teacher at one of Japan's most prestigious universities, has been married to Megumi for seventeen years. Five years ago, he moved out of the apartment he shared with her and their teenage daughter and has not returned. Though their marriage is beyond saving, Alan stays married for the sake of his spouse visa, which spares him the trouble of having to renew a working visa every year. (Spouse visas are good for three years.) In many ways, Alan feels his marriage was a total disappointment and blames himself for its failure. Megumi and he, as he later realized, are as different as night and day. "Had I learned more about Megumi and about Japanese culture, I don't think I would have married her," he says bitterly.

Alan met Megumi eighteen years ago in western France. He was twenty-two, she was twenty-five. Alan, a witty and humorous recovering alcoholic, says he was very shy and could not ask for a date before he had had a lot to drink. Megumi, who was studying in France and spoke excellent French, impressed Alan a lot. He found her exotic, bright, and strong-willed. The two married a year later. Alan was in between jobs and, hearing that the job situation in Japan was good, convinced Megumi that they should go to Japan.

Alan said he experienced a series of disconcerting surprises after coming to Japan. First, Megumi refused to work, although her French was good enough for her to become an interpreter. Alan felt forced into the role of being the sole provider. He said he did not realize that this is what a lot of Japanese women expect their husbands to do. He also felt that Megumi looked down on him because he didn't speak much Japanese and felt that she was resentful for his having become dependent upon her.

Alan also thought it was very hard to share things with Megumi, as she was very controlling. She liked to take care of everything and was very interested in keeping an eye on the bank book. Alan said that he felt like he was nothing more than a paycheck to her—while he was buying the gasoline, he says, "she was doing the driving."

A consummate romantic, although Alan had expected

Megumi to be someone with whom he could share intimate love and companionship, she remained rather cold
and unaffectionate. Alan says that sex was like an obligation for her. When evening came, she would routinely ask,
"Do you want to tonight or not?" Alan says this drove away
whatever romantic notions he might have had.

Emotional support, Alan felt, was also largely absent in
their relationship. In fact, Alan said Megumi never encouraged him to stop drinking, even after he started going to
Alcoholics Anonymous. Yet Megumi was very good at
creating the illusion that she was loving by stroking and
patting him in front of his friends. In reality, when they
were by themselves, Alan said she would not even touch
him. He saw then the clear-cut division of labor in Japanese
relationships, where the man is expected to be the "rice
winner" and the woman a professional housewife. There
seemed to be little room for love between them. Alan says,
sarcastically, that now he realizes why only mistresses and
bar hostesses talk affectionately to men—it's their job, and
the men pay for each loving word.

In retrospect, Alan thinks his relationship with Megumi
was doomed from the beginning because they both had a
lot of psychological problems and married for the wrong
reasons. To Alan, a Western husband–Japanese wife marriage stands little chance of working out because of the gap
in the concepts of love and marriage between the two
cultures. He warns against expecting a meek Japanese wife
because often the Western husband will find himself forced
into the role of a Japanese husband—that of the family
provider.

What Alan did not elaborate upon is the fact that when
the husband fails—in the wife's mind—to fulfill his responsibilities as dutiful breadwinner, she may nag and complain, even slapping her husband occasionally to make a

point (the "snap-and-slap" syndrome, as several friends of mine have ruefully put it), or she may totally ignore the husband and go her own way.

Some wives also command total say in how they want to raise the children if there are any. She will also resent any intrusion or suggestions her husband may make. One wife, for example, locked her New Zealander husband out of the house for two days for his interrupting of her scolding and hitting of their teenage daughter. The irony here is that he is a 250-pound six-footer and she is a frail-looking petite woman who appears very agreeable.

Although women like Alan's or the New Zealander's wife are not unique to Japan, the point here is that many Western husbands have fooled themselves into believing all Japanese women are compliant plum blossoms. That's why once they are married, they are caught sorely surprised at the absolute control their Japanese wives have at home.

Other Factors

Other factors contributing to the changing relationship in today's intermarriages have to do with the "travel and study abroad" boom, the declining birth rate, and the increasingly affluent, individualistic lifestyle of the Japanese.

1. Effects of the Travel and Study Abroad Boom

As mentioned in earlier chapters, the impetus to achieve internationalization created among young Japanese a travel and study abroad phenomenon, which began in the late 1970s. As growing numbers of Japanese women continue this trend, they acquire experience overseas, learn Western ways, and gain confidence about pursuing their own goals.

This exposure has contributed to a new sense of independence among those women who have intercultural relationships. The following account demonstrates this point.

• Bruce and Michiyo

Bruce and Michiyo live with their two daughters in a suburban city one and a half hours from the center of Tokyo. Bruce is a self-taught *shokunin* (craftsman) from Canada who makes a living by producing handmade *ukiyo-e* woodblock prints. Michiyo, forty-five, is a registered nurse and four years older than Bruce. A very determined woman who believes in self-improvement through education, she began attending a Canadian university two years ago and has since split her life between Japan and Canada. For nine months a year she studies in Canada, the other three months she returns to Japan to make more money for her tuition.

Since Bruce works out of their home, he assumes all responsibilities for the housework and care of their two daughters during Michiyo's absence, a situation he is not exactly thrilled about. Michiyo has recently declared that, after getting her college degree, she will go on to graduate school in Canada. Bruce says he doesn't know how long he can take this trans-Pacific kind of relationship.

The two met thirteen years ago in Canada. Michiyo, who was thirty-two at the time, had divorced her Japanese husband and was looking for a new life. She had traveled to Canada for a three-month English course at a community college. She instantly fell in love with the country and applied for immigration. Because she was a registered nurse, she had little trouble getting resident status. One day, she met Bruce at a train station and, after chatting with him at length, found herself drawn to his thoughtfulness and friendliness. Bruce, who admits he has always been attracted to Asian women, said he was taken by Michiyo's physical beauty, something he can't really explain. He later said it may have had to do with a subconscious reaction to his not feeling very much like a "he-man," an attribute he felt she could stimulate in him. The two soon started living together.

His relationship with Michiyo led Bruce into becoming interested in Japan. He was particularly impressed with *ukiyo-e*. His interest, in fact, became so strong that he persuaded Michiyo to return to Japan. Although life in Japan was fine for her, Michiyo never stopped thinking about returning to Canada to what she calls "a more challenging lifestyle." She had expected to return after just a couple of years. Bruce, however, had become very comfortable in Japan and had no intention of leaving. "North America depresses me. I'd rather live in Japan. I love the culture and the work ethic here. People are less selfish," he insists. After four years, Michiyo became impatient. That was when she decided to go back to Canada to pursue a bachelor's degree in medicine.

Although Michiyo is happy that she is able to continue her studies while Bruce stays home to take care of the children, Bruce clearly regrets the situation. "For Michiyo, partnership is not important. She wants to do her own thing," he says in front of her. (Michiyo just ignores the comment.) Bruce also says he wishes she would be more supportive of him by helping with translations and bookkeeping instead of his having to hire part-time help. At the time of the interview, neither Michiyo nor Bruce was sure of what would happen to their relationship. To Bruce, though, the only thing that was keeping the relationship from falling apart were the children.

Quite a number of Western men I interviewed complained about how self-centered Western women are, and how they are not family-oriented. Although some Western men think that Asian women are selfless and would even sacrifice themselves for their husbands and family, most at least feel that the collective or group orientation of Japanese women is a real plus in a marriage partner. Although Michiyo is a rather extreme example, she nevertheless represents a growing number of Japanese women who know their own minds and are beginning to place equal importance on their personal priorities. Unlike their predecessors, they would rather balance living for themselves with living for their husbands and children. Sometimes this makes for a tightrope walk.

2. Effects of Japan's Affluence and the Declining Birth Rate

Another theme that recurred throughout my interviews is that more and more young Japanese women are rejecting the traditional housewife role along with its domestic chores and family raising. These women, most of whom were born after 1960 and are often the only child in their families, were brought up in fairly wealthy surroundings and are used to being pampered and showered with attention. Consequently, they have little in common with their mothers or older sisters.

Akiko, the single daughter of a well-off family who is married to Nick, an Australian broadcaster, for example, will not get up to cook breakfast for her husband although she is a full-time homemaker. In fact, Nick cannot persuade her to have a child.

• Akiko and Nick

Nick and Akiko met in Malaysia seven years ago at a private leisure club. Akiko, now thirty-two, was taking an extended vacation from her work as a telephone operator.

Nick, now thirty-eight, was also on vacation from his Melbourne-based radio announcer job. Because Akiko had had two years of study in the United States, she spoke fluent English—a factor that helped a great deal during their initial courtship. The two hit it off immediately and were married sixteen months later.

After marrying, they lived in Australia for two years—an experience Akiko did not enjoy very much. Because Akiko is the only child of a very successful interior decorator and was raised very protectively, Nick says she is rather anti-social and does not like people much. When Nick's Australian friends proved to be overly friendly, knocking on the door, in her mind, whenever they pleased, Nick says she became tired of it. She finally convinced Nick to move to Japan, where he is now gainfully employed as a radio show announcer and news narrator. Akiko, meanwhile, has become a full-time homemaker.

Nick says Akiko chooses to stay home partly because of a chronic fatigue syndrome, which he calls the "yuppie flu," and partly because, in Nick's words, "she hates to work." I asked him about the stereotypical image of Japanese women. "Akiko? Submissive? Are you kidding?" Nick says Akiko never kowtows to anyone. Although she stays home everyday, Nick says she sleeps late and only cooks three days a week; the rest of the time they dine out. Their family life consists of walking the dog together and going to see a movie occasionally. Having children is not a likely option. "Akiko doesn't want to have kids because I already have one child from a previous marriage, so if we have one it won't be my first. And that, to Akiko, is an unbearable thought," Nick explains.

Because Akiko is very jealous, Nick says he cannot go out to meet his friends very often. Until recently, he says, he didn't have much of a social life. So far, Nick's only treat has been "to get jolly with my chums every few weeks at a bar."

His word of advice for men who anticipate marrying a Japanese woman is to not be misled into believing that they will put up with anything. Japanese women want security and to have their needs fulfilled, too.

3. Effects of a Widening Perception Gap

As one might expect, intercultural couples who base their attraction for each other on stereotyped images may be heading for disappointment. Many scholars found this to be the case among marriages between American servicemen and Japanese women during the 1950s. Describing this mutual disappointment, Hiroshi Wagatsuma says in his study, "The American man, expecting an 'Oriental doll,' finds himself married to a 'tough cookie.'" Meanwhile, "The Japanese woman, expecting a Western knight, finds herself tied to a weakling whose dependency disappoints and bothers her."[11]

If disappointment was commonplace in those days, contemporary couples may face even more disillusionment. One reason, as mentioned earlier, has to do with the dramatic socioeconomic changes that have occurred in Japan over the last few decades, which serve to exaggerate the perception gap. Some Western men who have not kept up with Asia's rapid economic rise, may still be under the impression that the Western standard of living continues to be superior to that of Asia and, therefore, Asian wives will not place any great material demands on their husbands. This was certainly the case with Matthew, the Ohio businessman mentioned in Chapter One. His underestimation of Fumiko's needs for material comfort, among other factors, eventually contributed to their divorce.

• Matthew

Matthew and his teenage son live in Kanagawa Prefecture, south of Tokyo. A forty-three-year-old former commercial airline quality controller from Ohio, Matthew now works as a professional civil servant for a U.S. military base. He came to live in Japan ten years ago because of Fumiko, his wife. Four years ago, he filed for divorce, ending the fourteen-year marriage.

Matthew met Fumiko in 1973 in Madrid. Fumiko, a flight attendent traveling with a girlfriend to Madrid, was in the same tour. Matthew, who admits he has always been attracted to Asian women, paid special attention to the two women. When he found out that Fumiko's friend had become ill, he volunteered to call for help. This led him to become acquainted with Fumiko. The two went out a few times while in Madrid and exchanged addresses. They kept in contact over the ensuing months and managed to visit each other over the next two years. In 1975, when Fumiko came to visit Matthew again in the United States, the two decided to marry. She was twenty-nine at the time and he was twenty-five.

Their marriage, however, was headed for a rocky start. At the beginning, things seemed fine because they were living in New York. In the second year, however, when Matthew had to move to Connecticut because of a new job assignment, things quickly started to deteriorate.

First, Fumiko didn't like American food and complained because there were no Asian food stores or restaurants nearby. Then she refused to play host to help Matthew entertain his business associates at home, saying that she was afraid of American people. She would not let Matthew's father visit them and their newborn son. In retrospect, Matthew thinks Fumiko, who was from a very wealthy family, behaved that way because she had never before lived away from home and had not learned how to assume responsibility.

Although Fumiko kept a very clean house at first, she soon became too stressed to do the housework. She also started to break things. To avoid direct confrontation, Matthew started staying out and drinking with his friends. When things got out of hand, Matthew filed for a divorce, but Fumiko persuaded him to wait a little longer, hoping that their conflicts could be resolved. Matthew arranged for Fumiko to return to Japan for short stays and had his mother take care of their young son. But things did not improve much, and Fumiko would neglect the housework and break things again. When there was no change in this pattern, even after the two returned to live in Japan a few years later, with Fumiko insisting on staying with her parents every weekend, Matthew once again filed for a divorce.

Thinking back, Matthew believes he and Fumiko never really knew each other. "I was as mystified by Oriental women as she was about Western men," he says. At the time, Matthew was under the impression that Western women were far more materialistic than Asian women and that Asian women were very compromising. He says he found this to be untrue. Fumiko, for example, was very stubborn and would sulk to get her way. As for Fumiko, Matthew believes she thought that all Americans were wealthy. Her perception was, he says, that American men were much more polite than the Japanese, so she was shocked by how crude and rude she found them to be after living in the United States.

Matthew also admits that he knew too little about the Japanese culture before committing himself to marriage. One thing he wished he knew more about is the subtlety between *hon-ne* (one's true intention) and *tatemae* (the outward appearance one shows). Matthew says he learned that there is often a big gap between what Japanese women say and what they think. He also thinks that his marriage might have been different if he had been able to speak more Japanese and if they had resolved their differences in common values and goals before they married.

As for advice, Matthew warns against the widespread belief that Japanese women are submissive. "The fact is, they (Japanese women) might be agreeable before marriage, but once married, it's *kakādenka* (a family where the husband is henpecked)," he says. He also points out that many Japanese women who think they cannot marry a Japanese man for one reason or another tend to fixate on Western men, which often creates unrealistic expectations.

A Success Story

Although the problems mentioned earlier may lead the reader to conclude that success is not very likely in an intercultural marriage, I do not intend, however, to suggest that Western–Japanese marriages are prone to failure. Instead, I hope to reveal how the problems within these marriages result largely from a general lack of understanding between partners of each other's culture and social circumstances. Worse yet, many couples also do not take the time to get to know the real person they are marrying. Instead, they often marry a set of cultural beliefs or conveniences that they think are automatically coming with the package. Just as the husband may underestimate the rising economic independence of the wife, so the wife may overestimate the socioeconomic power of the husband.

At the heart of the problem is the fact that people's perception of reality is still very much based on the mass media, which, unfortunately, has not kept pace with the rapid social changes in Japan and the West. Ultimately, people who choose a partner merely on the beliefs of his or her race and culture alone may be in for some sore surprises because the stereotype doesn't always fit.

Some couples I interviewed said that timing and luck are often important factors for a successful marriage. This may be true. The following story, however, illustrates how one couple has made their marriage work through conscious effort. Their success sheds light on the factors that make a successful intercultural marriage and, for that matter, marriages in general.

• **Dennis and Kumiko**

Dennis and Kumiko live near Yoyogi in west Tokyo with their five-year-old daughter. Dennis, age forty, owns a small PR firm while Kumiko, at forty-five, is a full-time homemaker after working for twenty years as a sales manager for a cosmetic firm.

Dennis and Kumiko met at a mutual friend's birthday party about ten years ago. Dennis, who came to live in Japan in 1977, speaks fluent Japanese. He was twenty-nine when he met Kumiko and had gone out with Japanese women before. He said the first things that struck him about Kumiko were her beauty and her maturity.

Kumiko did not make a big fuss over Dennis being an American with her friends, although he was the first foreign man she had ever gone out with. One day she called a friend from his apartment and started talking about her new boyfriend. She did not mention his nationality until she was asked about his name. Then she said, "Yes, he's an American." This impressed Dennis, he says, because it proved that his being an American was not important to Kumiko. This was completely different from what Dennis had experienced with other Japanese women, who invariably emphasized his foreignness and asked a lot of "Do Americans (fill in the blank)?" questions.

They soon started living together and a year later, they married. Dennis says they work well as a team. Until Kumiko quit working in the middle of her pregnancy, she worked long hours and came home around 8:30 P.M. Dennis always cooked dinner and Kumiko always cleaned up. They split the chores very well and there were no household hassles. Dennis also handles all the finances and is totally independent in his daily business dealings. Now that Kumiko is home full time with Jennie, their daughter, she does all the housework and most of the cooking. But Dennis takes care of Jennie on Sundays so that Kumiko has a free day.

Kumiko and Dennis have had very few fights. The only quarrels they had were when Dennis wanted Kumiko to take more leadership in the relationship. Looking back, Dennis says he realizes that Kumiko is not that way because she is Japanese, but because she is culturally Asian— more low key and "situational" than most Westerners. Dennis thinks that Japanese women are strong, but in different ways than Western women are. Through the Western cultural filter, however, they appear to be meek and submissive. Forcing her to be more expressive and socially aggressive, to Dennis, would amount to cultural chauvinism on his part. So he decided to just let her be herself.

Since the birth of their daughter, Dennis and Kumiko have been contemplating the idea of living in California when she reaches junior high school age. Since Kumiko has had little overseas experience and speaks only survival English, Dennis takes his family back home to San Francisco for two months every year to allow Kumiko to get accustomed to living there. While Kumiko says she is comfortable with the idea of moving back to the United States, Dennis says he knows Kumiko would always think about moving back to Japan. He is hoping to make arrangements so that the family can live in both countries.

As for why he and Kumiko get along so well, Dennis says it has much to do with the fact that he had already been in Japan ten years before he got married and so he speaks good Japanese. A fair fluency in Japanese and a good understanding of the culture, Dennis feels, are a must for anyone who anticipates marrying a Japanese. Dennis says foreigners often get married in Japan for the wrong reasons, because they are lonely or need someone to help them overcome daily difficulties. Without first becoming a mature and independent individual, it is difficult, he says, to lead a happy life with anyone.

Meanwhile, Kumiko says her secret to a happy intercultural marriage is not to think of it as being different from any other marriage. "I never thought of my marriage as a *kokusai kekkon* (international marriage) and I never saw Dennis as a foreigner. To me, he is an individual I happen to like." She said she never makes a big fuss about going to the United States or has the urge to make excuses for her nationality to her American relatives and friends every time a small crisis arises.

It seems clear that when the husband speaks the wife's language well, it tends to empower the wife, as he is more likely to cultivate a greater sensitivity to her culture and will be able to see things beyond the Western cultural filter he grew up with. This also reduces the chance that she will have to strictly follow his way of doing things.

When Couples Live Abroad

As mentioned in Matthew's story earlier, the perception

gap problem is one often encountered by many couples living outside of Japan. In the 1950s and 1960s, when Japan was still rebuilding its economy, the gap in living standards between Japan and the West was wide. Since the late 1970s, however, this economic gap clearly has been closing, so the claim of material superiority by Westerners has lost much of its merit. True, the U.S. and other Western countries still have much to offer in terms of gender equality and personal freedom. Yet if a Western man still thinks that he is "rescuing" a poor Japanese woman who, he hopes, will become grateful for having been offered a materialistically richer lifestyle in the West, he will no doubt be very disappointed.

By the same token, the Japanese woman will be equally disillusioned by what she has perceived to be the boundlessly rich and free Western world. This is particularly the case with women who have had limited exposure to the world outside Japan. Kayoko, a thirty-four-year-old Japanese woman residing abroad for the first time with her American husband in Morrison, Colorado, voiced definite disappointment.

Recalling a childhood fantasy she had about the United States, she put it this way, "When I was in elementary school, I used to dream of coming to the United States. I watched the TV series *Lassie* and saw a boy drinking milk from a gallon-sized container. Since I was drinking milk from a tiny glass bottle, I thought it would be great to live in a wealthy nation like that." But after arriving in the United States, she realized that wealth in the American sense is quite different from what it is for the Japanese. "In Japan, people wear name-brand clothes and stay at expensive hotels. Here in America," she says, "what you have instead is just a massive amount of land and food, that's all." What she leaves unsaid is that the quality of life in the

United States, as in many parts of Europe, has arguably deteriorated from its zenith during the fifties and sixties, especially in areas of safety, health, and education, compared to Japan. Today, Western economies are plagued by unemployment, crime, drugs, and other social ills.

Another perception gap has to do with how the Japanese wife sees her foreign husband before and after she goes to live in his home country. A number of Japanese women I interviewed admitted to me that when they married their Western husbands in Japan, they had overestimated their spouses' income potential and socioeconomic status. While in Japan, they say their Western husbands were typically regarded with deference because of the preferential treatment they receive from the Japanese. This, along with the women's general unfamiliarity with Western culture and limited social experience with Western people, prevented them from making realistic assessments of the strengths and weaknesses of their potential partners prior to marriage.

Mitsuko, a highly educated woman who married a former American G.I. after a brief romance in Okinawa, said that she did not know that she was "marrying down socioeconomically" until she arrived in the U.S. with her husband. While Mitsuko was ambitiously pursuing her MBA, she found her husband frustrated at not being able to hold down a steady job. She became disillusioned and lost her previous image of him. In the end, they had to go their separate ways.

Problems Facing Japanese Wives Living Abroad

Perception gaps aside, once the Japanese wife decides to live in the husband's home country, she must be psychologically prepared for the change in environment. Like the

Western husband living in Japan, the Japanese wife must be willing to make quite a few adjustments. Although some wives thrive in the individualistic climate of a Western environment, others are caught ill-prepared by the many unforeseen challenges of living outside the protected shelter of Japan. This naturally results in the loss of a certain amount of autonomy and mobility for the Japanese wife.

Other than the obvious issues of the language barrier and having to get a driver's license, another oft-cited problem is discrimination. A few Japanese women I interviewed mentioned discrimination on the job because they lack perfect English. One woman living in Southern California who not only speaks very good English but also holds an MBA from a major U.S. university, says she has been made to feel less competent in her job as a sales manager because she "does not speak English like a native." Before arriving there, she had dreamed of America as a land of freedom with abundant opportunities open to women. As an Asian, she feels she has a big handicap. "Americans, especially whites, claim that this country is free and open and anyone can become an American. That's a fat lie," she says. "White immigrants can become Americans as soon as they lose their accent, but non-whites never become Americans, no matter how many generations they go through." This has made her feel inept and inferior as an individual, which is a tremendous blow to her self-esteem. She says she is now looking forward to returning to Japan.

In an article published in the *U.S.–Japan Women's Journal*, Takako Day, a U.S.–based Japanese journalist, says that this kind of disappointment has to do with many Japanese women's hidden "aspiration to becoming like mainstream Western women."[12] But can Japanese women manage to become like Caucasian women in a Western country? Without a very high level of English and a firm grasp of the culture, Day argues that these women can't even hope to become equal partners with their Western husbands "with whom they can exchange their views freely and share a passionate, adventurous life together." They will find themselves "totally dependent on their husbands and subject to discrimination by the white-dominated society." To Day, unless Japanese wives wise up, their dream of emulating mainstream Caucasian women is doomed from the start.

Another problem has to do with a general lack of understanding by many Japanese of the physical realities of living in the outside world. While many Japanese travel outside of Japan, more remain ignorant of the real images of the West and continue to fantasize all Western cities to be just like New York, San Francisco, London, or Paris—images gained from movies and advertising. Japanese wives with these mistaken notions are thus often caught by surprise when they find themselves in the outback of Wyoming, for example, or in a remote town in Louisiana. In those circumstances, they are frequently distressed by the total lack of Asian restaurants and other Japanese with whom they can associate. Many women say they wish they had checked out their new environment before deciding to move with their husbands to their new homes.

Interestingly enough, the problems that many Japanese wives encounter in their husbands' home countries are mirror images of those faced by the Western wives of Japanese living in Japan. Their problems will be discussed in greater detail in the upcoming section on Japanese men and Western women.

 CHAPTER SEVEN

Japanese Men Today

Japanese women, encouraged by improved opportunities for higher education, better jobs, and a variety of new lifestyle choices, are changing rapidly. Far from yesterday's docile and submissive daughters, sweethearts, and wives, they have, in author Sumiko Iwao's words, been "winning an astonishing degree of freedom and independence" by way of a quiet revolution.[1]

But what has been occurring with Japanese women seems to be, for the most part, passing Japanese men right by. Even those men who do notice this trend seem to be bewildered by these changes. While Japanese women are marching into the work force in ever-increasing numbers, or are making waves by traveling overseas to advance their education, careers, or chances for romance, Japanese men, bogged down by corporate workloads, continue to be fourteen-hour-a-day salaried warriors who live and breathe their companies.

Meanwhile, Japanese women, unable to relate to their men, are increasingly shunning them by postponing marriage and initiating divorce. Fumiharu Yoshimura, president of the international dating service Dandies Minami

Aoyama, is amazed by the number of Japanese women who come to his agency in the hope of dating Western men. "While Japanese men sweat and bleed to build Japan's economic miracle, it's the women who are cashing in on the benefits of Japan's newly gained wealth. And now they are telling Japanese men that they are not good enough for them," he says. It appears that Japanese women are passing a powerful, if quiet, message to Japanese men: as far as a husband goes, a paycheck alone is no longer enough.

Not only are many younger women expressing clear dissatisfaction with today's Japanese men, many older women in their forties and fifties are also finding their husbands—most of whom have never lifted a finger at home—a nuisance. Older and retired men are called derogatory nicknames such as *nure ochiba* (wet leaves)[2] or *sodai gomi* (oversized trash) by some wives. In fact, the bargaining power of Japanese men in their relationships with women has become so weak compared with pre-war days that some social critics are calling the nineties "The era of the suffering male."[3]

The Suffering Japanese Male

To many foreigners, the image of a suffering Japanese male may seem absurd, particularly because Western media continue to perpetuate the fantasy of the sword-wielding samurai businessman. This image is evident in movies such as *Gung Ho*, which depicts ruthless Japanese corporate managers, and also in Michael Crichton's novel *Rising Sun*, that plays off the image of robotic and faceless Japanese businessmen. Westerners newly arrived in Japan who become instant experts on the culture persistently insist that Japan is a man's world, where most Japanese men routinely treat their women like slaves or servants. Consider this article, published in a local English newspaper in 1993 under the title "The Plight of Japanese Women":

> On the train from Narita Airport, I was surprised to see a Japanese man take the last available seat in the carriage, leaving his wife to stand.
>
> During the next few weeks I saw couples out walking, and quite often noticed that the man would walk a few paces ahead of the woman.
>
> One of the reasons men have an easier time as far as reputation is concerned could be because the Japanese believe that men are superior to women. This is reflected in day-to-day living. Men are the first out of elevators, they get served first in restaurants and are offered drinks first at parties. . . . [4]

The author's observations, though accurate, note a largely surface-only adherence to traditional roles. The forms remain while the contents have changed. Japanese men, forced to pledge their loyalty to their companies above all else, have been ignoring their families and are largely strangers in their own homes. The result is that they have lost power in their families and have seen their wives grow steadily more discontent. This is revealed in the rising divorce rate, which has doubled over the last two decades. According to Health and Welfare figures, in 1993, for example, there were 188,303 divorces, as compared with 95,000 in 1970. Of the divorces, the ministry notes that the increase has been particularly sharp among couples married for less than five years and for those married for more than twenty years.

What's more, a recent news story reported that divorce lawsuits in Japan has also risen rapidly. In 1993, divorces settled by family court went over 50,000 for the first time.

In addition, more than 70 percent of the suits were initiated by women.[5]

The Rising Divorce Rate

Japan's rising divorce rate, which has gone largely unremarked outside of Japan, has a great deal to do with changes in Japan's civil code. Until the late nineteenth century, Japanese women were denied the right to request divorces. In those days, if a wife wanted to leave her husband, her only option was to run away to a refuge or divorce temple (*kakekomi-dera*). During her stay in the refuge, she could neither remarry nor see her own children for three years unless she received consent from her husband to divorce. Neither could she receive custody of her children, who remained in the husband's *ie*, or family line.[6] Women were largely, as I explain later, "borrowed wombs." As such, when they married, they usually severed ties with their own families and were registered as part of their husband's family. From their lowly beginning as servant to the husband's family, they could only rise in status by producing children—including a male heir. The crown to a woman's life was to become mother-in-law to her son's wife. She could then lord her status over that of the new bride by criticizing the daughter-in-law's homemaking skills and generally making her life miserable.

Under the revised civil code passed in 1898, women could apply for legal divorce on the grounds of cruelty, desertion, or serious misconduct, but not for adultery. On the other hand, the code set the punishment for female infidelity at both divorce and a two-year jail sentence.

The postwar laws based on the new Japanese Constitution, which went into effect in January 1948, however, stipulates that "men and women are equal under the law and there shall be no discrimination on the basis of sex." In addition, the foundations of the family system and the patriarchal authority of the head of the house were also abolished. Under the present law, women have legal status as full and equal partners in marriage. This means that "an act of unchastity" on the part of the husband also became grounds for divorce.[7]

Divorced women are now entitled to a small public pension or a one-time alimony payment. In fact, in 1993, women who settled their divorces through family court on the average received a settlement of about ¥4.1 million, which is roughly US $41,000 when calculated at the rate of ¥100 to the dollar.[8] What's more, as recently as October 1995, there was a proposed revision to Japan's civil law for making de facto divorces possible.[9] If the law is revised as proposed, the court can grant a divorce for couples solely on the grounds that they have been living separately for five consecutive years. While people's opinions are divided about the proposal, some experts believe the law, if revised, would be good news for a growing number of women who are seeking divorce.

Although only one or two divorced women in ten are likely to receive regular child support payments, this has not deterred many from filing for divorces. Three out of four divorces today are said to be requested by the wife, who usually retains custody of the children, although she is legally bound to wait six months to remarry, to determine the paternity of future offspring.[10] The Justice Ministry, however, is now considering whether to shorten the six-month waiting period to 100 days.[11]

Other dramatic social changes have also contributed to the rise in divorce cases. For one, at least in urban settings, more and more people have come to accept divorce as a socially acceptable option, and divorced men and women bear less social stigma. According to a 1993 *Yomiuri Shimbun* nationwide survey on divorce, about forty percent viewed divorce as "unavoidable" if a marriage was not going well. Compared to a similar poll conducted in 1981, there was a decrease of twelve percent in the number of people who view divorce negatively. This shows a major shift in popular opinion about divorce over the past decade.[12]

Another factor that has contributed particularly to middle-aged divorces is the longer life expectancy. *Jinsei gojūnen*, or a life span of fifty years, was a Japanese catch phrase common during the immediate postwar period (1945–55). Nearly forty years afterward, Japanese can expect to live an average of 76.57 years for men and 82.98 years for women—the longest life-expectancy rates in the world—according to government figures for Respect-for-the-aged Day on September 15, 1995. Many wives do not anticipate enduring these added decades with a mate with whom they have little in common. The situation worsens if the wife, as in earlier times, is forced into caring for the ailing elderly in-laws. According to Madoka Yoriko, organizer of the *Niko-niko rikon kōza* ("Divorce with a Smile" course) designed to promote a better understanding of divorce, middle-aged couples are often under heavier financial and emotional pressure than younger or older couples as they are pinched in between the responsibility of putting their teenage children through university and the burden of caring for their elderly parents.[13]

Madoka also points out that because of the divided gender roles in Japan, where husbands and wives have very little to share, children often serve as the only common bond. When a couple approaches their late forties and the youngest child is grown, the meaning of their life together suddenly vanishes.[14] Compounding these issues is the widening gap of mutual expectations, a breakdown in male-female communications, plus the availability of more leisure and lifestyle choices. These points are discussed later in this chapter.

Marital dissatisfaction is not a phenomenon unique to middle-aged couples. Younger couples also seem to be following the trend. According to a 1990 magazine article published in *Spa*, a popular business, culture, and entertainment weekly for men, many businessmen in their thirties suffer from what is known in Japanese as *kitaku kyōfushō*, which author Iwao defines in her book *The Japanese Woman* as "the phobic inability to go home" syndrome. According to *Spa*, these men cannot communicate with their wives and become worn down by constant bickering about their meager salaries, lack of success at work, and not doing their fair share at home.[15] These men have developed the habit of frequenting bars until late into the night or dragging out their work so that by the time they arrive home, their wives will be asleep.

No doubt Japan is still very much a man's world, economically and politically. It is a country where men continue to run the businesses, earn more than women at the same jobs, and expect better opportunities for advancement. But when looking deeper into the social changes, it becomes apparent that women are the ones who have gained, as we shall see later, the real power at home. Japanese men are not nearly as in control as the Western media have painted them.

The Man Behind the Mask

In *Behind the Mask* (1984), Ian Buruma speaks of the gap between *hon-ne* and *tatemae*, or "real intentions" and "public posture." He explains the sexist behavior of Japanese men by saying:

> Foreigners who see how meek Japanese housewives are bossed around by loud-mouthed husbands incapable, or at least unwilling to do anything for themselves, often draw the conclusion that men are very much in command in Japan.
>
> In many cases, the meek, housewifely exterior is the public façade of a tough, steely wife and mother who is very much in control at home, while Dad's growling boorishness hides a helpless man clinging to his masculine privilege. The slave and sergeant-major are public roles that have little to do with actual strength of the individual. The wife shows respect for her husband in public because it is expected of her, but it is a respect for his role, rather than for the man himself. What happens in private is quite a different matter.[16]

Privately, many salarymen are happy to let their wives handle the home, children, and finances. They willingly hand their salaries to their wives and become "thousand-yen husbands"—a nickname based on the average amount of daily pocket-money granted to them by their wives. (Although today salaries are directly deposited into bank accounts of most workers, by having full access to the bank card, the wife continues to maintain the status quo.) Why doesn't this daily allowance business bother the Japanese husband? After all, he is the one who is bringing home the rice.

I asked this question to Kogo Tsuji, a professor at Tokai University in Kanagawa Prefecture, who admits to happily relinquishing his paycheck to his wife. Here's how he explains it: "In Japan, the family is seen as a unit, with the mother and the children as the core. And because the husband's concern for the family is more the home as a whole, he sees the arrangement of having the wife manage the family as being a fair division of labor and the only way to efficiently maintain the household."

He also suggested that Japan, as a group-oriented society, places a lot of emphasis on the importance of interdependence. This division of labor, or what Westerners call gender roles, is accordingly seen by society as desirable. As odd as it may seem, a married Japanese man stands a better chance for promotion because the assumption is that the wife will take care of his personal affairs at home, leaving him free to devote his full attention to work.

Perhaps this explains why 73 percent of all housewives in Japan have ultimate control of the household purse strings.[17] Meanwhile, on average, they give their husbands a monthly allowance of only ¥35,400 (US $350, at the rate of ¥100 to the dollar).[18]

The Rising Power of the Japanese Wife

It is important to clarify here that the wife's rising power at home is by and large a default, resulting from Japan's modernization. The rise of Japan's economy produced the salaryman household in which the father goes off to work for long hours and comes home late at night after the kids have gone to bed. Before World War II, when over 60 percent of all families engaged in home-based agricultural work, the husband was a figure of authority who commanded great respect from the children. Under the *ie* (household) system, the husband, as head of the household, was the first one to be served at meals and the first one to take a bath in the family tub.

Since World War II, however, with the rise of industrialization and the abolition of the family system, things have become quite different. In order to maximize labor in industries that were masculine-oriented (e.g., steel, chemicals, and construction), women were confined to the home to concentrate on child-rearing and housekeeping. This practice, which has continued for the last four decades, offers the wife tremendous power over domestic concerns. Not only does she control the family finances—a carry-over from farming households—it is also customary for the wife to handle the distribution of food. While the wife is still the social subordinate of the husband, she is the one who has the real say in the family. She makes important decisions, such as what neighborhood the family will live in, what furniture it will buy, and which school the children will attend.

This perhaps explains why quite a few Japanese women believe that their role as "assistants" to their husbands does not necessarily make them subordinate to them. Many housewives say they don't envy men and are happy to maintain the status quo of the separate gender roles. In fact, many wives feel lucky to have been spared the stressful company lifestyle of their husbands. Meanwhile, Japanese salarymen have had the most enjoyable part of their lives taken away from them—i.e., the respect (and the special treatment that comes with it) as a figure of power at home. Their only consolation at the end of a long, hardworking day is having a few beers at a Japanese bar or pub with a *mama-san* who lends a sympathetic ear to their gripes.

Japan's postwar economy has also led to a breakdown in the traditional family structure and a separation of the family from the company. While this separation is a common consequence of industrialization, Buruma argues that, for Japan, because the company is often regarded as another, larger family, the salaryman is put in the awkward position of being torn between two families.[19]

With the surge in economic growth that started in the mid-1950s, salaried workers were encouraged to become *mōretsu shain*, or "fiercely working employees." What they were promised in return was a house and the lure of promotions and annual salary raises under a seniority system. One Japanese salaried worker once told me that the dream of having his own house is effectively the dangling carrot that keeps the salaryman faithful to the company. In order to purchase a house, most salaried workers have to take out a company loan. In consequence, as soon as a salaryman has married and purchased a house through a company loan, his chance of receiving an undesirable assignment to a branch company away from home suddenly doubles. The company knows that the man is now under obligation and must pledge his utmost loyalty to the company by undertaking whatever duties he is assigned.

Shigeo Saito, a veteran journalist at Kyoto News Service and author of the award-winning book *Tsumatachi no shishuki* (Housewives' Blues), a report on social and family changes in postwar Japan published in 1982,[20] once told me that Japan was able to recover quickly from the two oil crises of the 1970s largely because salarymen were required to work extremely demanding schedules to raise their performance level. Their workload was so overwhelming that many suffered burnout and a few even died from overwork. This was how expressions such as *tanshin funin* (temporary transfer to a new post) and *karōshi* (death from overwork) came to be coined. These men had little energy left to keep up an active rapport with their families, so the wives filled the gap, picking up more of the husband's role at home. This followed along with the traditional concept of a clear separation between *uchi* (the inside), or family, and *soto* (the outside), or work. Japan's economic miracle, it is believed, was made possible largely because of this concrete separation of gender roles.

Ultimately, it is the family that suffers the most. Left to manage the household alone, the wife resents the husband's absence. Her frustration is compounded by the rise of the nuclear family, meaning she has no support from the extended family. Out of desperation, she invests all her energy and money in the children. Over the years, she learns to lead an emotionally independent life, socializing with other women, taking up hobbies, getting involved in community activities or, more recently, working at a part-time job to keep herself busy and add to the household income. She eventually learns to embrace the philosophy that *teishu genki de rusu ga ii*—a good husband is healthy and never home. Meanwhile, the gap between her expectations of what married life should be and the reality she faces continues to widen.

For the sake of the children, the wife puts up with a physically and emotionally unavailable husband. Life goes on until the husband retires. Because he has largely been absent and has contributed little more than a paycheck, the wife has become accustomed to having her own freedom. Now, suddenly the husband is home every day with nothing to do. To make things worse, he transfers his dependency on the company, which has been practically his whole life, onto his wife. Unwilling to suddenly have to put up with the hassle of taking care of an oversized, overaged "child," and resentful of the husband's intrusion into her autonomy, more wives end up demanding a divorce. This is naturally a shock for the husband, who has assumed that his wife would pamper him in his later years as a reward for all his labors.

Many Western scholars and authors, when writing about Japanese society, focus their criticism on how Japanese women are victims who are denied opportunities in society. Yet, ironically, it is the woman's "unequal" position that has spared her from the often strict restraints of Japan, Inc. This, as Sumiko Iwao pointed out, has allowed women the freedom to explore their individuality in ways that men cannot dream of. Tied to mainstream society and a steady income, men are afraid to leave the security of their company jobs. Tired and worn as they are from overwork, they do not, however, find peace at home. Instead they have to respond to their wives' expectations of their being good husbands and fathers. Accordingly, rather than sleeping in, they can be seen staggering through the parks with their children or unenthusiastically shopping with their wives on Sunday. Little wonder Sunday is known by the Japanese as "family service" day.

In this sense, Japanese men can be seen as being manipulated both by their companies and their wives. Rather than emphasizing the exploitation of women, it might be fairer to say that, in a society where individual rights are sacrificed for collective interests, neither men nor women win and both have made enormous sacrifices for the benefits of the economic miracle, perhaps the men even more so.

The Winds of Change

Surprisingly, it is Japan's ongoing economic slump that is creating a chance for these corporate warriors to sober up to their plight—and do something about it. With the nation in the grip of a recession since the early 1990s and companies desperately trying to cut back on their payrolls by chopping away at the working hours, Japan's Education

Ministry has decided the time is right to pull salarymen out of their offices.

All over the country, the ministry is sponsoring a series of experimental seminars at company conference rooms in praise of the wonders of family outings and home life. Topics include "The Changing Family," "Time for Father to Take Center Stage," and "Escaping from the Company-man, Company-first Rut."[21] One thing stressed at these seminars is the need to think about a life after work because of longer life expectancy. In fact, one lecturer warned her male audiences: "You have to live another twenty or thirty years after you retire. You will lose your title. You will lose your job. You will lose your business card. What is left? Only your children and your wife."[22]

Some social critics suggest that the ministry's "father-hood" courses have a "hidden agenda"—to reverse Japan's declining birth rate, which in 1995 stood at 1.5 children per woman. The theory goes like this: the birth rate is dropping because women are marrying later and returning to work. If men help raise children, the women will become less reluctant to have them.

Whatever the intention, evidence shows that some fathers, especially those in their twenties and thirties, are definitely changing their ways. A 1993 survey conducted by the Prime Minister's Office found that fathers below the age of forty were far more likely than those older to involve themselves in domestic life. In addition, of the three thousand people who responded to the survey, 70 percent also think the number of family-oriented men has risen from a decade ago.[23]

Some of the younger men, taking full advantage of the introduction of the five-day work week and the Child-care Leave Law enacted in April 1992, are also challenging the male-oriented society by refusing overtime in favor of family life or taking unpaid leave to be with their children. Mutsumi Ota, a thirty-four-year-old computer researcher, is one of the first men in Japan to have taken paternity leave. He later wrote a book about it. He said that in his father's generation, it was important for the father to work hard and earn a lot of money. He realizes that, in today's family, a paycheck alone is no longer enough.[24]

Daishi Kawabata, a thirty-three-year-old employee who works for a Japanese newspaper, is another father who decided to take advantage of the Child-care Leave Law to be with his newborn child. Yet others have been reticent to follow suit because Japan's corporate world is reluctant to cope with the changing environment. According to an *Asahi Evening News* article published in January 1994, Kawabata was only one of five fathers to take advantage of the leave during the first seven months after its enactment in April 1992, from among 3,131 workers at the 1,200 companies that had instituted it.[25]

As the article pointed out, what is keeping men from changing more quickly is not necessarily their own resistance to change, but rather "a lack of understanding among bosses and co-workers, (and) a shortage of labor at workplaces."[26]

Although this kind of family-oriented man is still rare, the current social and economic climates are now forcing workers to take a hard look at their lives. Many of them are seeing that Japan Inc.'s corporate-life-first mentality is coming to an end and they realize that they must do something to adapt to this development.

Japan's War of the Sexes

One may think that Japan would be an unlikely country for a gender war. Because of the clear separation of roles, men and women know their places and, for the most part, stick to them. True, compared to Western countries, Japan still boasts a very low divorce rate. According to the United Nations Demographic Book, in 1991, Japan's divorce rate stood at about 1.45 per 1,000 couples—roughly half that of the United Kingdom and only a third that of the United States.[27] Japan's divorce rate, however, has risen nearly 50 percent since 1970 and, as of the end of 1994, one in four marriages are ending in divorce.

In addition, the phenomenon of so-called *kateinai rikon*, or in-family divorces, where estranged couples may opt to keep up the appearance of marriage so that the wife can continue to benefit from the husband's earning power and the husband can avoid the embarrassment of being a social failure, is said to be widespread. Other signs point to rising tension between the sexes. The number of unmarried men and women above thirty, for example, has doubled over the last twenty years and is still rising. It appears that it is mostly women who are saying no to marriage. Even Japan's Crown Prince Hironomiya had a hard time persuading career-diplomat Masako Owada to marry him: It took him six years to convince her to agree.

In fact, younger women, especially those with careers, are challenging the centuries-old system of assuming their husband's name after marriage. In Japan, under the *koseki* (family registration) system, married couples are required to adopt a single name for their households. Although equality is, in principle, assured under the Civil Code, which allows a couple to adopt either the husband's or wife's name, in reality, 98 percent of all married women adopt their husband's name, due to the diehard paternalism of the Japanese family system that seeks to keep the family united under the authority of the husband or father.

This angers young women who feel it is unfair to have to

sacrifice their surnames, which often causes inconvenience and confusion in their workplaces. Consequently, as in the West in the 1960s, when women started actively demanding equal treatment, the call for the use of two different surnames gained such momentum in the second half of the 1980s that citizens' groups were formed in different parts of the country to advocate what is known as *fūfu bessei*, or different-surnamed husbands and wives. Some took their complaints to court, insisting they be given formal permission to use their own maiden names in the workplace. Others opted to marry and not register the marriage. So heated is this movement that the legislative council of the Ministry of Justice is now considering changing, or possibly abolishing, the family name system.

Not surprisingly, with men and women marrying later in life, the birthrate has also dwindled. As more than forty percent of all women are now part of the workforce, the perception gap between the sexes about courting and marriage has widened tremendously.

While Japanese men are continuing to look for "cute and cheerful but humble" housekeeper wives, as described in a news story,[28] many young women are casting a suspicious eye at their male counterparts, thinking them unreliable, self-centered, boorish, and predictable. At the heart of the problem is the male *maza-kon*, or "mother complex," a common description of how most Japanese men interact with the opposite sex; they expect to be spoiled and indulged by women as they were by their mothers. So common is this phenomenon that sociologist Chie Nakane, in her classic work *Japanese Society*, says that most wives adopt the role of mother rather than wife with their husbands.[29] Certainly, after a child is born, many couples begin using the names "mama" and "papa" among themselves, rather than the endearments they may have shared before. Although her book was published in 1974, the situation has changed little.

The Maza-kon Man

This complex has much to do with Japan's corporate success, where boys have grown up with little fatherly advice or influence, as their fathers are often absentee parents. This greatly contributes to their forming strong bonds with their mothers. As far as the spoiling goes, one proud mother, the wife of a high-ranking company executive, once displayed a picture of her eighteen-year-old son, saying, "This is my sweetheart." Of course she was joking, but there may have been a thread of truth to what she said. Because the wife receives little or no real attention—let alone affection—from her husband, she will often transfer her need to cuddle into coddling the male child, resulting in the development of a life-long interdependent relationship. This extends into marriage, with the average man looking for an obliging young wife who will become a substitute mother for him. The phenomenon was brilliantly captured in a popular 1992 Japanese soap opera *Zutto Anata ga Suki Datta* (I've Always Been in Love with You), in which the main character Fuyuhiko, a thirty-two-year-old banker, won't share the bed of his beautiful wife Miwa and throws childish tantrums. He predictably takes refuge in his butterfly collection whenever a marital dispute looms, and continues to seek moral support from his over-protective mother. In the end the wife runs away to be with her college sweetheart.

A recent *Newsweek* article offers its assessment of the mother-complex phenomenon in Japan: "In their childhood, most Japanese men are spoiled rotten by their mothers. All the signals that boys get growing up in Japan drive home a simple lesson—work hard in school, and someone will be there to take care of you on the weekends: Mom."[30]

Social critics have warned that unless Japanese mothers learn how not to discriminate in favor of their sons and start teaching them how to treat women as equals, Japan may soon face a war of the sexes as heated as the one currently raging in the United States. Some mothers, however, fear that if they start paying any less attention to their sons, they may be putting them at a disadvantage in the cutthroat competition of "male sphere" industries.

Even Yoriko Kawaguchi, who up until 1992 worked as the Deputy Director General for Global Environment in the Ministry of International Trade and Industry, said she is tempted to maintain the status quo. She is quoted as having said that although she tried not to differentiate between her son and daughter when they were young, she changed her mind midway because "he (her son) has to live in this society, and for his sake, I have to equip him for that."[31] Accordingly, the vicious cycle of young men being pushed to excel at school to prepare themselves to become tomorrow's corporate soldiers is perpetuated.

Less than fifty years ago, men had all the rights in marriage. Even now, some young, traditionally raised men are offended and angry about what they see as being a "feminine rebellion." I interviewed a twenty-seven-year-old salaryman working at a publishing firm who put it this way: "One of my female friends who admits to not knowing how to cook or do housework insists that her future husband be someone who comes home early from work, helps with the housework, and is sweet enough to tell her that she is beautiful. I have no time for a calculating woman who makes all these demands but has nothing to offer in return."

Below the surface of the gender war is the reality that

Japan is now faced with a generation of self-oriented, overprotected young people of both sexes who, used to having everything provided for them, are likely to struggle with give-and-take relationships and the sharing of responsibilities.

Some men, like their female counterparts, are beginning to eschew the idea of marriage. This, however, creates a dilemma in a culture that sees unmarried men as being immature and irresponsible, holding marriage as a prerequisite to social acceptance. Some bachelors, faced with the seriousness of the problem, are prompted to attend special courses such as those taught at the Bridegroom School in Tokyo, which opened in 1989. Here men learn how to become "good catches." Run by the marriage council division of Nihon Seinenkan, an organization affiliated with local governments, the school teaches the basics for becoming a good husband and father. Its curriculum includes subjects such as "What Kind of Men Do Today's Young Women Want?" and "Talking about Love and Sex."

Asian Brides—The Last Resort?

Even courses designed with the best intentions cannot come to the rescue of some bachelors. According to the Bridegroom School, farmers in small rural villages are having a particularly hard time finding wives. Likewise, certain men in urban areas also have a slim chance of finding a prospective bride, especially those who are engaged in the so-called "three-K jobs" (*kitsui- kitanai-kiken*, meaning physically demanding, dirty, and dangerous). Their job status is in direct contrast to the term of conditions that young women impose on their men, which are known as *sanko* (three highs): high education, high salary, and high stature or height. It is therefore small wonder that a 1993 Health and Welfare Ministry survey found that one out of every ten fifty-year-old men living in Tokyo is still single.[32]

Because of the desperation of single, middle-aged Japanese manual laborers and farmers, Japanese marriage brokers started "importing" women from poorer Asian nations to be matched up with clients. In 1986, the first batch of Asian brides was brought over to marry Japanese farmers in Yamagata Prefecture. The first such foreign brides were mainly from the Philippines. Recently, however, the range of Asian brides has expanded to include Koreans, Chinese, and women from Southeast Asia.[33]

In the past, the so-called mail-order brides were mostly imported to Western countries. Now Japan's affluence has also become a magnet for many women from the poorer parts of Asia. With Japanese women becoming increasingly selective, more Japanese men are turning to Asian brides for answers.

Although these marriages are helping to fill the gap, they are often associated with negative images. News about sham marriages and greedy brokers is common, particularly because international marriages have become a lucrative business, where matchmaking fees in big cities can run as high as US $20,000. Other scandals involve the exploitation and abuse of Asian women imported as marriage commodities because (in a reflection of the Butterfly myth) they are believed to be more docile than Japanese women.

In 1991, a twenty-seven-year-old Sri Lankan woman shocked the Japanese mass media by revealing how she was forced into marrying a Japanese businessman after being trapped in an Asian-brides-for-sale racket. She had answered a newspaper ad for computer training in Japan but was taken to a marriage broker directly from the airport.[34] In 1992, ten Chinese brides from Shanghai who had married Japanese men in remote Tochigi Prefecture through international marriage brokers disappeared together some time after coming to Japan.

Although there have been many successful marriages, disappointment is not uncommon as both marital partners have unrealistic expectations. For the most part, rural Japanese men, who are generally more traditional, may not view their foreign wives as being independent people with foreign backgrounds but "borrowed wombs" brought into the families primarily to preserve the family line—an expression that comes from the Japanese saying *hara wa karimono*, or "the womb is a borrowed thing." Many are accordingly very narrow-minded about cultural needs and differences (and this is hardly a surprise, since the women have literally been purchased). Even those who live in metropolitan areas tend to view their Asian wives as being second-class citizens and force them to adjust to Japanese ways. One Japanese man courting a Filipino hostess asked her to quit her job when they married. She then agreed to it on the condition that he would send money to her family in the Philippines. A few months after they had married, the husband reneged on his promise and stopped sending the money. When she decided to return to hostessing, he protested. In the end, she picked up her things and left.

In the book *Kokusai-kekkon—chikyu kazoku-zukuri* (International Marriages: Globalization on the Home Front), author Sachiko Ishikawa points out that one of her friends who was married to a Thai woman complained about his wife's inability to cook Japanese food. Ishikawa says he did not even think about the fact that she had never lived outside of Thailand. She likened his unrealistic demand that she cook Japanese food to "asking a fish to climb a tree."[35]

Many Asian brides, mistaking Japan's gross national product for their husbands' and believing that they have married into wealth, are disappointed when they discover their husbands are merely farmers or construction workers. In a local Chinese-language newspaper for Chinese students studying in Japan, one woman from Shanghai wrote in to reveal her shock about the Japanese husband she had met through a marriage broker. Not only was he not as prosperous as she had thought, but he also lived in a remote village in northern Japan. He was also very tight with his money and would not visit her in the hospital when she was ill. Months later, she decided to run away.

Many Japanese men, clinging to the sense of superiority they believe is their natural right, tend to think that because their Asian wives are from less advantaged countries, they will be amenable and pliant. Asian women, however, are proving to be less docile or accommodating than the common wisdom suggests. Makoto Endo, director of Shinjuku-based Absolute System Co., which specializes in brides from Korea, China, Malaysia, Australia, Sri Lanka, India, and Eastern Europe, was quoted as saying that Korean women have become "more choosy and will refuse to marry a Japanese if they have to live in a small apartment or if they have to share a home with the man's parents."[36] Another marriage broker also admits that Southeast Asian women as a whole no longer think that Japanese men are good catches, which is an indication of the improving economic conditions in Southeast Asia and concomitant improvement in the status of women.

Ironically, as instability and chaos continue to loom in Eastern Europe, many international marriage brokers are starting to import Western brides from Poland, Russia, and other East European countries. Many of these women, some as young as nineteen, readily take Japanese men as their husbands. Only time will tell how these marriages work out. Meanwhile, outside the broker's offices, there are signs of another growing trend—love and marriage between Japanese men and Western women, a result of more foreigners coming to study and work in Japan.

An American English teacher in his forties I was talking with at a conversation lounge became visibly upset when his English friend dropped by and mentioned to him that an acquaintance of theirs, an American woman, had recently married a Japanese. "But Japanese men are all chauvinists. What does she see in these men? She must be crazy," he said.

Comments of this sort are not unique. In fact, one American scholar at the University of Hawaii once told me that when she mentioned to Western males that her husband was Japanese, they told her that she must be "insane" and that she must be on the verge of divorce, or that she was lucky to have found one of the few, exceptional, Westernized Japanese men.[37]

Indeed, when speaking of Western-Asian relationships, the conventional assumption is that it only works the other way—when the man is Western and the woman Asian. This is because in international society, which often gives more weight to Western standards, Western men are invariably looked upon as being so much more cultured, considerate and thoughtful than their Asian counterparts. It should follow that Japanese men have little to offer a Western woman. But just how true is this assumption? This is the focus of the next chapter.

 CHAPTER EIGHT

Another Kind of Attraction

Many Western women I have talked to would not consider dating a Japanese man. In fact, quite a few of them admit to having had preconceived ideas about Japanese men before ever arriving in Japan. Twenty-one-year-old Monica, a scholar from Austria, mentioned during an interview that her parents had warned her not to marry a Japanese man. Why? Because, they said, they are all workaholics (an image well-publicized in the West).

Pam, twenty-six, a freelance television producer from America, says that when she first told her friends that she was thinking of going to Japan, they asked her why she wanted to go there "of all places." After all, they said, Japanese men are short, nerdy, and uniformly male chauvinists.

Alice, a thirty-two-year-old Canadian who works for a major financial news agency, also admitted that the thought of dating a Japanese man initially seemed far-fetched to her because, "I was expecting all Japanese men to be sexist and there was no way I would ever go out with one." That thought, however, quickly dissolved when she met her Japanese boyfriend Aki, a pop musician.

Stereotypes about the Japanese Man

If the Japanese woman is stereotyped as passive, feminine, and, good wife-material, the image of the Japanese man is close to the opposite end of the spectrum. Hollywood films, for example, depict them as ruthless samurai or conniving businessmen with productions like *Shogun* and *Gung Ho*. In both cases, they (and Asian men in general) tend to play sexually unappealing characters who never get the girl. They may also be depicted as gangsters or rapists with perverted sexual appetites, someone from whom women could be rescued by, say, a valiant white man. These images are found in movies like *Year of the Dragon* and the *Karate Kid* series. It is interesting to see that in such movies, a beautiful Asian woman is rescued from the hands of a dangerous Asian male or the Mafia by a gallant white man.

If these images were taken at face value, it would follow that Western women would see little reason to be attracted to or want to have a relationship with a Japanese man. Yet evidence is beginning to show that the attraction not only exists, but it is mutual. Marriages in Japan between Japanese men and non-Japanese women have increased dramatically in a matter of two decades. In 1971, for example, the marriage rate for Japanese grooms and non-Japanese brides was a mere 0.2 percent of the total number of marriages in Japan. By 1993, it had grown to 2.5 percent. Between 1972 and 1992, the number of Japanese men marrying non-Japanese increased 7.2 times.

Although over half of the foreign brides are from Asia, there are indications that marriages to Western women are also increasing. The annual number of American brides, for example, was a mere 75 in 1970. By 1993, it had risen to 244.

Another sign is seen in the growth of membership in the

Association of Foreign Wives of Japanese (AFWJ).[1] According to the group, at the end of 1993 it had a total of 578 members, as compared with only 41 in 1962.[2] Though these increases are still relatively small, they indicate that Japan has been attracting an increasing number of foreign women to work and study. Japan appeals to single, adventure-minded Western women as it is safe, and work opportunities are still plentiful for women. In the course of their stays, it is only natural that more are dating and marrying Japanese men.

A third indication is seen in the Japanese mass media. The *Nihon Keizai Shimbun,* a respected Japanese economic daily, ran a series of articles on couples comprising Japanese husbands and Western wives in March 1985. In September 1990, the *Japan Economic Journal* ran a full-length story on Japanese husbands and European or American wives. And in August 1991, *Across,* a monthly catering to young Japanese, ran a special on Japanese men dating Western women.

But perhaps more revealing of the rising trend of such romances is the recent publication of an autobiography by a British woman about her own romantic experience with a Japanese businessman. Published in Japanese, it is simply entitled: *Nihon no otoko to koi ni ochite* (Falling in Love with a Japanese Man).[3] In the book, author Catherine Macklon details her love affair with a married Japanese man whom she met in former West Germany. Although she herself was also married at the time she met him, the book describes how the two struggle together against all odds to finally be with each other.

Although Macklon's book is an account of a woman's battle against domestic violence and her own journey into finding herself, what is revealing about her book is her bold statement against the conventional belief that a West-

ern woman cannot possibly find a Japanese man attractive.
The irony here is that the author ran away from the abuse
of her British husband in order to find solace in the arms of
a Japanese man—the reversed scenario of a battered Asian
woman being rescued by her Western lover. The book thus
powerfully challenges the commonly held belief in the
supremacy of the Western male.

As mentioned earlier, the stereotypes of Japanese men
have been largely promoted in films and books on Japan. I
asked an American wife of a Japanese what she thought
could be the cause of the persistently negative image of
Japanese men. She said that it was because "most of the
books about Japan have been written by Western male
observers. And these men often listen to Japanese women,
who continue to tell them how terrible Japanese men are."

In comparison with Japanese women, Japanese men
have been changing relatively slowly because they have,
until recently, been tied to their work and have had little
time to become involved in life outside their companies.
However, more men are becoming aware of the need to
change and are making attempts to do so.

Japan: A Romantic Wasteland?

When I mention to friends and acquaintances that more
Japanese men are marrying foreign women, most express
disbelief. In particular, Western men seemed to have a
harder time understanding the phenomenon. "Is there such
a thing as a Japanese Prince Charming?" asked one American friend. "What foreign woman would want to marry a
Japanese man?" a male interviewee queried.

I asked women the same questions and was told by some
that they went out with Japanese men initially because
they were lonely and had given up on the local foreign

men. Japan, these women say, is a romantic wasteland because most Western men are involved with Japanese women, and are often said to be romantically unresponsive to Western women. An Irish artist who has been in Japan for six years says that her first four years in Japan, before she met her Japanese boyfriend, were a blank in terms of romantic involvement. An attractive Australian woman I interviewed says she became so frustrated that she finally decided to go out with a Japanese man because some relationship was better than no relationship at all.

One executive woman from New York who worked in Tokyo during the bubble economy years described Japan as a "golden handcuff" because, despite all the perks and money she was getting, she was frustrated about not having any real relationships. She eventually left Japan for home. An American editor in her early forties, who, after many unsuccessful attempts at romancing the local foreign men, summed up the situation by calling Japan a "sexual Siberia."

Joan, an American photojournalist from San Francisco, attributed the "sexual Siberia" observation to an Asian "fetish" held by the Western male. "Western men, because they are so popular with Japanese women, are like kids in a candy store," says a woman from Detroit. So upset is this woman about foreign men in Japan that she calls them "wimps turned pimps." Other women suggest that local Western men, spoiled by the ease of dating Japanese women, no longer want to bother with the courting etiquette of wining and dining the Western women. But more importantly, as one observant Canadian writer has pointed out: to many Western men, dating Japanese women is also an essential part of their "Oriental" experience.

A few of the men I interviewed, however, are quick to deny that they deliberately eschew Western women. Instead, they speak of having only limited opportunities to meet them. As long as they are in Japan, they say, it is only natural that they have more chances to meet Japanese women. Other reasons, as discussed in Chapter Four, include the practical need for an alliance with a local, who can help make the life of a foreigner easier in Japan.

More objectively, some foreign women also recognize that because Japan is a "revolving door," with people constantly coming and going, it is extremely hard for fellow foreigners to meet or enjoy long-term friendship with one another. "Besides, we didn't come here to be with other foreigners anyway," says a young management consultant from Boston. "We came here to work and to experience another culture."

Some of the women I interview say it is no great loss that foreign men are not interested, because many, they say, tend have an offensive or sexist attitude toward women. "The trouble with Western men in Japan is that they become so spoiled here by the attention they get that they are forgetting their manners," says a TV producer from Detroit. She continues, saying that many foreign men virtually ignore foreign women. These men find they can exploit the respect they receive from the Japanese merely for being a Western male, and treat foreign women with less respect than they would have to accord them at home. In fact, Western men can become easily influenced by the chauvinistic Japanese mind-set in the workplace. Suddenly, the producer says, they feel justified in not including their female colleagues at business luncheons and other meetings. These men, she says, look upon women more as objects or conveniences.

In a woman's eyes, the image of Western men in Japan varies greatly depending on who you talk to—whether she is Japanese or Western, or whether she has had a negative experience with them or not. Yet it is very noticeable that the hostility expressed by certain Western women toward foreign men seemed particularly heated during the bubble years of the Japanese economy. This was perhaps due in part to work and pay inequality between men and women, a difference which was even more exaggerated when the economy was booming.

That Western men in general tend to have an easier time meeting the opposite sex also contributed to the women's frustration. This is mostly because while there's almost an immediate attraction between Western men and Japanese women, many Western women continue to shun Japanese men. Held back by their own stereotypes, they too, like my American friend, cannot believe that there might be a Japanese Prince Charming. But then, many Japanese men, not having been trained to approach and charm a female partner, may also have not been very attractive to many Western women.

Yet this does not mean that all foreign women in Japan share the experience of "rejection" by Western men. In fact, I have talked with many younger women who say it is not any more difficult for them to meet the opposite sex in Japan than it is in their own countries. It might be because the younger women are more open-minded and more ready to try new things.

Women who complain about the unresponsiveness of Western men and would not consider going out with Japanese men, however, will sooner or later leave this romantic wasteland for a new destination.

Socioeconomic Status as an Attraction

Undaunted by traditional stereotypes, some foreign women are discovering more and more reasons to go out with Japanese men. One of these attractions, many are quick to admit, has to do with Japan's improved socioeconomic status.

This is precisely the point researchers and sociologists have been trying to prove for some time. In academic papers, experts argue that, for intercultural marriages, the ethnic background and nationality of a potential mate are often not as important for women as his social status and position.[4] Given this argument, it follows that the recent economic success of Japan has worked wonders toward creating a major shift of interest by Western women toward Japanese men as potential partners.

Professor Fumiteru Nitta, currently at Kibi International University in Okayama, points out that "When Japan's social status was lower, as until a few decades ago, Japanese men might not have been desirable marital partners. However, now that Japan has established a prominent socioeconomic position in the world, many Western women may feel less reluctant to choose Japanese men as marital partners."[5]

An American member of the Association of Foreign Wives of Japanese concurs: "Twenty years ago, Japan was still a poor nation and marrying a Japanese man would mean a step down for an American woman. But now, it's a real mixed bag, depending on the family background of the woman." An American teacher from Milwaukee who met her Japanese husband in Chicago also confided that she decided to marry him because he represented wealth and richness and she saw financial security in a liaison with him. The highly publicized Japanese purchase of Rockefeller Center in the late 1980s during the boom years clearly projected an image of wealth. This was illustrated by the release of the controversial, highly publicized murder-mystery film *Rising Sun* in 1993. One of the main characters is Eddie Sakamura, a rich Japanese playboy who buys the services of a naked blonde to use as a sushi plate.

As long as Americans and other Westerners are drawn to the image of a rich Japan, more and more of those who come to Japan are committed to longer stays. Says one American editor formerly married to a Japanese, "It used to be a big problem for Western women to bring their Japanese husbands home because of economic as well as racial prejudice. But the tide has turned and many foreign women see more economic opportunities in Japan and are becoming more open about marrying a Japanese and staying permanently in Japan."

Proximity Factor

Since the mid-1980s, foreign nationals have been arriving in Japan by the thousands. According to Ministry of Justice, in 1993, the number of foreigners living in Japan exceeded 1,320,000. Although the total number of men is greater than that of women in most age groups, there are indications that more and more women are coming to Japan, especially those in their early twenties. In 1993, for example, the number of women in the fifteen-to-twenty-four age group was about 40 percent more than that of men.[6] Once in Japan, they meet Japanese men at school and work, through parties and other encounters. In earlier chapters, I suggested that English lessons serve as an important venue for bringing Japanese women and Western men together. Likewise, these lessons also bring Japanese men and Western women together. Of the many foreign women I have interviewed, about a third say that they met their Japanese boyfriends and husbands through private and corporate-sponsored English lessons. Amid Japan's avid promotion of internationalization, eager English teachers and enthusiastic Japanese students have found a vital forum for mutual exchange.

The last two decades have also seen a veritable flood of Japanese traveling abroad, as mentioned in Chapter Four. Consequently, there are more opportunities for Japanese men to meet and interact with non-Japanese women. Although far fewer men than women travel abroad as tourists, according to statistics many more Japanese men than women travel overseas on business, rendering the combined figures for tourism-study and business travel for men far greater.[7]

In a survey conducted among 125 AFWJ members in January 1994, for this book, the two most frequently cited ways of initial contact between foreign women and their future Japanese spouses are introductory meetings on campuses (outside of Japan) or at work (both in and outside of Japan).[8] As sociologists have pointed out, shared status—such as being students or colleagues—may be more salient than either nationality or ethnicity when considering a marriage partner.[9] I therefore could not agree more with Cindy, a member of AFWJ who met her husband in the United States through work, when she insists that the recent trend in intermarriages in Japan has much to do with what she calls "the invention of the airbus."

The Curiosity Factor

Although quite a few women I spoke with, especially those in their thirties, say they started dating Japanese men mostly by accident, quite a few of the younger women interviewed said they had half expected to go out with Japanese men. "Before I came to Japan, my only encounters with Asian men were with American Chinese and American Japanese, so I was curious about what real Japanese men were like," said a twenty-ish American woman who works for a local publisher. Mary, an English teacher from Canada, also admits to having gone out with a student in her company class. She says she finds his dark eyes and dark hair very mysterious, and very attractive. Other women also say that Japanese subtlety can be a turn-on. "Because his personality is not on display, it makes you want to discover the man behind the mask," says one American woman of her Japanese boyfriend. Thus the old saying "exotic is erotic" also applies to Western women and Japanese men.

Another factor that has contributed to the exotic factor of Japanese men is the change in their physiques and appearance, which have improved greatly since the war. More dietary protein in the form of meat and dairy products has resulted in an increase in average height. With the affluence of today's society, many Japanese men, especially in their twenties and early thirties, are also more fashion-conscious. Several women I interviewed commented on the nice taste Japanese men have in clothes and they used such adjectives as "elegant," "cool," "slim," "tight," and "clean-cut" to describe their sense for fashion.

The Changing Attitudes of Japanese Men

Physical attraction and exotic appeal aside, many foreign women also find younger Japanese men to be a far cry from the old male-chauvinist stereotype. A common remark among Western men in Japan is that "Japanese men are much more sexist than we are." But are they? To many women who belong to the AFWJ, they are not. In fact, these foreign wives often mention how much their Japanese husbands deviate from the stereotypical Japanese man in that they treat women with respect, show more sensitivity, and help more with the children and around the house than many of the Western men they know.

The conventional stereotypes of Japanese men have not caught up with the changing times. As mentioned in Chapter Seven, the younger Japanese men of today are very different from their fathers and even their elder brothers. They are far more likely than men in their forties and fifties to value family outings, celebrate family birthdays, and help out with child care. Judging from the current trend, it appears that more and more younger Japanese men are beginning to accept and adjust to the concept of sexual equality.

"The relationship between husbands and wives in Japan is definitely changing for the better," says Rebecca, a twenty-eight-year-old American staff member at a job placement firm, who two years ago married a Japanese colleague one year her senior. "Because my husband grew up knowing that his mother, a working woman, did not appreciate the way she was treated by his father, he has learned to be more respectful and considerate of women," she says. Aside from helping with the chores at home, one thing Rebecca says she particularly likes about her husband is how open he is about showing his affection. He is not inhibited about kissing her in public, which is still rather uncommon.

Several Western women I interviewed have voiced similar sentiments. One British woman who works for a securities firm says that her husband is very romantic and tells her he loves her every day. Admittedly, her husband has had extended experience living abroad. Still, the hard fact is that younger Japanese men, like Japanese women, are changing as Japan opens its doors wider to the outside world.

Less exploited than their fathers and elder brothers by Japan's corporate society, younger Japanese men are also more relaxed about life and more eager to try new things. Given the recent push from the government to take longer vacations from work, in addition to the availability of child-care leaves from work, Japanese husbands are slowly getting more involved with the family and housework. As Japanese lifestyles continue to diversify and the recession and crumbling lifetime employment system force salary-men home earlier, the old stereotypes about Japanese men as workaholics who don't lift a finger at home may soon become obsolete.

Cultural Attractions

Although many Western men claim that Western women who go out with Japanese men must be drawn to their "Westernized manners," not a few of women I talked to insisted that it is the "Japanese qualities" that first attracted them to their Japanese partners. These include the following:

1. The "Feminine" Qualities

Perhaps most surprising is that many foreign women claim they appreciate qualities about Japanese men deemed "feminine" in the West—a seeming contradiction to the notion of Japan as one of the most male-dominated cultures on earth. Women I have talked to or interviewed repeatedly say how they find the non-confrontational manners of Japanese men refreshing, although the men these women refer to are in their early thirties or younger. Their discussions with Japanese men, many claim, are friendlier and much less potentially antagonistic than those they have with Western men, although this may be due partially to the polite attitudes of the Japanese and partially to the language barrier. Says a private satellite television producer, "Discussions with Western men here often earn me a feminist label, but I'm just expressing my opinion."

Going out with a Japanese man can thus effect an escape from the "gender war" between Western males and females that may become heightened in Japan because of the different treatments men and women tend to receive. Many women actually say that when they are with Japanese men, they feel relieved from the "oppressive feeling of power" that men are often viewed as having over women in Western countries. This feeling, many women say, comes from a sense of competition Western women often feel with Western men. In Japan, however, because of the clear separation of gender roles, this kind of competition between the sexes is largely blunted. Perhaps this is why Japanese men, it appears to the Western women, feel less need to prove their masculinity .

Even the tendency for Japanese men to want to be mothered, which so many Japanese women scoff at as a sign of weakness, is seen by some foreign women as "an adorable quality if brought out in a positive way." Such women might even embrace the tradition of Japanese girl-friends, making a boxed lunch for her boyfriend, laying out his work clothes the night before, and allowing him to put his head in her lap. Pam, whom I mentioned earlier in this chapter, says she really appreciates this need to be mothered in her three-year-live-in Japanese boyfriend. She says it shows her his open and honest need for her love. "Tell me, how many Western men would admit openly that they need me?" she mused.

Though this shy little boy image may not appeal to every Western woman, it definitely has its attraction for some. One AFWJ member, whom I also mentioned earlier in the chapter, says, "Japanese men's come-ons are much quieter—it's appealing because it's not as intimidating.

Because the lines Japanese men use on women are often so unsophisticated and transparent, they are refreshing and cute." One New York woman who works as a computer engineer also suggested that many women are fed up with the blatant type of "slam, bam, thank you ma'am" sexual overtures quite common in pre-AIDS America.

2. *Family Commitment*

Living with the husband's family and tending to its needs is something many young Japanese women want to avoid at all costs. However, more than a dozen foreign women I came across said they have lived with their husbands' families, and quite a few of them said that they did not mind this traditional arrangement.

Then there is the example of Jeannie Fuji, a twenty-eight-year-old English teacher from California who has made quite a name for herself for helping her Japanese husband's family run a traditional Japanese inn in the town of Ginzan in the remote mountains of Yamagata Prefecture in northern Japan. She has become an overnight celebrity as the country's first blue-eyed *okami*, or female concierge, who works as chief cook and bottle washer, providing guests with old-fashioned and labor-intensive personal services.

What could motivate a liberated, Western woman to want to take on a traditional role like this? When I mentioned this to a Canadian English teacher in her early forties, she explained that some Western women find a strong appeal in being closely involved with a Japanese family. This woman, who married a Japanese salaryman three years ago, says she was initially attracted to her husband because of the closeness of his family—something she says she always wanted for herself. "Because my parents divorced while I was still very young, I have always wanted to experience the intimacy of a family. And when I saw how close my husband was to his mother, with whom he lived, I really wanted to be a part of that family." She said she enjoyed doing all the Japanese things, as well as the housework and going shopping with her mother-in-law.

Beyond the family, other women speak highly of their Japanese husbands' sense of responsibility. In a survey I conducted of AFWJ members, respondents repeatedly used words such as "reliable," "responsible," "stable," "trustworthy," and "dependable" to describe what they liked about their spouses. Says an English teacher from New York who recently married an elite Japanese businessman and moved to Philadelphia with him, "I dated many guys back in New York and most of them were flaky and unreliable. They were either into drugs or were emotionally noncommittal. But I know I can count on Masaru, who takes life very seriously."

3. *The Amae Factor*

Another attraction that some Western women feel toward being part of a Japanese family or community is the feeling Japanese call *amae*—a concept introduced by translator John Bester in Takeo Doi's classic *The Anatomy of Dependence* as "the desire to be passively loved"; "the feelings that all normal infants at the breast harbor toward the mother—dependence"; and "the unwillingness to be separated from the warm mother-child circle and cast into a world of objective reality."[10]

Several women have mentioned that after living in Japan for some time, they begin to enjoy the comforts of interdependence. Says one high-profile radio personality from Wisconsin working in Tokyo, "In Japan, once you are accepted in a group, you are accepted for life, whereas in the West, people tend to be very critical of each other. There, I am made to feel that I am being judged all the time and that if I don't live up to their expectations, I will be dropped right away." In Japan, she says, she can indulge in the love of her Japanese friends and community and is made to feel that she occupies a secure and respected role within the group.

One pressure this woman says she felt from her peers in the United States was to appear to be strong at all times. Women friends at home, she says, brag about not cooking for their husbands. Admitting to doing household chores would amount to admitting to being weak and backward. "But here I can be weak when I want to and I can let my hair down without feeling bad," she adds.

This view is readily shared by the Canadian English teacher I mentioned earlier, who also expressed relief at being able to let her weaker, more passive side out into the open. She says she is tired of having to be "politically correct" all the time and actually enjoys being a full-time housewife here—something that her friends and family members frown on back in Canada. They told her that she had become "really conservative and uninteresting."

Being in the group-oriented society of Japan, where the emphasis is on harmony, is thus a relief for some foreign women who tire of having to fend for themselves in the highly competitive societies of the West where personal success is given priority over the need to strike a balance as a member of a unit or group.

4. Access to Japanese Culture

The added bonus of being romantically involved with a Japanese national, many women also point out, is the access to insights into the Japanese culture. "My boyfriend has opened up a whole new facet of the Japanese world that I wouldn't otherwise have had access to," says Alice, who has been living with her Japanese boyfriend for the last three years. Alice said with Aki's help, she has learned to understand the language and the Japanese people at a much deeper level. Through touring Aki's hometown in Hiroshima, for example, she said she got to see how the Japanese live and relate to one another—an experience she no doubt would have missed without Aki as her personal guide to Japan.

Women also voice a feeling of closeness they experience with the Japanese community when married to a Japanese. "It can be hard to get close to Japanese people heart-to-heart," said Rosanna Fukada, an international business consultant from Pennsylvania, in a 1990 article for the *Japan Economic Journal*. "But if I say my husband is Japanese, I move one step closer to them." This statement is readily agreed with by Ruth, a New Zealander married to a Japanese. She speaks of sharing a comradeship with Japanese housewives with whom she laughs as they joke about their Japanese husbands.

The Rising Interest of Japanese Men

If some Western women are finding good reasons to approach Japanese men, they are rewarded with a keener interest in return. As Professor Nitta puts it, "American and other Western men have been marrying Oriental and other non-Western women for their 'exotic' and other qualities in the past. This does not mean that Japanese men were not interested in marrying non-Japanese women. There simply was not much opportunity for most of them to meet such women until a couple of decades ago."[11]

Even if Japanese men did have the chance to meet Western women, it was not likely that the encounters could have resulted in romance. Indeed, though American women were the first Western women to come into close contact with Japanese men during the Occupation years, the impact was negligible. This was because, as Sheila Johnson, author of *The Japanese Through American Eyes,* pointed out, "Most American women in Japan during the immediate postwar years were either in uniform themselves or were civilian employees of the Occupation, and it is not likely that a man from a defeated country would have dared to make advances to a woman so clearly above him in status."[12]

The war experience was not the only reason that kept Japanese men from approaching Western women. In an interracial marriage study, Hiroshi Wagatsuma pointed out that Japanese men have long suffered from an inferiority complex toward Westerners and see Western women as being inaccessible. "When Japanese men feel a vague sense of discomfort at the sight or notion of a Japanese woman marrying a white man, especially an American, the feeling may be related to their unconscious understanding that a Japanese woman, by choosing a white man, is challenging their worth as men and their virility."[13]

During World War II, some Japanese soldiers in Manchuria were said to have purposely sought to sleep with Russian prostitutes to redeem their virility because, as Wagatsuma asserts, "Actual sexual experience with a white woman may help some Japanese overcome such feelings of inferiority toward Caucasians."[14]

This may explain why Western women have always been treated as favorite subjects for sexual fantasies in Japanese men's magazines. This may also explain why foreign women living in Japan when Caucasian foreigners were still relatively rare were occasionally accosted by explicit sexual overtures from *chikan,* or perverts. In the late seventies, when I first came to live in Japan as a student, I recall many occasions when American and other Western women friends complained about Japanese men suddenly exposing themselves in front of them on streets and in elevators. On one occasion, one American friend said that while commuting late one evening on an empty train she was interrupted by a young salaryman who exposed himself and demanded, "Would this do for you?"

Now that foreigners are a common sight in the bigger cities of Japan, fewer of my women informants have recounted such extreme encounters. Japanese men with this type of complex, however, are still grappling with their sexual virility in other ways. Recently, for example, a young British woman told me that she was approached by a young Japanese man on the street who simply pleaded, "Look, can you help me out, I've never slept with a white woman. Would you go to a hotel with me?"

The Impact of Internationalization

Younger Japanese men, armed with new confidence by their nation's rising economic power and, thanks to the efforts of *kokusaika* (internationalization), not as tongue-tied as they once were, are becoming bolder and more direct in their approaches to foreign women. What's more, according to some international dating services, more Japanese men are expressing interest in meeting and possibly marrying Western women. According to Miharu Kobayashi of Inter-Connect System, an international dating service based in Tokyo, there is a rising trend in Japanese men wanting to meet Caucasian women, particularly European women. Most of these men, Kobayashi said, are in their early thirties, speak fluent English, hold executive-level positions and command annual salaries of more than

US $80,000. What attracts them to Western women? Aside from their curiosity about foreign cultures and the cliché that they are looking for free English lessons, there are other, sounder reasons.

1. *The Bridge to Freedom*

If foreigners living in Japan are looking for an "in" into the closed Japanese society, then Japanese men, much like their female counterparts, are searching for an "out" from the rigidity of their culture. Foreigners, who epitomize internationalization, fit the bill. Aki, the pop musician involved in a three-year relationship with his Canadian girlfriend Alice, said that although he did not consciously seek to go out with her, he found that he was initially excited about learning about North America and was glad that he was able to travel to Canada with her on several occasions, his first trips out of Japan.

Other Japanese men, however, are more conscious about looking for an access to the outside world through marriage to a foreign woman. As Miharu Kobayashi puts it, "The kind of adventure and tension that comes along with a bicultural relationship is a great way for them to stay within mainstream Japanese society while maintaining their own individual lifestyle." These men, Kobayashi added, are tired of being the same as everyone else.

A forty-something Canadian woman from Toronto who recently separated from her Japanese husband after four years of marriage, said she sees a lot of truth in this assertion. While she was still living with her husband, she said he often complained about being bogged down by the responsibilities of work and home. He had dreamed of buying a second house in Canada and leading a freer lifestyle with her. She felt that she was essentially "a bridge to freedom" for him.

2. The Trophy-wife Syndrome

Aside from the excitement and freedom rendered by such relationships, Kobayashi also spoke of a more unconscious motivation that involves the Japanese man's sense of status and oft-noted inferiority complex toward Westerners. Some Japanese men want to marry a Western woman because having a Western wife, Kobayashi said, would make them look good in the eyes of their colleagues. According to Kobayashi, while a bride from a developing Asian country is likely to put a dent in a man's social status, a wife from America or Europe is likely to enhance it. "To many of my clients, marrying a Western woman is like owning a Porsche—it's a status symbol." This is why Inter-Connect System, Kobayashi explains, is doing good business matching up Russian and European women with Japanese businessmen.

What Kobayashi did not mention is that having a Western wife also gives a Japanese man a slight edge over others because, as one foreign wife put it, "People at work become a little more understanding when my husband explains that he has to go home earlier because his wife is a Westerner."

Evidence shows that the trophy-wife mentality is quite common among a certain type of Japanese man. Throughout my research, I have been repeatedly told by women that their businessmen boyfriends or husbands take them out to public functions and business meetings just so that they can be seen with them. Many women say they don't see the point in it, as they say they don't understand much Japanese and are made to feel like a doll sitting on a shelf.

Opposites attract, and my observations have shown that Japanese men seem to have a particular obsession for blondes—an influence that has perhaps come from the Hollywood stereotype, or the fact that they are about as different as possible from the Japanese. One Japanese male friend, however, insists that he is not influenced by the public message that blondes are more desirable than brunettes. Instead, he explains his penchant this way, "I like women with long, blonde hair because their hair is so much softer and is so beautiful. It is so different from Asian hair. Women with blonde hair remind me a lot of goddesses." As hard as he tries to prove his point, his argument rings rather hollow.

It is hardly any wonder that blondes should be singled out for special attention in *gaijin* hostess bars and clubs in Japan's big cities. An attractive bar hostess from Australia with long, dark hair said she was once approached by a Japanese client who wanted to be her patron on the condition that she dye her hair blonde. She was so upset that she refused the offer.

Some of the women interviewed say it bothers them that they are treated like objects, or are liked only because they resemble the images men have seen in magazines. Other women, however, say they appreciate the extra attention they get. Says an American language-school owner in her forties, "I like being the center of attention; it's good for my ego. I was back home for a few years after an extended stay in Japan and was really depressed to find that I was . . . just like everybody else." Although she said that she knows the attention she is getting is all on the surface, she likes it because it helps build her confidence.

3. *The Search for an Equal Partner*

It would be unfair to say that most Japanese men who go out with Western women do so for reasons of "*gaijin* tokenism," as one American wife puts it. Some are sincerely looking for what they believe to be a more ideal and equal life partner. Many find the Western woman's sense of self and purpose in life refreshing. "It's a relief to know women whose goals in life are not limited to just marriage," says a Japanese editor in his thirties who has traveled extensively in Europe and the United States. What is left unsaid is that Western women, in general, are also more willing to contribute their share toward the household income, thus freeing the men from the role of having to be the sole bread-winner.

Denny, a twenty-four-year-old Japanese who works for a foreign-capital chemical firm also points out that European and North American women generally seem to know what they want and are good about taking the initiative in making decisions. This, he says, contrasts with Japanese women who are "wishy-washy and won't tell you what's on their minds." He continues by saying, "A guy going out with a Japanese woman always has to make a lot of decisions like where to go or what restaurant to go to because she doesn't tell you what she wants. This places a big burden on a guy because you only know so many places."

Denny also says he thinks that Western women are more honest about what they are thinking about and are therefore a lot easier to understand. "If they have boyfriends, they will tell me straight out. But Japanese women won't tell me directly because they don't know how to say no to a man." On a deeper level, Denny says the indirectness of Japanese women may also have to do with their wanting to weigh the situation to best suit their own personal interests. He added, however, that Japanese men may also have the tendency to avoid being straight when things are not going well. This, he admits, amounts to "wimping out of a confrontational situation" in the Western sense. But he said he himself does this with Japanese women—something he is not proud of but feels trapped into "because this is the way they do things here." It is therefore refreshing for Denny to date a Western woman as he feels liberated from such confusing courtship games.

This theory is confirmed by a young New Zealand wife of a Japanese who wrote and said that the non-Japanese-ness of foreign women offers Japanese men "more leeway in terms of what they can do and say without making the long-term commitment that perhaps a Japanese woman would expect." Since foreign women are not a part of the strict social code that regulates a relationship between two Japanese, men may feel less pressure when the relationship they are in is intercultural.

4. *The Lure of "Otherness"*

Because of the intangible social pressure on the Japanese to conform, less courageous people may be at a loss about how to lead their own individual lives. It is much easier for them to keep to the accepted pattern. In an intercultural relationship, however, the "otherness" provided by a foreign partner often serves as a catalyst or stimulant to the Japanese partner, thus hastening the process of change.

The foreignness between couples also appears to create a freshness that helps mute the heated friction that sexes of the same culture often experience in modern society. An American wife of a Japanese herbalist calls this attraction to a different culture the lure of the "otherness." "In my (American) culture, couples that have similar professions are having a harder time getting along with each other because there is simply too much 'sameness,' which creates a lot of competition," she explains. But when couples come from different backgrounds, their "otherness" tends to balance things between the two partners, thus creating a more harmonious relationship.

Ironically, many of these men say they are not interested in marrying a typical Japanese woman because these women are not independent-minded enough for them.[15] Japanese men, speaking in the same tone as their female counterparts, say they also aspire to a partnership fashioned after the Western model. Rather than working together with their own female counterparts to cope with recent social changes, some Japanese men, like some Japanese women, find it easier to seek an alternative through the "outside" stimulation provided by a foreign spouse.

Tetsuya, a handsome, well-traveled salaryman in his thirties from Hiroshima who recently married Kate, a New Zealander from Wellington, says he chose to marry her instead of a former Japanese girlfriend because, "As a third son, I cannot expect any inheritance from my parents and I must start things from scratch. I need a partner who is willing to contribute financially toward a future together." With a Japanese wife, he says he would be afraid that she might gravitate toward the traditional role of being a full-time homemaker. Kate's foreignness, however, provides her an excuse not to conform to the traditional wifely role.

Judging from Tetsuya's case, it can be assumed that some of the more forward-thinking Japanese men tend to "defect" from relationships with Japanese women in order to gain a measure of personal freedom, which is not unlike the Japanese women who marry biculturally and biracially to throw off the traditional burdens of society.

Problems in International Dating

Despite the mutual appreciation, going out with Japanese men is still frustrating for many foreign women. For one thing, many women fixate on the romantic notion they grew up with of a knight in shining armor. "Japanese men are still very shy and lack social skills. They don't open the door for you. They don't wait to help you on with your jacket. They just don't know how to charm and sweet-talk a woman the way a Western man does," insists a corporate editor from Southern California. Here, however, she may be imposing her own cultural bias.

Pam, the American television producer I mentioned earlier who has been living in Japan for six years, thinks that courting in Japan is an entirely different ball game. Women cannot expect to wait for the romantic phone call and roses on a second date and must take a lot more initiative in approaching men. She said it took her eight months to woo her current live-in artist boyfriend, whom she literally had to seduce. The Irish artist I mentioned earlier in this chapter also points out that it is unrealistic to impose expectations on someone that are based strictly on one's own culture. "I think that there is a lot to be learned from stepping out of your own cultural boundaries," she says.

People make a lot of assumptions based on their own cultures. In intermarriages between Japanese men and Western women, what are some of the common gaps in their mutual expectations? And what can they do to survive the pitfalls? These are some of the questions that will be discussed in the next chapter.

 CHAPTER NINE

Japanese Husbands, Western Wives

Stepping out of one's cultural boundaries involves being able to recognize one's own culturally biased views of other cultures. For a Western partner involved with an Asian, this may be easier said than done, for in international society, there is a strong tendency for Westerners to judge non-Western cultures strictly by Western standards.

Eurocentricity

This cultural bias, referred to by some critics as Eurocentricity, can often be found in the mass media. The *1993 Romance Report*, a survey of fourteen nations by the Harlequin Enterprises of Toronto, a Canadian publisher of romance novels, concludes that Japanese men rank as the least romantic.[1]

The survey, conducted in Australia, New Zealand, the United States, Canada, Japan, and nine European nations, asked female respondents to rate their mates. Japanese women typically ranked their husbands or boyfriends very low in response to questions concerning romantic behavior and attitudes. Yet the questions only voiced Western social concerns and the more traditional, chivalrous conduct, such as if men remember important days like wedding anniversaries and birthdays, whether they know their loved one's preferred perfume or lingerie size, and whether they buy their girlfriends or wives flowers.

The truth is, the Japanese have seldom celebrated occasions such as wedding anniversaries. Media-produced events such as St. Valentine's Day are imports that have only become popular in the last ten years. The idea of "romance" between men and women, after all, is intrinsically Western. If Japanese men are slow at catching on giving their loved ones flowers, it could be because they never saw their fathers or romantic heroes in Japanese movies and television programs do the same.

Japan was the only Asian country included in the Harlequin survey, so it is not surprising that Japanese men should seem sadly lacking in the comparison, which was based strictly on Western romantic ideals (and of course Harlequin would have a certain bias anyway).

Yet these comparisons, unfair as they may seem, are in fact encouraged by the Japanese themselves. In the nation's craze to emulate the Western world, Japan shows a strong inclination to subordinate both its political and social standards to those of the West. Not only has this tendency toward Eurocentricity, or more precisely, "Americentricity," gone largely unchallenged, it has actually been reinforced by Japan's own mass media.

A 1993 survey by Kokusai Denshin Denwa, Japan's largest overseas telephone company, conducted to determine the differences between Japanese and American husbands, is one example that demonstrates how the Japanese force Western comparisons onto themselves. The study, released in June 1993, found that nearly two-thirds of the American husbands (out of 105 surveyed in the U.S.) said they went out with their wives at least once a week, where-as only 14 percent (out of 110 surveyed) of the Japanese men said they did the same.[2] Eighty-eight percent of the American husbands said they always give their wives presents on their birthdays, in contrast to only 28 percent of the Japanese husbands.

The study makes no attempt to explain the vast differences between the two cultures. Birthday presents, for example, are not a Japanese tradition; it is only recently that Japan's expanding commercial interests began to promote this practice. Taking the wife out every week is also more American than Japanese, though more young couples are dining out occasionally—on the infrequent occasion the husband has time to do so. After the children are born, Japanese couples always take the whole family out together. Babysitters are still rarely used, as most Japanese do not like to leave their children in the care of non-family members.

The study continues to say how 33 percent of the American fathers said they are actively involved in teaching their children at home, while only 10 percent of the Japanese fathers said so. It reports that 48 percent of the American husbands regularly share housework with their wives while only 15 percent of the Japanese husbands said they did the same.

Again, there is no mention in the study of the more positive traits of Japanese husbands, such as their strong commitment to work in order to support the family. Nor does the study acknowledge the long working hours put in by most, who may not be able to make it home until 9:00 or 10:00 P.M. The more important point here is that most Japanese salarymen still count on overtime pay to supplement their incomes in the high-priced cities of Japan (which many, during the current recession, no longer receive, though they may continue to have to work overtime).

Survey of Western Wives Shows Unexpected Results

Because Japanese husbands appear overly traditional and overly preoccupied with their work by Western standards, many people, both Westerners and Japanese, expect Western wives to regret having married a Japanese. Are they really all that unhappy? I set out to find the answer by polling 360 members of the Kanto Chapter (which includes Tokyo and the Yokohama area) of the AFWJ in a survey conducted in January 1994, and received a few unexpected replies.

1. High Satisfaction Rate

In the survey, I asked the wives how happy they were in their marriage and of the 125 women who responded, 82 percent said they were either "Very Happy" or "Fairly Happy."[3] Admittedly, many who responded positively had been married for a relatively short period of time.[4] Still, this overwhelmingly positive rating contradicted the common assumptions.

One possible reason for the positive replies could be that unhappy wives did not respond to this survey. Another more certain reason is that many Western wives, after having lived outside of their own cultures for some time, have come to realize their own cultural biases and learned to evaluate their husbands by a more inclusive set of standards and priorities.

While it is true that some foreign wives responded by confirming the typical stereotypes of Japanese men—that their husbands are workaholics, poor partners, and inattentive fathers—many more wives responded positively. Included in the survey I sent out to foreign wives was the international Kokusai Denshin Denwa survey mentioned earlier in the chapter on the differences between Japanese and American husbands. I received quite a few comments saying how "unfair and dangerous" the comparisons were. One British woman in her forties wrote, "My husband leaves home 7:20 A.M. and returns about 10:00 P.M. Just how much housework can he be expected to do?"

She continued to say how "none of us realizes how totally and completely we are brainwashed by our own cultures until we have lived out of that culture for many years. Even then, some people never lose their bias that Western culture is somehow intrinsically better, and is thus the norm by which to measure all other cultures. Thus, we generally measure how far Japanese culture deviates from Western culture when we look at Japanese males, marriage, etc. It is inevitable that Japanese men will appear to be sadly lacking, and a marriage to one somehow inferior in quality to our ideal, which is usually the Western ideal."

2. *The Hard-working Provider*

Although many people expect that it would be the Japanese men with Western traits that Western women would find more attractive, about half of the respondents said that they are more charmed by their husbands' Japanese qualities. Many wives said they really appreciate their husbands' willingness to assume the role of steady bread-winner, a quality many Western wives say is becoming harder and harder to find among today's Western males. Quite a few candidly told me that they are truly "relieved and overjoyed" about the arrangement, as it frees them to take on a "more traditional role" as mother and wife—a role that they say they cherish and are glad to be able to assume in 'a country where it is not frowned upon. This may explain why the majority of Western wives rated their Japanese husbands extremely high as providers. Out of the 125 respondents, 59 percent rate their partners as a 9 or 10, 10 being highest in this category.

Interestingly enough, most wives also indicated that they are either "full-time" homemakers or are only engaged in "part-time work" around the house so that they can be close to their families. Only 20 percent said they have full-time jobs. Considering that 71 percent to 74 percent of American women remained working full-time during their prime child-bearing years,[5] their job participation rate is indeed very low. This may suggest that many Western wives of Japanese follow the path of a Japanese wife more than that of a Western one. Yet the question still left unanswered is, did most of the Western wives consciously choose the full-time homemaker lifestyle or did it happen that way because their Japanese husbands expect them to stay home?

3. *The Not-so-average Japanese Man*

Some of the women surveyed also suggest that the high rating they give to marital satisfaction may have to do with the fact that the kind of Japanese men who wish to marry Western women are not likely to be average. My survey seems to support this. About 49 percent of the Japanese husbands surveyed have graduate degrees or Ph.Ds. Fifty percent have lived in a foreign country for more than three years. In general they also speak very good English: 60 percent of the women surveyed rated their partners' English ability as "fluent."

The high education rate of Japanese husbands perhaps can be explained in part by the fact that the better educated the men are, the more likely they are to be sent to work overseas. This makes them more likely candidates to inter-marry than those without the higher degrees.

In addition to being better educated, 45 percent of the wives surveyed also rated their husbands either "perfect" or "near perfect" as fathers. They also indicated that their husbands help to discipline the children and prefer to come home early to be with the family rather than social-ize with colleagues.

One twenty-eight-year-old British woman who works as a researcher for a Japanese firm also said that her hus-band calls every evening from work to let her know what time he will be home—something he said he wouldn't do if she were Japanese. That Japanese men are likely to behave differently when their spouses are American or European, the woman suggested, could be because "they know they cannot get away with the sexist attitude they apply toward Japanese women."

Sexist or not depends very much on how one interprets the circumstances. Most Japanese wives would not bother their husbands at work—not out of fear of their husbands, but more because they understand this is the accepted social norm in Japanese society. Besides, they also want their husband to work overtime to earn some extra cash for the family. This is why they not only accept the status quo, but actually welcome the idea that their husbands work late. Yet it is undeniable that Japanese men are more likely to bend the rules if their wives are Western, and especially if they are from advanced Western nations. This is so because Japanese still harbor certain complexes toward Westerners. These predispositions, along with the eco-nomic leverage that many Western nations have with Ja-pan, often helps to tilt the power balance more in favor of the Western wives in their relationships with their Japa-nese husbands.

This difference in attitude also extends beyond the cultural response that Japanese men do not make "good lovers." In the survey, for example, 36 percent of the wives gave their husbands a 9 or a perfect 10 as "good lovers," while another 35 percent rated them as average. Yutaka Masuda, a Japanese sex counselor who runs a clinic in Shinjuku, Tokyo, said in an interview that while Japanese husbands of Japanese women may have a bad reputation as lovers, they are likely to improve when they have Western partners. "Given Japanese men's inferiority complex toward Westerners, Japanese husbands tend to try harder to please their foreign wives," he said.

Why the Persistent Belief in a High Divorce Rate?

Despite these positive responses about Japanese husbands, there is a widespread belief that the divorce rate of Japanese husbands and Western wives is high.[6] An American friend of mine once told me how she was warned against marrying a Japanese man by an official at the American Embassy when the two went to register their marriage. Many people I interviewed also suggested this repeatedly. Why does this belief persist? I have come to see that there is some practical reasoning, not just sheer prejudice, behind it.

Western wives living in Japan, for one thing, have greater adjustments to make than Japanese wives of Western husbands, mainly due to the issue of turf. If Japan-based intermarriages are allowing Japanese women more and more autonomy and power in their marriages to foreign men, then Western wives of Japanese living in Japan must learn to cope with the cultural differences of living in a foreign country that may make them feel extremely incompetent, helpless, and marginalized at times.

The inability of many Western wives to speak the language, to begin with, remains a major stumbling block to making a better adjustment to life in Japan. One thing I noticed in my survey is that most wives say that their Japanese ability is limited. English appears to be the main language of communication between Western wives and their Japanese husbands. In my survey, for example, 58 percent of the wives say they only speak adequate or survival Japanese. Four of them even said that they speak no Japanese at all, despite the fact that they all have spent at least four years in Japan. One wife who has been living in Japan for ten years says, "Every day is a struggle. Even when the phone rings, I feel I have to make a tremendous effort." This is why 45 percent of the wives responded that they communicate all or mostly in English with their Japanese spouses. Only 41 percent say they communicate half in English and half in Japanese, while a low 10 percent say they communicate only or mostly in Japanese.

This is in direct contrast to my survey of Western husbands. As I mentioned in Chapter Six, of the thirty Japanese wives surveyed through the Association of Multicultural Families, 34 percent said they communicate only in Japanese with their husbands, 30 percent said they communicate half in Japanese and half in English while another 30 percent said they communicate only in English. This suggests that more Western husbands speak Japanese than Western wives.

One reason accounting for the small percentage of Japanese-speaking Western wives may have something to do with what Professor Fumiteru Nitta of Kibi International University calls the "male-female difference" in his comparative studies on the differences between international couples. In his study, Nitta found that while most foreign men meet their Japanese wives in Japan, most Japanese husbands meet their foreign wives outside of Japan—something he believes is due to the fact of there being a general tendency in most societies for men to travel more than women.[7]

Their lack of practical living experience in Japan may mean that many foreign wives are ill prepared to make the necessary cultural adjustments. In the following section, I will touch on, through case studies, some practical problems that Western wives often face when living in Japan. Later, I will describe some possible solutions as illustrated through two success stories.

When Western Wives Live in Japan

Not only are Western wives less likely to speak Japanese than their Western counterparts (i.e., Western husbands of Japanese wives), they are also less advantaged than the Western husbands in terms of adjustment. If most Western husbands can count on their Japanese wives to maintain the household while they work fairly comfortably in an office where help is provided in the form of Japanese-speaking secretaries and colleagues, many Western wives are stuck at home alone to take care of practical matters and the daily drudgery. This means, for example, facing the many day-to-day hazards of dealing with neighbors and the public at the bank, post office, school, ward, and tax offices—a situation that could be overwhelming for someone who does not speak adequate Japanese and is unfamiliar with the social system.

Wives with children particularly feel the crunch. From taking the children to the hospital when they are sick, to helping them with their homework, many wives say they feel particularly helpless and incompetent. This often adds to the burden of coming to terms with the foreign culture they have married into. They speak of losing confidence and self-esteem. Many wives who try hard to integrate into Japanese society also say they feel they are losing their identity by giving up or having to change their way of thinking and doing things.

One American wife from Oklahoma said that after years of living in Japan, she came to realize that "the most intractable problems (of mixed couples) stem from living here rather than differences between partners. If we did not have to invest so much emotional energy in simple survival, we would have more left over to deal with the ordinary troubles that arise in any marriage."

1. The Need for a Supportive Husband

Invariably, foreign wives find they have to look to their husbands and in-laws for help to cope with daily survival. Surprisingly, several wives have mentioned that their husbands appear not to understand their need for emotional support. These husbands appear not to want to help the children with their homework or assist the wife with other daily chores such as banking and taxes. In fact, many husbands, who are preoccupied with their own work, automatically expect their foreign wives to handle the household and the education of children single-handedly, as would a Japanese wife.

Below is an example of a not-so-supportive husband, told through the story of Lisa, an American wife from Kansas City, Missouri.

• Lisa's Case

Lisa, a mother of two, has been married for eight and a half years and is a full-time homemaker. Although she is fairly happy about being with her children and not having to worry about juggling work and child care, she says she often feels frustrated with Yoshi, her husband. He is a gentle man and a hard worker. The problem is, she finds him unsupportive and sometimes unresponsive to her needs. "I can't get him to help me learn Japanese. When I asked him to help me learn, he would just tell me it's too troublesome. In fact, he doesn't much like the idea of me learning Japanese," Lisa says at her Chiba home.

Lisa met her husband in the United States. He was sent there to do business in Kansas City and she was hired to work as his assistant. Although their mutual attraction was not immediately obvious to her, after a year of working together when Yoshi was due to return to Japan, he proposed. Lisa was shocked, but as she had always considered him attractive, she said yes.

The two came to Japan to marry. It didn't take Lisa long to find out that Yoshi had a stubborn streak. When they would decide to go out to eat, for example, Lisa would make a suggestion. If Yoshi liked a restaurant she suggested, they would go and all would be fine. But if he didn't like it, he would make excuses and try to change her mind without telling her straight out that he didn't like the place. If Lisa put her foot down and insisted on her way, he would make things difficult by pouting during the entire dinner.

Lisa, since she can't read Japanese, became dependent on Yoshi for information. Although he sometimes complained to Lisa that being married to a *gaijin* was a big hassle, he did routinely read the mail every day after work. Lisa, feeling trapped in the house with their children, always looked forward to taking part in some outside activities. Yet Yoshi seemed more interested in having Lisa stay home and would hide information about such activities from her. Lisa did not find out about this until she was told later by friends about several activities that she had missed. This made her very angry. When she confronted Yoshi in search of an explanation, he became very evasive.

Lisa also had to look to Yoshi for support with the children's homework. But Yoshi had a demanding managerial job at a trading company that kept him very busy, and when he finally got home, he was not always in the best mood to help. Lisa was made to feel guilty and helpless. Yet she did not know what else to do.

At times, Lisa feels very lonely and wonders if she really knew Yoshi well enough when she decided to marry him. In retrospect, she feels she was too young and had taken a lot for granted. Had she known more about herself and what she wanted from life, she says, she probably would not have married Yoshi. But now that they have two children, Lisa is determined to make it work.

Lisa's determination is finally beginning to pay off. After years of working long hours at his job, Yoshi plans to quit and move the family to Hiroshima to take up a teaching position at a college. She hopes this means that he will be able to spend more time with her and the children. Lisa says she hopes she and Yoshi will learn how to support each other more and that they will get to know each other better.

As shown by Lisa's situation, the support a foreign wife receives from her husband can make a huge difference. This is particularly the case during the adjustment period. Unless the husband is sympathetic to the difficulties his wife faces living outside of her own element and unless he makes an effort to work with her as a team to handle some of the basic day-to-day matters, the marriage will most likely suffer.

2. Husband's Job Makes a Big Difference

The overworked Japanese salaryman's life is another

reality that many foreign wives do not foresee when they marry a Japanese and live in Japan. Quite a few of these wives expressed their frustration about how wrapped up their Japanese husbands are in their companies and jobs. It is not that they are too busy socializing with their colleagues after work at *aka-chōchin* (Japanese-style bars) or karaoke bars, as many say their husbands prefer to stay at home with the family after work. The problem is more that they can't break away from work or that their commute to and from work is too "horrifyingly" long.

This means that the husband does not return home until 9:00 or 10:00 P.M. Naturally, the wife cannot look forward to his sharing some of the child-care and household chores, much less any romantic conversation or emotional support, which she may badly need as she struggles to adjust to her new environment.

According to comparative figures provided by the Ministry of Labor in 1994, the average Japanese salaryman worked a total of 1,904 hours, or about 400 hours more than Germans and Italians, and 300 hours more than French workers.

Tammy's husband is a typical example of an overworked Japanese salaryman.

• Tammy's Case

Tammy is a thirty-year-old mother of two from Colorado. Married to her Japanese husband, Shinji, for eight years, Tammy says that her marriage is less than satisfactory. In our interview, she told me that she was unhappy with her husband mostly because of his working conditions. "It's not that he has extremely long working hours," she explained. As a draftsman working for a construction company, Shinji works an average of nine to ten hours per day, which is less than what most salary men endure. The problem is his long commute to and from work. Living in a suburban town on the outskirts of Tokyo, he has to travel one and a half hours each way to and from his office in Tokyo. This condition worsens when he is sent on special assignments to more remote sites.

"Until a few months ago, my husband had to travel from our home in Hachioji to Chiba every day; that's a three-and-a-half-hour train ride each way!" Tammy said. By the time he got home, it was midnight. Tammy says he was so dead tired he barely had energy to drag himself to bed. The situation lasted for nearly a year, and to Tammy, who was trying to go to college while tending their two young children and keeping up with the housework, it was simply too much.

Not able to count on his help and having to deal with the language handicap and every day frustrations of being a foreigner, she ended up with an ulcer. While she was hospitalized, her mother came from the U.S. to help with the children. In the end, Tammy was forced to quit college altogether.

Now that her husband has finished with the Chiba project and Tammy has recovered from her illness, things have improved. But things are still far from ideal. Living far away from the city, although she is happy to be closer to nature and a more people-oriented lifestyle, she does feel very lonely to be so far from the support of other foreign wives. She longs for the moment her husband gets home because he is usually very helpful and supportive. Besides, she says there just does not seem to be enough time to talk about things, except on Sundays. Tammy loves Sundays. She even composed a song in their praise:

On Monday, everything is fresh;
On Tuesday, well, the feeling is still there.

When Wednesday comes, the memory begins to fade;
On Thursday, it is hardly there.
Friday is when things begin to get in the face,
Saturday is when we'll have our fights;
And on Sunday, yes, that's when we shall kiss and make
up.

Tammy says she realizes it is the harsh demands that Japanese society and Shinji's company place on him that makes life so difficult for the family. But at this point, circumstances can't be improved. She dreams about the day when she can go back to college. "Perhaps I can go back when my children are grown," she muses.

Meanwhile, she is trying to improve communication with Shinji with the help of a tape recorder. She speaks into the recorder, telling him how she feels and asks him to listen to it later. She has also decided to become less dependent on her husband for emotional support and is beginning to seek new friendships with Japanese and other foreigners in her neighborhood.

Tammy, like many other foreign wives, is caught in the dilemma of wanting her husband to come home early but not wishing to jeopardize his chance for a promotion.

Companies have such control over their employees' lives that some wives may find themselves forced into the role of helping to support their husbands' careers. One wife, for example, told of how she had to play the demure wife when her husband's boss visited. She served tea and kept quiet, as dictated by social rules, to keep the proper decorum and impress the boss.

Although some wives say that their husbands change and completely relax outside of Japan, other wives say they continue to suffer from being psychologically "shut-in," even after they have moved from Japan. In the July-September 1991 issue of the *Japan Quarterly*, for example, one foreign wife living in New York recited her experience of being forced to quell her strong urge to dance to street concert music by her Japanese husband who was afraid that she might be seen by his Japanese colleagues.

Because of the power companies have over the lives of their workers, which is still supported and adhered to by the employees themselves who fear criticism from their peers as well as their superiors, many wives warn Western women who are thinking about marrying a Japanese man to understand and consider their future husband's job situation before committing themselves to marriage.

From what I gather through these interviews, most of the happier wives are those married to academics, artists, entrepreneurs, and other professionals whose workload is more autonomous. They also tend to live outside of the big cities where the pace is hectic and living quarters can be oppressively tight.

3. *The Problem of Living with In-laws*

The percentage of Western wives living with in-laws is relatively low. Only 18 out of 125 AFWJ members surveyed said they have lived or are currently living with their in-laws. But several expressed shock when they found they have to live with their in-laws. Many parents continue to play a dominant role in the lives of their sons even after they have married and it is not uncommon for sons to be asked to live with the parents, especially the eldest son. In some cases, this is due to the convenience and practicality of sharing a larger house, particularly if the husband is still financially dependent on his parents. In other cases, it is due to the need to care for a widowed mother or ailing father. In Japan, homes for the elderly are still a fairly new idea. Government-subsidized homes are few and many

Japanese are still averse to leaving their parents in such institutions.

This necessitates the wife's having to deal with live-in in-laws—a custom foreign to many Westerners. In such cases, foreign wives will be forced to deal with situations which many may find very unpleasant and stressful. This causes many problems later on. The following is the experience of Carol, an American wife from Long Beach, California.

• Carol's Case

Carol, who is in her forties, married a Japanese student she met at a Tokyo English-language school where she was teaching about eight years ago. Her husband Toshi, who Carol thought was cute, ran a beef cattle farm for his family in a rural part of Chiba. A year after dating her husband, Carol found herself pregnant and the two decided to get married. Since he was living at his family's house, it was only natural for Carol to join him there. That was when she said she discovered the difficulty of living so closely with her widowed mother in-law.

Carol felt a sense of helplessness and powerlessness whenever she was around the mother-in-law, who seemed to have absolute control over the household and the family business of which she owns a major share. As his mother knew a lot about its ins and outs, Toshi spent a lot of time with her talking about the business. Since Carol spoke little Japanese, she had only a vague idea about what was going on and felt totally left out. The mother-in-law also had absolute control of the money, which made her son dependent on her. This made him seem unconditionally yielding to the mother, and Carol resented this.

Although the farm house was very spacious, the sharing of living quarters was another major problem. "It was her kitchen, her house," Carol said. As a newcomer to Japan, Carol did not know how to cook Japanese-style food. This made her feel very inadequate. Her lack of language skills meant there were a lot of day-to-day chores she could not do very well. The mother-in-law invariably took control. To make things worse, Carol's husband would not stand up for her and wouldn't eat the food she cooked. Carol felt as though her husband and the mother-in-law were ganging up on her.

When their twin sons started school, Carol felt she had lost another battle. Because of Carol's language handicap, it was the mother-in-law who ended up helping the sons with their homework. The situation went from bad to worse. Finally, when Toshi suggested that she have another baby, she said she would on the condition that he build a separate house for her.

Now Carol has her own house next to the mother-in-law's. She has her own car, her own bank accounts, and takes her own vacations, making her life easier. Although her husband eats at the mother-in-law's and their two sons still sleep there, Carol feels that at least she finally has her own space.

Carol says she could be happier with her marriage. She said she had entertained the thought of divorce, but is too afraid of losing her two sons completely to the mother-in-law.

In retrospect, Carol thinks that she was naive about what marrying a Japanese farmer would involve. She was almost certain that Toshi would have had more trouble talking a Japanese woman into marrying him, given his living situation. She also says she wishes she had known more about the culture before agreeing to marry Toshi. "Had I known more, I would have insisted that he live on my turf in the U.S. instead," she says.

As seen in Carol's case, living in close quarters with in-laws can create a lot of stress and conflict. Sharing the same kitchen is often cited as the worst possible arrangement, especially if the mother and daughter-in-law come from vastly different backgrounds and have very different ways of cooking. Raising the children is also a source of serious conflict.

Many foreign wives say that this arrangement is impossible for them and that even Japanese daughters-in-law are refusing to live with their mothers-in-law these days. Some wives have even joked half seriously that this is the reason their Japanese husbands have chosen to marry a foreigner. Most agree it is best to live separately. If this is not possible, the next-best situation is set up a household next to or nearby their in-laws' house.

In some cases, the neighboring household arrangement has proved to be a nice set-up for mutual support, especially if the foreign wife works or is still unfamiliar with her surroundings. One wife, who lives next to her in-laws in Chiba, says after years of experience she has come to appreciate the positive aspects of what Westerners term an "inter-dependent relationship" in Japanese society. She drives her in-laws into town whenever they need to run errands. In exchange, they help her look after the children when she and her husband want to spend a night out.

The Success Stories

Despite the problems mentioned earlier, which may seem hard to resolve at times, some couples have found ways to lead a more fulfilling life together. How do they do it? I looked for answers through interviews with couples who, after at least ten years of marriage, say they are "very happy." I have chosen to include two of the foreign wives who have managed to resolve the above-mentioned problems successfully through their own efforts and the support of their husbands.

• Silvia and Tomoharu's Case:

Silvia and Tomoharu have been married seventeen years and have two teenaged children. The two met in Japan at a college in Chiba where they were both teaching—he was teaching ceramics, she was teaching English.

Silvia, now in her late forties, is an easy-going American from Idaho with a great sense of humor. She came to Japan to teach EFL nineteen years ago. Tomoharu, armed with a master's degree in ceramics from Long Beach State University, speaks fluent English. Silvia, who described her Japanese ability as "adequate," says Tomoharu's English ability was part of her initial attraction to him. Tomoharu is also a very supportive husband. He helped run errands and entertain while I was talking with Silvia who was nursing a bad back. The two were talking about taking a family ski trip together and Silvia was determined to get her self back in shape for the trip.

Thirteen years ago, at his parent's request, the two moved near them in Chiba, where the parents own some land. His parents helped them build a spacious Western-style house next to their Japanese farm house and they have lived there ever since. They lead a very non-conventional life. Tomoharu has a large kiln in their yard where he practices his ceramics. He also works as a pottery teacher for Japanese and foreigners in the community and owns a *juku* (cram-school) for junior high school students where Silvia helps teach.

Silvia says living close to her in-laws has not been a problem at all because she has learned to make it a mutually helpful relationship. She says she is not a great Japanese cook so is always pleased to be able to get some *miso* soup from them for her husband's breakfast.

Silvia says foreign wives who have troubles with their in-laws tend to be those who are very defensive, "unbendable," and want to compete with the mother-in-law for the husband's attention. What she found helpful was to give the mother-in-law the satisfaction of maintaining the position of authority in the house. She also learned to have respect for the *senpai-kōhai* (senior, junior) system[8] and respect for the elderly. Silvia says there is a "testing period" for an outsider who enters a Japanese family. Once they find that you have embraced their ways, she says they will accept you and let you have your way. Given that you have established a give-and-take relationship with the in-laws, they can be, in Silvia's words, "wonderful built-in baby-sitters." Having a good sense of humor, Silvia says, has also been a tremendous help. Silvia learned to laugh off a lot of the things that seem ridiculous to her.

Without Tomoharu's generous support, no doubt life would have been much harder for Silvia. Tomoharu says he does all the banking, correspondence, and household finances because he knows how hard it would be for Silvia to do these things. He also helps their children with their homework when he comes home at night and, thanks to his flexible schedule, has always managed to be around the house when Silvia really needs his help.

Silvia and Tomoharu also have great respect for each other's cultures. Silvia, for example, says she would like Tomoharu to be a little more affectionate in public. But she realizes this is not a part of Japanese culture and that she can't force or change him.

Silvia is aware of the problems many women face with the indirect way of communicating in Japanese and how unresponsive their Japanese partners can be to their needs.

But she feels there is a danger of blaming too much on cultural differences: "There is a basic difference in how men and women communicate. Men, for example, are said to be doers, while women are talkers," she says, citing an example from the book *You Just Don't Understand*, by Deborah Tannen.

She also thinks Western men and women place too many expectations on marriage. Her advice to Western women married to Japanese is to develop an interest and life outside of their spouses' and learn to become more emotionally independent. She thinks it would be a great help for the couple to spend a few years in each other's countries before they decide to marry.

As for Tomoharu, he says that in general, he does not recommend intercultural marriage because "it takes a lot of work and energy." He feels that only people who are very flexible and can handle a great deal of stress will be successful. He thinks that his marriage has survived and thrived basically because he and Silvia have both been very flexible and easy-going.

• June and Takeshi's Case

June and Takeshi live in a beautiful Western-style house at the foot of Mount Fuji in Yamanashi Prefecture above Lake Yamanaka. Takeshi is a university professor who teaches linguistics at a local university. June is a full-time homemaker who is constantly running around picking up after their three teenaged children. They have lots of space to themselves at home and are surrounded by nature. The children, all home-educated through a special American school correspondence program, are also very active outdoors. The family has a cheerfulness that is infectious. On a drive to a play in Tokyo, they sang together in melodious harmony the whole way. June and Takeshi, who are obviously very much into their family and each other, said they have become truly happy after twenty years of marriage.

June and Takeshi met at a party at the University of Hawaii twenty-one years ago. She was a graduate student in Asian Studies, while he was a graduate student in linguistics. June says they had an instant attraction for each other and became inseparable almost from the start.

Almost two years later, when Takeshi was to return to Japan, the two decided to marry. At first, they lived in a small town in Miyagi Prefecture. Those were hard times for both of them. Takeshi taught at a high school and returned home rather late every night. June, trapped in a small Japanese apartment in a conservative community, tried her best to adapt to a country and lifestyle she found so totally different from what she was used to. They were very unhappy initially and realized they had to do something about it.

When a visiting couple told them about a world tour they had taken together, June and Takeshi brightened up. They planned a one-year trip around the world and Takeshi quit his job at the high school at age twenty-nine—a move most Japanese would try to avoid at all costs. This upset the school so much that he was told by the administration that they would make certain he would never teach in Japan again.

In retrospect, June says that was a crucial move for their marriage as Takeshi had to confront his fears about throwing everything away, just as she had to when she decided to come to Japan. They traveled through twenty-two countries together, learning that there isn't any one way to do things right. They gradually learned how to share things in a way that was comfortable for both of them.

Returning to Japan, Takeshi started teaching part-time at several universities and slowly worked his way to a tenured position at a local university. But there was another hurdle to overcome when the two started living with Takeshi's widowed mother. Although a kind-hearted wom-an, Takeshi's mother had a lot of things to say about the way June is dressed and about how she should raise her children. She also controlled the kitchen and cooked all the meals. June felt she could never do anything right around her and the two built up a lot of resentment.

Takeshi tried to smooth things out by listening first to his mother's complaints about June for an hour, and then spent another hour listening to June's complaints about his mother. He thought that by being understanding, things would improve. They didn't, and June remained very un-happy. Finally, it dawned on Takeshi that he was trying too hard to make a Japanese wife out of June and that he was not "allowing her to be herself." He found he was suppress-ing her cheerfulness—the very quality that had initially attracted him to her. In the end, he had a heart-to-heart talk with June and told her that what he wanted most was a happy wife. He told her to be herself and do what she felt was natural.

June says she was pleasantly surprised by Takeshi's ges-ture. She felt as though he had given her the "permission" to be who she was. She felt she no longer needed to engage in a doomed battle of trying to be someone she could never be—someone who never made waves, someone who never stuck out. She also saw that she was trying too hard to be Japanese and that she was limiting herself by striving too hard to do things the Japanese way.

This realization helped her create the space necessary for her to allow her real self to emerge. She began to regain confidence about expressing herself. She also learned that she could maintain outward social agreements without sacrificing her sense of self. With that knowledge, she saw that what was most important between her and her mother-in-law was not who was right and who was wrong, but how things could work in a peaceful, harmonious manner. The question she began to ask herself was, "Do I want to be right or do I want to be happy?" It took her thirteen years to finally make the shift.

June's life with Takeshi's mother ended seven years ago when Takeshi and June decided to build a house near Mount Fuji. Takeshi's mother thought the move would distance her from her friends and the conveniences of the city, so she found her own house. June's relationship with her mother-in-law has since greatly improved. Now they visit each other with greater respect and appreciation.

As for advice, June says for those who have trouble living with in-laws, one thing she learned in the past was not to disagree with her mother-in-law. "I would agree with her verbally 100 percent and then turn around and do things differently right in front of her. She didn't get mad, but loved the fact that I had agreed and respected her opinions," she said. Learning where her mother-in-law was coming from and realizing that she was from a different era and had had only limited exchanges with other cultures also helped June become more understanding.

June and Takeshi, meanwhile, say they have never been happier. They say the secret to their happy marriage is their devotion to their partnership and their commitment to their mutual growth as human beings. Even today the two set aside an afternoon each week for a date. This is their time together to talk openly about their feelings without any mention of the children or other family business. They say their international marriage has created more opportunities for their mutual growth than they had ever imagined.

 *Conclusion*

Despite the drastic socioeconomic changes Japan has undergone since Western influence found its footing, Western men dating and marrying Japanese women continue to be heavily influenced by the *Madame Butterfly* myth of a demure and selfless but exploitable Japanese woman.

This image, however, is a far cry from current reality. Not only is the modern Japanese woman less likely to be the self-sacrificing butterfly type, but she is probably demanding a major shift in gender roles. When dating cross-culturally, she is more likely to be the one to pursue a Western lover, both in and outside of Japan. Once married, she is also likely to have more say in deciding where the family should live, what car to buy, and what school to send the kids to, particularly when she and her foreign husband choose to stay in Japan.

Another myth widely circulated in the West is the image of the spineless workaholic salaryman or arrogant Japanese male who mistreats women and consequently does not have what it takes to attract the attention of a foreign woman. "Is there such a thing as a Japanese Prince Charming?" not a few foreign interviewees mused. Prince

Charming or not, Japanese men are currently three times as likely to marry interculturally than Japanese women. Although over half of their non-Japanese wives are Asians, the number of Westerners is also steadily increasing.

A Limited Western Perspective

At the core of these myths and prejudices is the persistence of Westerners to interpret Asian culture through Western cultural viewpoints.

Western scholars and writers have continuously either lauded or criticized Japanese women for meekly allowing men to boss them around. But long-timers in Japan would readily disagree, as would many of the foreign men who get to know Japanese women intimately through relationships and marriage.

In her foreword to *The Japanese Through American Eyes*, Sheila Johnson argues that, "While many of my colleagues were still bemoaning the low status and powerlessness of Japanese women, I became convinced that Japanese women actually had a great deal of power and independence in the management of their homes and families."

It is true that by American standards, the position of Japanese women remains low outside the family realm. Yet as long as there is no stigma attached to being a full-time homemaker in Japan, and as long as they continue to maintain covert dominance over their husbands whose back-breaking salaryman lifestyle they have no desire to emulate, they will happily accept their status as "domestic finance ministers."

What is more, all signs are pointing in favor of younger Japanese women gaining greater social equality with men in the future, particularly in the workforce. True, in the wake of Japan's prolonged recession, many Japanese women new to the job market are being discriminated against. But there is clear evidence that Japan will experience a continuing shortage of labor into the next century as a quarter of the population turns sixty-five or older while the birth rate continues to dwindle to an all-time low.

In addition, Japanese women's high levels of education and increased experience with independence and freedom will make them less likely to remain victims of social discrimination. As one American journalist puts it, the Japanese woman is a genie in a bottle and "once out, you can no longer put her back . . . " Japanese women have made and will continue to make great strides, but in their own way, and not to satisfy the agenda of a few Western critics. Besides, as Sumiko Iwao noted in her book *The Japanese Women: Traditional Image and Changing Reality*, "the traditional female is becoming but one of several breeds of women in a society that is growing increasingly pluralistic." There is, accordingly a great need to look at women from a new point of view.

Meanwhile, the Western image of an insensitive, boorish Japanese husband who has no consideration for his wife is proving to be more of an outmoded Western interpretation of things Japanese. As many Western wives have pointed out, although Japanese businessmen do not hold doors open for women, this does not necessarily mean that they are sexist or rude, as this type of courtesy has never been a Japanese social custom. Yet many people, including the Japanese themselves, have been led to believe that the Western standard is somehow intrinsically better than their own and other cultures.

As I have shown, the Japanese man is far from being a powerful figure, and he has actually lost much of his influence and privilege at home, as the result of fulfilling his obligations to his company. While change may be slow in coming, Japanese men are waking up to the unreasonable sacrifices they have made on behalf of their jobs and companies. Now that the economic bubble has burst and companies have begun to change their management style (which up to now has centered on lifetime employment and seniority), salaried workers who have devoted their souls and bodies to their companies are finding themselves betrayed.

Belatedly, they realize it is time for Japan to change its society so that the individual's values are given more weight in relation to the needs of the employer. These days, rather than striving to carve an important position at work or gaining more material wealth, more men are aspiring to a fulfilling life with personal interests. It is perhaps this realization that is beginning to make Japanese men more attractive as human beings and as potential marriage part-ners for some Western women.

Seeing a foreign culture from a Western perspective can be very misleading. Western perceptions of the Japanese as feminine enigmas or male-chauvinist tyrants, as author Kittredge Cherry observed, "Have more to do with what's happening in our cultures than in Japan." It is only through understanding the Japanese in the context of their own culture that one can expect to gain a more realistic picture.

The Changing Landscape

Not only are Western stereotypes of the Japanese prov-ing to be outdated and inadequate for understanding inter-cultural relationships, there have also been some notable social changes—particularly during the past decade—that are quickly shifting the entire power base. Perhaps the most obvious has to do with Japan's rising socioeconomic status.

1. Socioeconomic Status

Japan's rise as a world-class economic power has had a great impact on how intercultural partners relate to each other. Thirty years ago, when Japan was still struggling for a place in the world economy, the kind of foreigners living in Japan were limited to the eccentric scholar, artist, missionary, and diplomat settled in Japan. Meanwhile, Japanese who traveled to the affluent West during the sixties were instilled with strong feelings of inferiority when they experienced the luxurious social freedom and wider living space of the Western world, not to mention the relative material wealth. Since the 1980s, with the burgeoning economy and the Japanese government's stepped-up efforts to internationalize the country, a host of job opportunities, particularly in language-related fields such as English teaching and editing, were created for foreigners. Suddenly Japan became the golden land of opportunity where foreigners, particularly North Americans and other English-speaking Caucasians, could earn a good living and lead a comfortable life in the relative safety of Japan's tight society and crime-free streets.

Although Japan has suffered a serious recession since the beginning of the 1990s, as long as employment opportunities continue to outweigh the bleak job prospects at home, many foreigners married to Japanese have chosen to stay in Japan. This is indicated by a continual increase in the number of foreign nationals living in Japan in the nineties.

This gives both the Japanese husband and the Japanese wife greater power and autonomy in their cross-cultural relationships. They are on their own turf and, subsequently, have more control. The woman's situation is far from that of a war bride of the 1940s or 1950s who was forced to settle outside of Japan and walked in the shadow of her

Western husband. Ironically, half a century later, the war-bride syndrome is now being experienced by foreign wives of Japanese who encounter similar difficulties and disorientation when they settle in Japan.

Helping to boost the confidence of the Japanese partner of today is the power of the yen. In the 1970s, when the exchange rate was about 360 yen to the U.S. dollar, visitors to Japan felt rich. In the 1990s, with the dollar dwindling to only a third of its previous value, it is the Japanese who feel the strength of their economy and the purchasing power of their currency when traveling overseas. This has given them a new sense of pride, which helps to put them on more equal footing in their relationships with Western partners.

In the late 1980s, many Westerners, under the wide publicity of the Japanese purchase of properties and businesses overseas, saw most Japanese as being rich. Some Western wives interviewed admitted to agreeing to marry Japanese initially because of this image of wealth and the concurrent security it provides.

2. *Growing Independence*

Another change closely connected to the rising yen has to do with the growing social independence of the Japanese, especially that of the women. As recently as twenty years ago, most Japanese could not afford to travel outside of Japan. Women who aspired to lead a richer, more fulfilling lifestyle would have to depend on a Western boyfriend or husband to literally take them to the affluent West. And if their Western lover then chose to abandon them, they were placed in a position of great disadvantage. The myth of the passive butterfly was rooted in the Japanese woman's lack of economic resources and independence.

Today, backed by this economic strength and employed

at jobs with little responsibility, many young Japanese women travel abroad as tourists, for study and employment opportunities. This mobility provides them not only with opportunities to learn about the outside world, but also with a chance to meet potential Western boyfriends and husbands. With their new power, the once unattainable "American Dream" of more personal freedom is suddenly within their grasp, giving them more control over their relationships. The once passive maiden of the Orient has emerged from her chrysalis, transformed into a butterfly who can now flutter to wherever—or whomever—may take her fancy.

Changing Motivations

Not only is the balance of power in these relationships shifting, but the motivations for having them are also undergoing changes.

Chance and availability of course continue to be very important factors in bringing cross-cultural couples together. But there are other reasons, too.

1. *Japanese Women and Western Men*

As in any marriage, the motivations behind intercultural couplings are manifold. Some marry for love, others for more practical reasons. If poverty-stricken Japanese women married American GIs during the Occupation because they wished to improve their economic status and gain access to material comfort, then the affluent Japanese woman of today is motivated by the desire for social and emotional fulfillment.

Many Japanese women, locked into the expectations of their society, feel they are facing emotional starvation. But whereas their mothers and grandmothers had to stifle their emotional needs (thus adding to the stereotype of the quiet, suffering Japanese woman), today's women are beginning to feel they can do something about it. The rise of Japan's economy has indirectly boosted the social status of Japanese women. Better educated and economically more independent, they are beginning to demand a different kind of partnership with their male counterparts—one that incorporates greater respect and more emotional and practical support at home.

But most Japanese men have not kept pace with these changes. Still confined to strict, unwritten corporate and social rules, they have neither the time nor energy to attend to women's needs. In frustration, the women may look to Western men, known for their relatively polished social skills and romantic gestures, in the hope of finding better mates. Furthermore, these women may seek relationships with foreigners in their search for even greater individual expression and a desire for a personal anonymity they cannot find in their own society.

There are also some Japanese women who are motivated by the image and status of being married to a "white" husband. As long as most parts of the world continue to be subject to the heavy influx of Western images via television and movies, Japanese women will see Caucasian men as the ultimate "dream relationship" for which to aspire.

In the 1950s and 1960s, Japanese women marrying American GIs faced a strong social stigma and the possibility of being disowned by their families. But since the 1980s, with the government's push for internationalization and with more and more Japanese traveling to the West, a certain glamour has developed around those who are in a relationship with a Westerner. In fact, the expression *koku-sai-kekkon*, or international marriage, has become a buzzword among young Japanese women. While marriages to other nationalities and races continue to meet with opposition, marriages to Western Caucasians are receiving increased acceptance by Japanese society.

Although the motivations behind the attraction of Japanese women to Western men is fast changing, the attraction Western men have for Japanese women has remained more constant over the years. There is no proof that most Western men who date and marry Japanese women are necessarily avoiding Western women; however, this practice suggests a definite undertone of frustration with feminism. Many Western men are prone to describing Western women negatively, saying that they have become too aggressive and competitive and too desirous of having their own careers and lifestyles.

Charmed by the small, delicate appearance of Japanese women and their quiet, non-intimidating demeanor, many of these men are hopeful that they may still find a modern-day "Miss Butterfly." They still tend to see Japanese women as expecting less and as having a better appreciation of men than do many Western women. This way of thinking is particularly strong among North American men who have grown all too weary of the explosive social issues of sexual equality and sexual harassment back home.

But the modern-day Japanese woman has also gained a new popularity with Western men as a symbol of the economic vitality, intelligence, and energy of the Pacific Rim nations, which makes her an object of their desire for a woman of status.

2. Japanese Men and Western Women

Some Japanese men are also influenced by a Eurocentrically biased standard of beauty, and want to find a "white" wife who looks like a Barbie doll. Success as portrayed in Hollywood movies is not just defined by the man's material possessions, but also by the status of his woman—especially as defined by her appearance. In the 1950s and 1960s, when Japan was emerging from the rubble of World War II, few Japanese men not among the elite could attract the attention of a Western woman. With the rising socioeconomic status of Japan, Japanese men not only have more confidence about approaching Western women, but have more access to them because of an influx of foreigners coming to work in Japan. For them, these women are like unattainable prizes finally within reach.

Although Japanese men are slower in catching on to the many changes occurring around them, some are also beginning to seek greater freedom of individual expression. Some of these men date and marry Western women in the hope of being able to create an alternative lifestyle while, at the same time, maintaining a mainstream life within the confines of society.

Ironically, the more liberal Japanese men tend to date cross-culturally, which makes it more difficult for Japanese women to capture these more desirable Japanese mates.

A friend once asked me what my most surprising finding had been. I told him that Western women appeared to be drawn to Japanese men for the same reason that Western men are drawn to Japanese women. What I meant to say is that if Western men are attracted to Japanese women because they think the women are more family-oriented, then Western women are drawn to Japanese men for the very same reason.

To put it another way, as much as some Western men are glad to find that they can still have the traditional lifestyle of marriage and family, with the man being the breadwinner, by marrying a Japanese woman, then some Western women seem to be happy playing the more traditional role of a wife by marrying a Japanese man. But this kind of woman, among Westerners, is still very much a minority. Frustrated by sexual confusion, disintegration of family, and fast-changing gender roles at home, some American women complain about how difficult it is today, in their words, "to meet a sincere man who is free from drugs, not prone to violence, and committed to having a relationship and a family." This makes the industrious, marriage-minded Japanese man seem like a prize to them.

Some Western women even find that being a full-time homemaker in Japan is a refreshing change from the career-and-family superwoman promoted by the American media, an archetype of perfection who is made to feel inadequate if she can't juggle a full-time job with running the home and family.

3. The Ultimate Attraction

The ultimate attraction of a cross-cultural romance, most couples say, lies in its "otherness." The idea that "exotic is erotic" is not only stimulating in a physical sense, but also allows an intercultural couple a chance to step outside the boundaries of the their own social codes to experience a fresh way of relating to the opposite sex. This has the same effect on a relationship whether that relationship is Western man–Japanese woman or Japanese man–Western woman.

The relationship provides both partners with an opportunity of seeing new possibilities while also allowing them the chance to create their own unique paradigm outside the strict confines of their cultural norms.

As the gender war in North America continues to intensify and gender roles in Japan stretch to meet new challenges, the "otherness" will no doubt become a bigger driving force to bring more and more Westerners and Japanese together.

The Age of Romantic Confusion

Japan's cross-cultural dating scene, however, is becoming more confusing and potentially more heart-wrenching than ever. This is in part because the myths and cultural beliefs that Japanese and Westerners have about each other have never been more exaggerated. There are some sound reasons behind this.

1. Prevailing "Western Misconceptions" about the Japanese

Not only are many Westerners prevented from obtaining a more realistic understanding of their Japanese partners because of their tendency to interpret things strictly from a Western perspective, but their view is further obscured by the promotion of exaggerated and dated images. The image of the self-sacrificing Madame Butterfly, for example, dates back to 1904.

This stereotype, however, persisted through to the late twentieth century through Western mass media, particularly films and musicals, perpetuating the image of a passive, exploitable Japanese woman. In fact, here at the dawn of the millennium, the image of the Japanese woman as Madame Butterfly was updated recently in an American musical mega-hit, *Miss Saigon,* in which the Asian woman commits suicide after being abandoned by her American lover.

Seldom challenged and corrected, this stereotype in turn, has helped create the prevailing Western image of the East. In fact, the image of the victimized Japanese woman is so powerfully imprinted in the minds of most Westerners that many cannot comprehend the possibility of a non-victimized Asian woman. This tendency underestimates the power and influence of Japanese women, keeping them subservient to fantasies imposed by the West, thus undermining a more accurate, up-to-date understanding of the Japanese.

2. Japanese Complexes about the West

In many ways, the insecurity of the Japanese in their relationship with the West has also invited misunderstanding at their own expense. In their enthusiasm to internationalize, Japanese have employed many "Western experts." Their awe of the West has, in part, been responsible for the high salaries they offer—two or three times those of the regular Japanese salaryman. English-lesson fees can go as high as $100 per hour, while English "consultants," and relatively inexperienced English-speaking bankers and stock traders could earn $10,000 or more a month during the bubble economy of the late 1980s.

As observers note, many Japanese tend to view Westerners as "mini gods." "Token gaijin-ism" of the 1980s is an exaggerated form of their admiration for the Westerner. Foreign models with blond hair and blue eyes also proved to be more popular than some of their own top idols.

As long as Japanese fail to see the person behind the glamour of the *gaijin* privileges they themselves have accorded to Westerners, they can't expect to cultivate enduring relationships with them. On the other hand, as long as Westerners receive preferential treatment, many will exploit their privileges, even to the point of discounting Japanese society as a whole.

There are a number of signs that the Japanese attitude toward Westerners is changing. Now, with the new confidence of the Japanese, and the abundant availability of English-speaking workers, the notoriously high salaries once taken for granted by *gaijin* workers are fast dropping.

Not only that, but an increasing number of companies are requiring that their English help also be competent in reading and writing Japanese.

3. *Projection of Cultural Beliefs in Gender Role Confusion*

The 1990s is a confusing time for cross-cultural relationships. This is so because both Japanese and Westerners are experiencing frustration and confusion due to changing roles both at home and at work. When they encounter culturally different societal behaviors, both the Westerners and Japanese tend to attach special meaning to them that may have more to do with their own anxiety than with reality.

An American man, frustrated with what he sees as the aggressively strong American woman, may come to Japan in the belief that he can still find a "nice" Japanese woman who is quiet, demure, and non-competitive. He may take a bowed head or silent answer as deference or submission, rather than as the Japanese woman's polite attempt not to cause the man to lose face by directly giving him a contradictory response. Even a gift presented by a Japanese for a home visit—a common custom in Japan—tends to be interpreted by Western men as a gesture unique to the thoughtful, gentle Japanese women. The bottom line is: People see what they want to believe.

Similarly, a Western woman, frustrated with her uncommitted male counterparts, may welcome a Japanese man's quick offer of marriage and interpret his ensuing emotional dependence as a sign of his love, rather than as general societal responses.

Meanwhile, Japanese women, disappointed in the obsession of Japanese men with their work and their seeming indifference to women's needs, are primed to be unduly charmed by what is to Western men a routine display of social etiquette. The pulling out of chairs and opening of doors—gestures that have long been taken for granted in Western societies—are quickly misperceived as being a special kindness and expression of caring.

These responses are due to overinterpreting routine social gestures, a mistake that creates unrealistic expectations on both sides and later leads to disappointment. Central to all this confusion are the vastly different views on the meaning of love and marriage held by Japan and the West, a state of affairs further exaggerated by the language barrier.

4. *Cross-cultural Love and AIDS*

One important issue that is raising heated concern is that many intercultural couples are caught unprepared, or choose to ignore, the reality of AIDS. This is particularly true about the Japanese partners, who generally lack proper AIDS awareness and receive little sex education at home and school.

According to Megumi Baba, of the Waikiki Health Center in Hawaii, the use of condoms during intercourse is viewed by most Japanese men only as a birth control practice. This is why they only use them with their wives and seldom for casual sex with professional women at massage parlors or the like, where it is seen as the women's job to protect themselves from pregnancy. Baba says she has counseled many Japanese businessmen who have contracted sexually transmittable diseases or suspect that they might have been infected with the deadly HIV virus through casual sexual encounters at tourist destinations.

The situation with young Japanese women is equally alarming, if not worse. Lately, there has been a lot of publicity about Japanese women having risky sex during overseas travels. What makes the situation even worse for these women is their own denial of the problem. Until Japanese women come to terms with the existing problem by doing something about it, they may well become the worst sacrifices in the confusion created by the changing sexual roles in Japan.

Secrets of Success

Despite the potential hazards, intercultural relationships are not doomed from the start. Many of these relationships do lead to very happy marriages. One major key to happiness, as many of my informants have confided, involves being able to constantly step outside one's cultural boundaries and, at the same time, it is equally important to not impose one's own cultural values onto the partner. In our Western-oriented international society, there is a strong tendency of imposing Western values onto all other societies. Not doing this requires the Western partner to adopt a more sensitive and objective attitude toward the Japanese spouse's culture.

One thing that helps cross-cultural partners to cultivate a more objective and realistic understanding of each other is when they can arrange to live for a time in the other's country, either together or separately, before committing to a long-term relationship.

Most of the happy couples I have talked to are those who have done just that. The Japanese spouses usually have had experience studying at a North American or British college or have spent time working in the West, while the Western partners also tend to have had prior experience living in Japan before meeting their Japanese spouses.

Another point that was made repeatedly is that it is important for both partners to engage in candid communication so that they can discover a fresh approach workable for both of them. This is critical because people in a cross-cultural relationship don't have a ready-made blueprint for coping with problems. The two individuals must, therefore, be creative and open to various approaches.

Learning to speak the partner's language also appears to be extremely important to the success of an intercultural relationship. It is amazing how many intercultural couples are not able to speak each other's language well and consequently can only maintain a very basic level of communication. Language is not only a crucial tool to better understanding, but an essential source of insight into the partner's culture and way of thinking.

Speaking the language also allows the foreign partner a greater sense of autonomy and independence. Without autonomy, many spouses may later develop resentment toward their partners for their dependency. Sometimes they are also made to feel inadequate or helpless, which may in turn affect their self-esteem. This feeling was cited by many Japan-based Western spouses of Japanese, particularly the foreign wives. Trapped in the house while their Japanese husbands are away working, they become frustrated by the difficulty of managing the household and taking care of the children without knowing the language. As more intercultural relationships become Japan-based, there will be an increasing necessity for the Western partner to acquire a better proficiency in Japanese.

But none of these efforts will help unless the intercultural partners learn to see each other as individuals beyond the cultural boundaries. Cultural behavior, after all, has nothing to do with the substantive quality of an individual, which is ultimately more important. Yet many people continue to confuse culturally learned behavior with personality. It is only after they are married that many intercultural couples say they realize that it is the personality that counts. Happiness, as one woman puts it, "is not about having the car door opened for you." So even if an American man opens doors for women, it does not necessarily make him a kind and considerate person. And even if a Japanese man leaves elevators ahead of women, that does not necessarily mean that he is haughty and inconsiderate.

In my interviews, many insightful couples or previously married partners have pointed out time and again that cultural differences were not the ultimate underlying factors behind the success or failure of their marriages. Beyond the cultural issues, they say, lies the more important basic issue of man and woman, individual and individual.

Looking into the Future

One thing is for sure, Japan's new cross-cultural romances will continue to grow and expand into the twenty-first century to involve ever-greater numbers of Japanese men and women.

In the past, Japan's intercultural relationships were cultivated amid strong disapproval and, sometimes, deep hatred. There also tended to be a vast gap in the balance of power between international partners, such as during the Occupation years. Thanks to Japan's economic success of the 1980s, those days are no longer. The massive cultural and intellectual exchange resulting from Japan's subsequent internationalization efforts, along with the rising self-confidence of the Japanese, has led to a small explosion of a new intercultural marriages that are showing greater equilibrium and diversity. *Kokusai-kekkon* has never looked more positive.

There are, however, bound to be a few mistakes along the way, simply because of the lack of any model to follow.

The eighties, after all, gave more Japanese than ever before an opportunity to explore the outside world. This is also true for many young Westerners, particularly North Americans, for Japan's open-door policy toward the West meant a chance to live and work in the affluent, exotic Orient for the first time. No wonder Japanese and Westerners alike have been, until now, reacting to each other emotionally based on images projected by the mass media. In essence, the mass-media-created images produce a "false familiarity" about other cultures, causing many to form preconceived impressions.

Fortunately, the continued popularization of the "air bus," and the ever-growing flow of exchanges between Japan and the West is bound to promote better mutual understanding in the long run. After the initial excitement has quieted down and there has been time to experience other cultures first-hand, couples from vastly different backgrounds will eventually come to see each other as who they are, not as they are imagined or stereotyped.

One thing that is helping to put the "enigma of the Westerner" into perspective is Japan's prolonged economic downturn. Because of harder times, fewer *gaijin* are being hired at the magnificent terms once accorded to them. As a result, Japan is becoming less a target for those only interested in coming to make easy money. What's more, as of the late 1980s, in order to receive a working visa in Japan, one must have proof of a university-level degree. These days, the kinds of Westerners who come to Japan are more likely to speak Japanese because of greater demand for Japanese skills on the job. This tendency will no doubt help cultivate more in-depth understanding between Japanese and Westerners.

Meanwhile, as Pacific Rim nations continue to gain more importance in the world economy, Asia is beginning to gain a greater voice in an increasingly multicultural mass media. This can be seen in the rise of Asian films and other performing arts in international markets. In addition, Japan is stepping up efforts to promote better understanding of the country by setting up special organizations devoted to cultivate exchanges with overseas countries. One such organization is Association of 100 Titles from Japan—an organization that makes its goal the promotion of translation of Japanese literature and non-fiction titles into English and other foreign languages. Established in 1992, the organization was formed to counterbalance the overwhelming number of Japanese translations of European and American titles that continue to bombard the Japan market. By encouraging foreign-language translation of Japanese titles, the organization hopes more foreign readers can gain a more realistic understanding of Japan.

One important point about the emergence of an Asian influence on the international mass media is that Asian images as portrayed by Asians are bound to offset the many outdated myths produced by the West that continue to meet the public eye. This trend, hopefully, will help curb the Eurocentric perspective of other cultures on the one hand, and boost the confidence of Japanese and other Asians on the other hand. From there, perhaps a more balanced, non-biased picture of Asia will emerge, which, to be sure, will help further mutual understanding between the East and the West.

 *Notes*

INTRODUCTION

1. Ann Kim, "For the last time, gosh darn, I am not a mail-order bride," *The Japan Times*, October 25, 1990.

CHAPTER ONE

1. This quote is from a U.S.–based Japanese language newspaper, the *Hokubei Mainichi*, Saturday, June 15, 1991. Japanese synchronized swimming star and Seoul Olympics medalist Mikako Kotani attended the meeting as a Japanese Olympic Committee member in Nagano, Japan's bid to host the 1998 Winter Olympics.

2. Yoshi Kuzume, "Images of Japanese Women in U.S. Writings and Scholarly Works, 1860–1990: Formation and Transformation of Stereotypes," *U.S.–Japan Women's Journal*, English Supplement, No. 1, 1991.

3. Sheila K. Johnson, *The Japanese Through American Eyes*, Tokyo: Kodansha International, 1989, p. 79.

4. *Ibid.*, p. 76.

5. Leonard P. Sanders, "'Reiko' Lets Love Conquer All," *The Japan Times*, February 18, 1992.

6. Mike Steele, "The Other Side of the Story: Miss Saigon Hit a Nerve among Asians," *Star Tribune: Newspaper of the Twin Cities*, January 9, 1994.

7. Akira Sato, "*Ajia miayamatta 'datsua nyuo' no riron, 90 nendai mo nokoru,*" ("The 'Deserting Asia and Joining Europe' theory that mis-

reads Asia remains in the '90s"), *Asahi Shimbun Weekly Aera*, September 15, 1992.

8. Masaaki Tonedachi, *"Shimei hikkurikaesu Nipponjin no fushigi,"* ("The Incomprehensible Practice of Japanese in Reversing the Order of their Family Names"), *Asahi Shimbun Weekly Aera*, September 15, 1992. This is a related article to Sato Akira's mentioned above.

9. *Ibid.*

10. This data is based on an article by Sam Jameson, "Internationalization—It's Slow Going but Japan's Getting There," *The Japan Times*, January 12, 1987.

11. Ian Buruma, *God's Dust: A Modern Asian Journey*, London: Vintage, 1991, p. 28.

12. Sumiko Iwao, *The Japanese Women: Traditional Image and Changing Reality*, New York: The Free Press, 1993, p. 269.

CHAPTER TWO

1. Edwin Reischauer, *The Japanese Today, Change and Continuity*, Tokyo: Tuttle, 1992, p. 175.

2. Although as of 1993, compared with women, twice as many men entered four-year colleges, the number of women pursuing junior-college educations exceeded that of men nearly twenty-fold, i.e., 24.4 percent versus 1.9 percent. ("Education Continuance Rate," *Japan Almanac 1995*, Asahi Shimbun Publishing 1994.) This makes the combined rate of women receiving a tertiary education higher than men. In 1994, 45.9 percent of women and 40.9 percent of men went on to college and university after graduating from high school. (Mihoko Iida, "A Woman's Work is Never Done," *Nikkei Weekly*, Mar 20, 1995.)

3. For a detailed account of the recent history of female employment in Japan, *see* Frank K. Upham, *Law and Social Change in Postwar Japan*, Harvard University Press, 1987, pp. 124–65.

4. "Labor Force Population Employment by Age and Sex," *Japan Almanac 1995*, Asahi Shimbun Publishing 1994.

5. "Electronics Firms Agree to Offer Maternity Leave," *The Japan Times*, April 6, 1990

6. "Hard Times for Job Info Magazines," *Asahi Evening News*, February 2, 1992

7. According to Recruit, a research company, in the summer of

1992, the ratio of job offers to job seekers was 0.93 times for women due to graduate from two- and four-year colleges in the spring of the following year, as compared with 2.22 jobs for each male graduating senior. (In Japan, job applicants begin processing their employment applications roughly a year before graduation.) Yayoi Uchiyama, "Hard Times Make Job Hunting Even Tougher for Women," *Asahi Evening News*, June 12–13, 1993.

8. *Ibid.*

9. "Women in the Firing Line," *Asahi Evening News*, April 14, 1993.

10. Takie Lebra, "Gender and Culture in the Japanese Political Economy: Self-Portrayals of Prominent Businesswomen." Shumpei Kumon and Henry Roskovsky, eds., *The Political Economy of Japan, Vol 3., Cultural and Social Dynamics*, Standard University Press, 1992.

11. The figures are quoted in "Big Spenders in Japan: The Young Adult Female," *Honolulu Star-Bulletin*, May 14, 1990.

12. Hideko Takayama, "Japan's New Woman," *Newsweek*, January 15, 1990.

13. Teresa Watanabe, "Doing Business: Ferraris, Sexy Ads Help Tokyo Language Schools Sell ABCs," *Los Angeles Times* "World Report," April 25, 1992.

14. Hideko Takayama, "Japan's New Woman," *Newsweek*, January 15, 1990.

15. Takie Lebra, "Gender and Culture in the Japanese Political Economy: Self-Portrayals of Prominent Businesswomen." *The Political Economy of Japan, Vol 3. Cultural and Social Dynamics,*

16. Susan Imrie, "Job Shortage Forces Women to Try on New Hats," *Mainichi Daily News*, September 20, 1994.

17. According to a Ministry of Labor survey, male employees between the ages of 20 and 24 make roughly $1,900 a month, which is about 10 percent more than their female counterparts in the same age group. As the age advances, the gap in pay between the sexes widens. (Ministry of Labor, "Basic Survey on Wage Structure," 1992.)

18. "*Mikon, kekkon, shigotokan,*" ("Views on Staying Single, Getting Married, and Working"), *Mainichi Shimbun*, July 19, 1990.

19. "Lost Art of Motherhood," *Mainichi Daily News*, June 10, 1994.

20. "*Tokai no shinguru-raifu tsumashiku: hitorizumai no dokushin-josei kaishain kyuyo takaiga kakei wa akaji,*" ("Living in the City as a Single Means Living Frugally: Single Female Employees Living Alone are

Well Paid but Unable to Balance Their Books"), *Asahi Shimbun*, May 3, 1994.

21. This is based on figures from a 1990 national survey conducted by Altmann, a marriage research institute. *Altmann's White Paper on Marriage*, Altmann Research Center, 1990 edition. However, a 1991 *Newsweek* article put the estimate of surplus in men to as many as 2.5 million. "Land of the Lonely Hearts," *Newsweek*, February 11, 1991

22. The conventional wisdom in Japanese society has it that while Japanese men and women may prefer the three-year age gap when choosing a marital partner, as they become older and realize that their options are gradually decreasing, they may become less choosy and look more to those from their own age groups.

For more details, *see* Chizuko Ueno, *"Kekkon senso sabaibaru sakusen,"* ("Surviving the Battle of Marriage"), *Hanamuko gakko: Ii otoko ni narutame no jussho* (Bridgegroom School: Ten Chapters on How to be a More Polished Bachelor), Keiko Higuchi, etc. al., eds., Tokyo: Sanseido, 1992.

23. Quoted from a group discussion on the problems of marriage. *"Tokushu: gendai no kekkonko,"* ("Special Edition: Studies on Modern Marriages"), *The Community*, No. 97, The Community Study Foundation, Tokyo: 1992

24. Karen Ma, "Japanese by Numbers: the 1-2-3s of OL Lingo," *City Life News*, March 1992.

25. This is according to the Statistics Bureau of the Management and Coordination Agency. *"Nagaku naru dokushin jidai,"* ("The Prolonging Single Age"), Mariko Banto, ed., *Nippon no josei detabanku*, (Japanese Women's Databank), Ministry of Finance, 1992.

26. According to Ministry of Health and Welfare figures, in 1994, Japanese women married at an average age of 26.1, while their counterparts in Britain married at 25.5 (according to *Britain: 1994: An Unofficial Handbook*, Central Office of Information, London; 1993) and those in the U.S. married at 24.5 (according to the U.S. Department of Commerce, Economics and Statistics Administration, Bureau of Census, 1993).

These figures echoed the findings of an international survey conducted by *Mini-World*, a Tokyo-based magazine. According to that survey, in 1993, Japanese women married at an average age of 25.9, while their counterparts in England and Wales married at 24.2

and those in America at 24.3. "Data File-Opinions About Marriage in Japan, the U.K. and the U.S.A.," *Mini-World*, June-July 1993 .

27. "Is Housework a Wife's Job?" *Altmann's White Paper on Marriage*, Altmann Research Center, 1990 edition, p. 39.

28. "Japan's Working Wives Burdened at Home Also, Survey Shows," *Asahi Evening News*, April 5, 1990.

29. "Marriage No Longer Priority for Working Women," *Asahi Evening News*, January 10, 1991.

30. Sumiko Iwao, *The Japanese Woman: Traditional Image and Changing Reality*.

31. *"Monoiri kurisumasu: Okurimono kokyuka, hoteru ni gaisha—wakai dansei niwa junan?"* ("Large Christmas Expenses: Gifts are Getting More Luxurious, Hotel, Imported Cars—Is this a Suffering Season for Young Men?"), *Asahi Shimbun*, December 21, 1990.

32. *Ibid.*

33. Masumi Mori, "Evaluating the Effectiveness of the Equal Opportunity Law," *Economic Eye*, Winter, 1992.

34. *Ibid.*

CHAPTER THREE

1. "Yellow Cabs," *Transpacific*, July–August 1993

2. Shoko Ieda, *Yellow Cab*, Tokyo: Koyo Shuppansha, 1991.

3. Shoko Ieda, *Genshoku no ai ni dakarete*, (Resort Love), Tokyo: Seishun Shuppan, 1992.

4. This is quoted in a *Japan Times* article. Janet Ashby, "'Yellow Cab' takes a walk on the wild side," *The Japan Times*, April 3, 1992.

5. Brian Covert and Hiroaki Wada, "New York residents call *Yellow Cab* author a fraud," *Mainichi Daily News*, June 8, 1993.

6. "Sex, lies, and faked scenes on TV Asahi," *The Daily Yomiuri*, September 1992.

7. *"OL joshidaisei ga kaigairyoko no seika hokoku,"* ("OL, female college students overseas travel sex report"), *Shukan Hoseki*, September 11, 1987.

8. This is quoted from a speech given to the Japan Afro-American Friendship Association in October 1993, during which Karen Kelsky claimed that she had met about thirty beach boys who made their living off sexual encounters with touring Japanese women.

9. "Female tourists said at risk—ignorance seen leading to care-

lessness in Thailand," *The Japan Times*, August 9, 1994. A related article appeared in the *Tokyo Weekender*. David Tharp, "You, me, AIDS, sex and the devil," *Tokyo Weekender*, August 19, 1994.

10. Karen Kelsky, "Postcards from the edge: The 'Office Ladies' of Tokyo," *US–Japan Women's Journal*, English Supplement, No. 6, 1994.

11. *"Joseishi no sekkusu tokushu daikenkyu,"* ("Reading special editions on sex in the women's magazines"), *Flash*, September 29, 1992.

12. *Ibid.*

13. "Government Must Keep Up with Public Views on Sex," Editorial, *Asahi Evening News*, August 21, 1994.

14. This is quoted in a *Tokyo Journal* interview with Amy Yamada, in which the interviewer noted "After your book was published, there was a big increase in the number of girls who started hanging around the bases." *Tokyo Journal*, March 1991.

15. Mark Cote, "The English Teaching Business," *City Life News*, December 1992.

16. Yumiko Ono, "In Japan, English Classes Aren't All Tongue in Cheek," *Asian Wall Street Journal*, January 14, 1992.

17. Blake Gray, "Hello, I Love You," *Tokyo Journal*, July 1993.

CHAPTER FOUR

1. *"Nihon josei no meiruoda romansu"* ("Japanese Women's Mail Order Romances"), *Shukan Hoseki*, April 2, 1992.

2. *Ibid.*

3. Also *see* Michiko Yamamoto, *Amerika gurashi no ikikata bijin: kyuku-tsu na nihon ni sumanai onnatachi*, (The Beautiful Lifestyles of Women Living in America), Aki Shobo, 1993; and Kurihara Nanako, *Nyu yoku jibun sagashi monogatari*, (Looking for Myself in New York), Wave Shuppan, 1994.

4. This is from a 1989 survey conducted by the Center for International Cultural Studies and Education (ICS), an educational counseling service based in Tokyo. From the roughly 6,000 women who used ICS's services, the survey found that more than 60 percent went to the United States. This was followed by England, Australia, and Canada.

5. Naomi Imamura, *"Nyu yoku yumin ni natta nippon josei,"* ("Japanese Women Becoming New York Drifters"), *Spa*, July 29, 1992.

6. Sumiko Iwao has an excellent explanation of this typical non-verbal type of communication between Japanese couples in her book, *The Japanese Woman: Traditional Image and Changing Reality*, Chapter 4.

7. Shoko Ieda, *Genshoku no ai ni dakarete* ("Resort Love"), Tokyo: Seishun Shuppan, 1992

8. *"Nihon josei no meiruoda romansu"* ("Japanese Women's Mail Order Romances"), *Shukan Hoseki*.

9. In general, the term *kokusai-kekkon* refers to any intercultural marriage involving a Japanese and a non-Japanese. It can have either a romantic or a negative image. A pairing between a Western man and a Japanese woman is often seen as being romantic. But a pairing between a Japanese man and an Asian woman can have a negative image. In the latter case, some might think that the Japanese man married a bride from a poorer Asian country because he could not find a Japanese bride.

10. Kaori Kawatake, *Kokusai-kekkon monogatari*, (Tales of International Marriages), Tokyo: Koseido, 1992., Preface.

11. Sheila K. Johnson, *The Japanese Through American Eyes*. .

12. This figure is somewhat misleading as second- and third-generation Korean residents born in Japan continue to be regarded as foreign nationals by Japanese law.

13. Boye de Mente, *Bachelor's Japan*, Tokyo: Yen Books, 1991.

14. Lafcadio Hearn, *Japan: An Attempt at Interpretation*, Tokyo: Tuttle, 1955.

15. This appeared in the first edition of Boye de Mente's *Bachelor's Japan*, Tokyo: Tuttle, 1962, p. 121.

16. Rich Angell, "Letters to the Editor," *The Daily Yomiuri*, November 20, 1992.

17. Boye de Mente, *Bachelor's Japan*, 1991.

18. Hiroshi Wagatsuma, "Some Problems of Interracial Marriage for the Japanese," In I.R. Stuart and L.E. Abt, eds., *International Marriage: Expectations and Realities*. New York: Grossman Publishing, 1973.

CHAPTER FIVE

1. Takakazu Kaneko, *"Ai o tenidekinai zainichi gaikokujintachi,"* ("Foreign Residents of Japan Who Are Missing Out on Love"), *Crea*, November 1991.

2. According to international surveys, compared with Americans and Britons, more Japanese tend to shy away from physical contact with partners where love and marriage possibilities are absent. In a 1993 comparative survey conducted by the Management and Coordination Agency on views of marriage and love held by young people, while 30.6 percent of Britons and 13.8 percent of Americans between the ages of 18 and 24 said they were prepared to engage in a physical relationship with a partner in the absence of love, only 3.8 percent of Japanese said they would do the same. *Sekai no seinen tono hikaku kara mita nippon no seinen* (Japanese Youngsters Seen through Comparison with Other Youths from around the World). Youth Affairs Management and Coordination Agency Administration, ed., December 1993.

CHAPTER SIX

1. "Readers' Forum," *Pacific Stars and Stripes*, July 28, 1993.

2. According to Ministry of Health and Welfare figures, in 1965, three times as many Japanese women than men were married to non-Japanese. Of these women, 51.5 percent were married to Americans, 36.5 percent to Koreans, 5.1 percent to Chinese, and 6.8 percent to those from "other foreign countries."

3. Fumiteru Nitta, *"Kokusai-kekkon:* Trends in Intercultural Marriage in Japan," *International Journal of Intercultural Relations*, Vol. 12, 1988, pp. 205–232.

4. These four categories: "Korea," "China," "U.S.A.," and "other foreign countries" were the only ones included in Ministry of Health and Welfare statistics until 1991. In 1992, the "other" category was further broken down into "Philippines," "Thailand," "Britain," "Brazil," "Peru," and "other." In some ways, the "Korea" figures are somewhat misleading, as many of the Koreans were born and raised in Japan.

5. According to Ministry of Health and Welfare, in 1992, 54 Japanese women were married to foreign men from the Philippines, 13 to those from Thailand, 168 to those from Britain, 152 to those from Brazil, 56 to those from Peru and 1,065 to those from "other." In 1993, those married to British grew to 220 and those to Brazilians dropped slightly to 146. Meanwhile, those married to men from the "other" category continued to grow to 1,129.

6. "Association for Multicultural Families," P. H. Ferguson and Thomas Boatman, *Networking in Tokyo: A Guide to English-speaking Clubs and Societies,* Tokyo: Tuttle, 1995.

7. Sheila K. Johnson, *Japan Through American Eyes.*

8. G. J. Schnepp and A. M. Yui, "Cultural and Marital Adjustment of the Japanese War Brides," *American Journal of Sociology,* No. 61, 1955, pp. 48–50.

9. P. H. Ferguson and Thomas Boatman, *Networking in Tokyo: A Guide to English-speaking Clubs and Societies.*

10. "Students Abroad Studying Japanese Triple in 10 Years," *The Japan Times,* February 17, 1995.

11. Hiroshi Wagatsuma, "Some Problems of Interracial Marriage for the Japanese," *Interracial Marriage: Expectations and Realities.*

12. Takako Day, *"Nihon josei no kokusai-kekkon: amerika de ikiru ajiajin josei no shitenkara,"* ("International Marriages of Japanese Women—from the standpoint of an Asian woman living in the United States"), *U.S.–Japan Women's Journal,* Japanese Supplement, No. 11, 1992, pp. 17–31.

CHAPTER SEVEN

1. Sumiko Iwao, The *Japanese Woman: Traditional Image and Changing Reality,* p. 2.

2. The term implies that such husbands, after their retirement, tend to cling to their wives like "damp, dead leaves."

3. From a collection of essays included in *Dansei junan jidai—menzuribu kara hyuman-ribu e,* (The Era of Suffering Men: From Men's Liberation to Human Liberation), Koichi Ichikawa, ed., Tokyo: Shibunto, 1992. This expression soon caught on and began to appear in popular magazines such as *Spa* and *Asahi Shimbun.*

4. Simone Cave, "The Plight of Japanese Women," *Tokyo Weekender,* January 29, 1993.

5. "Divorce Lawsuits in Japan Rose to Record in '93," *Nikkei Weekly,* June 27, 1994.

6. Kittredge Cherry, *Womansword,* New York: Kodansha America, 1987, p. 56.

7. Joy Hendry, *Marriage in Changing Japan,* Tokyo: Tuttle, 1986, p. 26.

8. "Divorce Lawsuits in Japan Rose to Record in '93," *Nikkei Weekly.*

9. "Groups Opposed to Revision of Civil Law on Divorce," *The Japan Times*, October 13, 1995.

10. Kittredge Cherry, *Womansword*, p. 57.

11. "Draft on Sexual Equality in Marriage Approved," *Mainichi Daily News*, July 13, 1994.

12. "Survey: 40 Percent View Divorce as Unavoidable in Certain Cases," *The Daily Yomiuri*, June 13, 1993.

13. *"Kanashiki chukonen rikon yobigun,"* ("The Sad, Middle-aged Candidates for Divorce"), *Nikkei Shimbun*, January 22, 1993.

14. *Ibid.*

15. *"Ie ni kaeritai noni kaerenai 'kitaku kyofusho' ni ochiiru otokotachi,"* ("They Want to Go Home But Can't—Men with the Phobic Inability to Go Home Syndrome"), *Spa*, December 12, 1990.

16. Ian Buruma, *Behind the Mask*, New York: Random House, 1984, p. 198.

17. This is according to a survey conducted in 1994 by the Institute for Household Economy. "Wives Control the Finances in Most Single-earner Homes," *The Japan Times*, October 5, 1994.

18. *Ibid.*

19. Ian Buruma, *Behind the Mask*, p. 202.

20. Shigeo Saito, author of *Tsumatachi no shishuki* (Housewives' Blues), won the Japan Press Club Award in 1983 for his outstanding journalism. *Tsumatachi no shishuki*, Kyodo Tsushinsha, 1982.

21. "Classes May Help Harried Fathers," *Asahi Evening News*, October 6, 1993.

22. David Sanger, "In Japan's Astounding Future: Life With Father," *New York Times International*, November 12, 1993.

23. "Men's Lifestyles Polled: Men Said to Be More Domestic," *The Japan Times*, Feburary 28, 1994.

24. Teresa Watanabe, "In Japan, They're Now Making Room for Daddy," *Los Angeles Times*, July 10, 1993

25. This is according to a Labor Ministry survey of 3,131 workers from 1,200 companies published in March, 1993. "The Month that Dad Took Child Care Leave," *Asahi Evening News*, January 12, 1994.

26. *Ibid.*

27. The data are provided in *Japan 1994: An International Comparison*, Keizai Koho Center, Japan Institute for Social and Economic Affairs, ed., 1993.

28. "Japanese Businessmen Prefer Humble Women, Survey Shows," *Asahi Evening News*, March 7, 1992.

29. Chie Nakane, *Japanese Society*, London: Penguin Books, 1974, p.132.

30. Kay Itoi and Bill Powell, "Take a Hike, Hiroshi," *Newsweek*, August 10, 1992.

31. Robert Christopher, *The Japanese Mind: The Goliath Explained*, Tokyo: Tuttle, 1987, p. 67.

32. "Survey: Japanese Favor Marrying Later in Life," *The Daily Yomiuri*, April 8, 1993.

33. Kyoko Shukuya, *Ajia kara kita hanayome* (Brides from Asia), Tokyo: Akashi Shoten, 1988.

34. "Where Want Ads Are Bait and Weddings Forced," *New York Times International*, April 12, 1991.

35. Sachiko Ishikawa, *Kokusai-kekkon—chikyu kazoku-zukuri* (International Marriages: Globalization on the Home Front), Tokyo: Simul Press, 1992, p. 99.

36. Kennosuke Funakoshi, "When No One Else Will Have You," *Mainichi Daily News*, July 2, 1991.

37. Karen Kelsky also related her experiences in a letter published in the *Daily Yomiuri*. "Letters to the Editor," *The Daily Yomiuri*, March 3, 1994. A Ph.D. candidate in anthropology, Kelsky conducted field work in Tokyo in 1994 on young Japanese women's myths and images of Western men.

CHAPTER EIGHT

1. The Association of Foreign Wives of Japanese (AFWJ) is the counterpart of the Association of Multicultural Families (AMF). The former is a Japan-wide organization of non-Japanese women married to Japanese men, while the latter is a nationwide group of Japanese women married to foreign men. Over 80 percent of AFWJ members are from Western nations such as North America, Europe, Australia, and New Zealand.

2. Both the 1969 and 1993 figures were provided by AFWJ in December 1993.

3. Catherine Macklon, *Nihon no otoko to koi ni ochite* (Falling in Love with a Japanese Man), Soshisha, 1994.

4. In a cross-cultural study, Kikumura and Kitano argued that the

comparably high intermarriage rates of male and female Japanese Americans in Los Angeles could be a result of the economically secure and successful status of the male. A. Kikumura and H. H. L. Kitano, "International Marriage: A Picture of Japanese-Americans." *Journal of Social Issues*, No. 29,1973, p. 67–82.

5. Fumiteru Nitta, *"Kokusai-kekkon:* Trends in Intercultural Marriage in Japan," *International Journal of Intercultural Relations*, pp. 205–232.

6. This is according to the Ministry of Justice "Statistics on Foreigners Entering and Japanese Leaving Japan in 1993." The total number of foreigners entering Japan in 1993 was 3,747,157. Of this number, 57.6 percent were men. Yet the number of women between the ages of 15 to 24 was 247,872, which far surpassed the 151,437 men in the same age-bracket. What's more, in the two-year gap between 1991 and 1993, there was a marked increased in the number of young women in the 20–24 age group coming from Europe and Canada. In 1991, the number of women in that age group coming from the UK was 3,059, those from Russia was 562 and those from Canada was 2,427. In 1993, however, the numbers jumped to 3,358; 1,258 and 2,773, respectively. These numbers all surpass those of men in the same age-bracket by nationality.

7. This is according to Mariko Banto in *Nippon no josei detabanku* (Japanese Women's Databank). Of the roughly 11 million Japanese who traveled abroad in 1990, 6.7 million were Japanese men. Among them, 38 percent were tourists and 22 percent were business travelers. These figures are calculated from 1991 figures provided by the Justice Ministry and the Japan Travel Bureau, a major travel agency in Japan.

8. Of the 125 members polled, 21 said they had first met their prospective husbands on campus, followed by 20 at work, 18 through friends, and 10 through language schools, etc.

9. A. E. Imamura, "Ordinary Couples? Mate Selection in International Marriage in Nigeria." *Journal of Comparative Family Studies*, No. 17, Vol 1., 1986, pp. 33–42.

10. Takeo Doi, *The Anatomy of Dependence*, Tokyo and New York: Kodansha International, 1973, p. 7.

11. Fumiteru Nitta, *"Kokusai-kekkon:* Trends in Intercultural Marriage in Japan," *International Journal of Intercultural Relations*, pp. 205–232.

12. Sheila K. Johnson, *The Japanese Through American Eyes*, p. 83.

13. Hiroshi Wagatsuma, "Some Problems of Interracial Marriage for the Japanese," *International Marriage: Expectations and Realities*. pp. 247–264.

14. *Ibid.*

15. This tendency has been confirmed by a study conducted by Dr. Diane Fujino, a psychologist based in the U.S. According to an article published in *The Japan Times*, in her 1989 Los Angeles survey, Dr. Fujino found that while a substantial percentage of second- and third-generation Asian American women are marrying biculturally and biracially, more and more Asian-American men are also dating interracially, making it more difficult for Asian-American woman to find an Asian-American mate. "Asian-American Women Throw Off Traditional Burdens," *The Japan Times*, March 10, 1994.

CHAPTER NINE

1. "Love Report: Japanese Men Tops at Being Least Sexy," *Asahi Evening News*, February 4, 1993.

2. "Japanese, American Husbands Live by Different Priorities," *Asahi Evening News*, June 22, 1993.

3. Out of 125 respondents, 50 answered "Very Happy" and 53 answered "Fairly Happy," 13 answered "So-so," 7 answered "Not Very Happy," and 2 answered "Miserable."

4. Of the 50 who answered they are "Very Happy," 25 were married for less than four years. Among them, four were married for less than a year and two had just registered their marriage. Only 11 of the women have been married for more than 10 years. The 53 who answered they are "Fairly Happy" represent a more balanced picture—they are made up of women married anywhere between 16 months to 36 years. Only 11 women in this category have been married for four years or less.

5. These figures are based on the Japan Institute of Labor's *Year Book of Labour Statistics*, 1988, reprinted in *Japanese Working Life Profile, 1990*, Tokyo: The Japan Institute of Labor, 1990.

6. The divorce rates of intermarried couples have been difficult to determine as such figures have been so sparsely recorded. There is no easy way to confirm if the divorce rate of Japanese husbands and foreign wives is indeed higher than Japanese-Japanese or other marriages. Until 1992, the Ministry of Health and Welfare kept no

data. The latest figures for divorces of mixed couples are from 1993. In that year, the total number of registered marriages between foreign women and Japanese men was 20,092. In the same year, there were 5,987 divorces between foreign women and Japanese men. Meanwhile, in the same year, 6,565 Japanese women were married to foreign men, while 1,610 such marriages ended in divorce.

7. Fumiteru Nitta, "Kokusai-kekkon: Trends in Intercultural Marriage in Japan," *International Journal of Intercultural Relations*, pp. 205–232.

8. The *senpai-kohai* system, according to sociologist Chie Nakane, is a Japanese social ranking system based on vertical relationships. The system is divided into three categories—*senpai*, or seniors; *kōhai*, or juniors; and *dōryō*, or colleagues. The system is based more on duration of service within the same group and on age, rather than on individual ability. This system remains very important in today's Japanese society as a way of maintaining the social order and as a measure of individual social values. *See* Chie Nakane, *Japanese Society*, London: Penguin Books, 1973, pp. 26–42.

 *Index*